Postmoderns

The Beliefs, Hopes, & Fears of Young Americans (1965–1981)

by Craig Kennet Miller

DISCIPLESHIP RESOURCES
MATERIALS FOR GROWTH IN CHRISTIAN FAITH & LIFE
— NASHVILLE, TENNESSEE —

Library of Congress Catalog Card No. 95-83705

ISBN 0-88177-157-0

DR157

INDEX TO SURVEY RESULTS, CHARTS, AND GRAPHS

Below is listed an index to results of the Spring Break Survey (SBS) and graphs based on national demographic information (Demographics) available from such sources as the U.S. Census and the Justice Department. National demographic information for 1995-1996 is published by the government in *The American Almanac: Statistical Abstract of the United States: 1995–1996*, (Austin, Texas: The Reference Press, Inc., 1996), and was a valuable resource for this project.

A C K N O W L E D G M E N T S

any hands and feet went into the development of this resource. Teachers, young adults, high school students, and ministers all played a part in obtaining the data used as the basic research for this book. My thanks goes to people like N. Adiel a. De Pano and Bill Mayhew in National City, California; Lowell H. Shisher in Las Cruces, New Mexico; Eugene Bates in Warner Robbins, Georgia; Rob Winger in Tarkio, Missouri; George Acevedo in Fort Lauderdale, Florida; Dan Jones in Houston, Texas; Vicki Hildreth in Glendora, California; Nicole Bray in Arcadia, California; Victor Quon in San Jose, California; Randy Rowland in Seattle, Washington; Connie Bickford and Theodore Lockhart in Boston, Massachusetts; Larry Stoterau in Chandler, Arizona; Bob Clo in Cincinnati, Ohio; Rob Weber in Shreveport, Louisiana; Paul Marzahn in St. Paul, Minnesota; Scott Miller, in Atlanta, Georgia; and many others across the country who were captured by the vision of listening to members of the Postmodern Generation.

Thanks goes to Rod Redman and students in my 1992 class on "Ministering to the Baby Boom and Baby Bust Generations," at Fuller Theological Seminary who helped me capture a vision for the book. Pastors like Tim Celek, Dieter Zander, and Randy Rowland were instrumental in helping me understand the need for the church to understand and to welcome Postmoderns into their congregations. Thanks as well goes to my colleagues in the Discipleship Ministries Unit at the General Board of Discipleship of The United Methodist Church who have shared their insights as I have shaped this resource.

Two people deserve a lot of credit for helping me pull together the survey material used in this book. Carol Tempelton was instrumental in processing the survey data, and Robbie Jones processed data and transcribed the many interviews that we used in the book. Thanks also goes to Craig Gallaway for editing the manuscript, Sharon Anderson for her graphic design, and to the staff at Discipleship Resources for keeping me on track as the resource was developed.

Finally thanks goes to my wife, Ivy, and my daughter, Jasmine, for their support, nurture, and patience as I wrote this resource.

In many ways this book is the result of the work of a team of people who realize that in order to move into the future, we must move together. Their gift of time and support is a gift to all of us as we seek to follow the One who calls us to love.

Craig Kennet Miller
December 1996

here is no question that change is in the air. From corporate downsizing, to digital integration, to the remodeling of the family system, the world is seemingly on the brink of ruin or on the verge of utopia, depending on your point of view. Since the 1950's we have seen dramatic culture shifts that have moved us from the heyday of the modern, industrial age to the birthpangs of the postmodern, digital age. While all of us have felt the effects of these changes, no one has felt them more than those born from 1965 to 1981, the group I am calling the Postmodern Generation.

Many names have been postulated for this diverse group of young Americans. The Lost Generation, Generation X, Slackers, Survivors, the Gap Generation, and the MTV Generation are just a few that come to mind. But none of these terms comes to grips with the part this generation is playing as we enter a pivotal point in history. The term "postmodern" captures the mood and the reality of a generation caught between the modern age and the future yet to be born.

In the springs of 1993 and 1995 I initiated two national surveys of the Postmodern Generation. Using a network of contacts, high school students, college students, and teachers across the country, I probed the concerns of this generation. In some cases surveys were taken in high school classes by teachers, in others cases

Spring Break Survey

1993 & 1995 Combined

Breakdown of those surveyed (total: 600)

African American (black)... 9%	In High School 43%
Asian American 8	High School Graduate......8
Euro-American (white) 64	In College 39
Hispanic/Latino American ..12	College Graduate 6
Multiethnic 6	In Graduate School.......4
Native American 1	
American-born...........88	REGION OF COUNTRY (by Time Zones)
Foreign-born.............12	Pacific 39
	Mountain................12
Males...................48	Central..................32
Females.................52	Eastern..................17
AGE GROUPS	Conservative.............29
Born 1965-1970...........17	Moderate 52
(ages 23-28 in 1993, 25-30 in 1995)	Liberal 19
Born 1971-1976............50	
(ages 17-22 in 1993, 19-24 in 1995)	Atheist 5
Born 1977-1981...........33	Agnostic 6
(ages 12-16 in 1993, 14-18 in 1995)	Seeker 10
	Believer 79

youth surveyed people in malls. In one instance, a college group conducted surveys on the beach during spring break. Other college students set up tables on campus asking people to fill out the survey as they went by. In all instances those responsible for conducting the survey were instructed to take random samples of people they did not know.

Three hundred face-to-face surveys were taken each time, for a total of six hundred. Respondents were asked to fill out the surveys, seal them, and then return them to the persons taking the survey. The information was kept confidential and was not opened until it was added to the data base for this project. After having taken the survey, respondents were asked if they would like to make additional comments.

As you will see, results of the research consistently show results similar to other national surveys. What this survey includes that most others do not, especially phone surveys, are various quotes and comments that focus on the issues most important to this generation. The surveys are supplemented by conversations and interviews I have had with Postmoderns from around the country.

Of those surveyed, 64% were Euro-Americans (whites), 12% were Hispanic/Latino Americans, 9% were African Americans, 8% were Asian Americans, 6% were multiethnic, and 1% were Native Americans. Additionally 88% were born in the United States and 12% were born in other countries. The results listed include all racial categories unless otherwise noted. All results include both American-born and foreign-born Postmoderns as well. Immediately this speaks to the great diversity of this generation.

What emerges from the research is a picture that is somewhat different from the media hype of the goateed, grunge-impaired, hat-on-backward image of a young adult who seems to have no future. Instead of the stereotype we find a diverse group united by a single theme: "How do I make it in a world with no rules and no blueprint for the future?"

Rather than a generation who has given up, they are the generation who has had to endure increasing violence in their schools and communities, a loss of job security in the changing marketplace, the constant barrage of new computer-driven consumer devices from video games to the laptop computer, and the results of their parents' experimentation during the sexual revolution. Teenage pregnancy and suicide are not uncommon among their numbers. AIDS is a specter that clouds their desire to form new long-lasting relationships.

But theirs is a generation that wants more than mere survival. They are ready to have their say about the world we are now creating. They too have their American Dream. They too look to form new families. They too want a better future for themselves and their children.

In the following pages we will examine the nine culture-shifts that have molded the Postmodern Generation's view of the world. The first three culture-shifts—*from order to chaos, from the atom to the bit,* and *from one truth to many truths*—explain what it means to be postmodern. The next three culture-shifts—*from the war out there to the war right here, from the traditional family to the multifamily,* and *from the job to the task*—examine this generation's greatest fears and challenges in a world that seems increasingly frightening and unsettled. The next two culture-shifts—*from one way to diversity* and *from religion to spirituality*—look at their strengths and hopes for the future. The last culture-shift, *from the modern to the postmodern church*, looks at the church and its relationship to this generation.

Throughout the book you will find quotes from Postmoderns and results from the surveys. These tell a story within themselves. *(Note: Some names have been changed to protect the privacy of those individuals who participated in the surveys and the interviews.)* Where possible, results from other national surveys are referenced to add additional weight to the insights given.

I am indebted to all of those who contributed their voices to this book. As I wrote these pages I saw the faces of Postmoderns from around the country with whom I have talked. I remember the young woman at Harvard whose friend had just been murdered in a drive-by shooting, the thirty-year-old pastor from New Mexico whose mother was in her third marriage, the twenty-eight-year-old computer hacker who landed a job at a new Internet coffeehouse in Boston, the high school athlete from Texarkana whose greatest fear was getting caught in the middle of a gunfight between rival gangs, the fourteen-year-old girl from Arizona who had lived with a different relative each of the last four years because of her parents' divorce, the twenty-year-old unmarried father carrying his child in a mall in Alexandria, Virginia, and the twenty-nine-year-old veteran of the Gulf War whose

call to ministry compelled him to seek *shalom* in a world desperately needing peace. These faces are not part of a nameless group of *Xers*, but are real individuals whose voices all Americans, regardless of their generation, need to hear.

As I reflect on what I have learned, I realize that each generation has its own story to tell. As a Baby Boomer I have wrestled with whose voice needs to be heard in this book. My voice? Their parents' voice? The voice of older generations? No doubt all need to be heard in some way, but above all the voice that needs to be heard is that of the Postmodern Generation.

The postmodern story is one that in many ways is hard to hear because it tells us so much about where we as Americans are hurting. I do not believe you will get through this book without at least once feeling that the voice is hitting too close to home. The situation that many Postmoderns face is at a crisis point. Their issues are America's issues. To deny them is to give up the ability to listen and to heal.

Yet the Postmodern Generation is not content to gripe about their problems. Instead they bring to us a resilience of strength and character, an unapologetic realism and spirituality that we all need as we career into the 21st century. This book is as much their book as it is mine. Together we offer it to you as a way to understand the beliefs, hopes, and fears of a generation who is ready to take their place in history.

For Mike, Nancy, Nicole, Wes, and Amy:
May the future be yours.

From Order to Chaos

Sometime in the late 1960's the modern era died. We are not so certain of the exact time, but we do know why: The underlying belief system of the modern era had lost its credibility. Since the turn of the 20th century in 1901, the Western world had operated on the modern notion that through the application of scientific reasoning, humanity was guaranteed unlimited, unending progress. At first the advancements of the modern world were quite dramatic. The invention and eventual widespread use of electricity, the telephone, automobiles, and airplanes created a world in which anything seemed possible. People were able to communicate faster, were able to travel farther, and were able to create whole new industries like the automobile and the movie industries. These advancements seemed to prove the validity of the modern perspective, that through the rational use of the five senses—hearing, seeing, touching, tasting, and smelling—anything was possible.

But an unintended result of modern progress was the ability to kill people in greater numbers than ever before imagined. This began to happen as people came head to head with other cultures and perspectives. Two World Wars, countless genocides, and civil wars in countries throughout the world decimated huge populations of civilians caught in the cross fire of ideas and convictions backed up by progressive weapons like tanks, aircraft carriers, and, eventually, nuclear weapons.

While the modern era was successful in producing a wide variety of new technology, it has been unsuccessful in producing a better human being. No matter how technologically advanced people became, they still had to deal with the age-old human problems of hate, anger, jealousy, greed, and the quest for power. While science was able to make people better on the outside, it

---

Birth year events of Postmoderns: 1965-1981

1965-1967:
Civil Rights Movement
Women's Liberation Movement
Escalation of War in Vietnam

1968-1969:
Assassination of Martin Luther King, Jr.
Assassination of Senator Robert Kennedy
First Landing on the Moon
Woodstock

1970-1973:
Kent State Students Killed in Vietnam War Protest
Voting Age Lowered to Eighteen
Abortion Legalized
Supreme Court Orders Busing for Desegregation
Nixon Goes to China
Patricia Hearst Kidnapped

1974-1978:
OPEC and Oil Crises
Nixon Resigns
U.S. Pulls Out of Vietnam
Carter Elected President

1979-1981:
Iran Crisis
Reagan Elected President
Reagan Shot
Pope John Paul II Shot
Sandra Day O'Connor First Woman on the Supreme Court

proved unable to change what was on the inside. People still needed something to believe in, something that had lasting meaning, something that moved people from mere comfort to making a difference in the world for good.

By 1965 the promises of the modern era were falling short. After the assassination of President Kennedy in November of 1963, young American Baby Boomers began to question the beliefs and values of the older GI Generation who had lived through the Depression, was victorious in World War II, and who had enjoyed the postwar economic boom of the 1950's during which time the United States was the prime economic leader of the world. Born from 1908 to 1926, the GI Generation was the glue that held together the institutions of society.

In contrast, the younger Baby Boomers were raised with the specter of nuclear destruction. Born from 1946 to 1964 they came into a world that could be blown apart at any minute. Rather than enjoying the fruits of unending progress, Baby Boomers pushed against the norms of modern society in an attempt to find meaning.

From 1965 to 1981, Americans found themselves in the midst of a cultural revolution that pitted the older GI Generation against the younger Baby Boomers. This conflict brought to light many of the injustices that were buried under the surface of American society. The norms that seemed to govern life in the 1950's were questioned at every turn and many groups in society sought to change the nation so that they could have their place at the table.

Whereas Baby Boomers experienced the events of the late sixties and the seventies in their youth and young adults years, Postmoderns were born into them. Postmoderns were the ones caught in the middle of the many ideological wars and social changes that marked their birth years. As the country was experiencing profound doubt about itself, potential parents of Postmoderns questioned the advisability of raising children in an unstable world in which values and beliefs were undergoing remarkable cultural shifts.

One result of this questioning was a lower number of births between 1965 and 1981. Starting in 1965, births dipped below four million, breaking a ten-year run of over four million births that began in 1954. This decreased birth rate continued a downward trend that bottomed out in 1973 when the number of births hit a low of 3,136,965. Over the course of twenty years—from 1953 to 1973—the birthrate went from 25.1 to 14.8 per 1,000 people.

The drop in births can be partially attributed to two important factors. First, by 1965 the birth control pill had obtained a wide acceptance among women who, for the first time, were able to make choices about when to have children. Second, the legalization of abortion in 1973 meant that from 1973 to 1981, one fourth of the Postmodern Generation was aborted.[1] In 1972, the

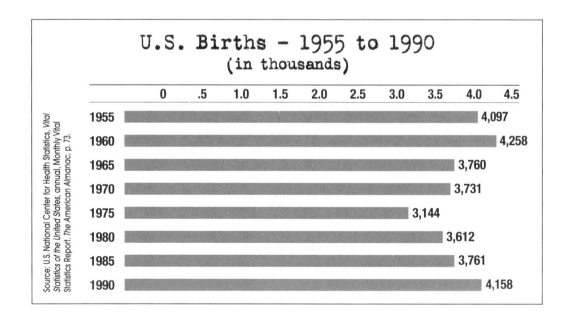

U.S. Births - 1955 to 1990
(in thousands)

Source: U.S. National Center for Health Statistics, *Vital Statistics of the United States*, annual, Monthly Vital Statistics Report. *The American Almanac*, p. 73.

Year	Births
1955	4,097
1960	4,258
1965	3,760
1970	3,731
1975	3,144
1980	3,612
1985	3,761
1990	4,158

first year abortion was legalized in all fifty states, 587,000 abortions were performed. By 1975, the number had doubled to 1,034,000. By 1981 it had tripled to 1,577,000.[2]

In contrast to the post-World War II baby boom, which ran from 1946 to 1964, after 1965 men and women decided to wait and see what was going to happen before they brought more children into the world. They had to get their lives together. Or they were starting their careers. Or one child was enough. Or they were getting a divorce.

The Post-1965 Revolution Has Us Living in a State of Chaos

The one word that best describes the post-1965 revolution is chaos. Gone are the quiet, orderly ways of the past. In the fifties and early sixties, there was a sense of order to life that everyone could pretty much agree with: You finished high school. You went into the military or to college. You got a job. You courted. You got married. You had children. You matured in your work and received promotions, getting a bigger paycheck in the bargain. You raised your kids until they left home to do as you did. They were to get a job and start a family. Then you retired.

Life was simple. Life was orderly. Regardless of economic status, there was this image of the American Dream that

offered people the hope of doing better than their parents had done. It is this dream that has brought immigrants from around the world to the shores of America throughout its history. While the dream was not true for all, in 1963 most Americans held these basic beliefs: Work hard and you will be rewarded. Be loyal to your family and to your employer or employees, and you will be treated fairly. Be faithful to your God and church and you will have a good life. Trust your government and give to your community. Join the PTA and give back to your kids. Life is good. Enjoy it.

But as the 21st century dawns, it is not so easy to plan optimistically for the future. Increasingly Americans live with a sense of chaos. They do not trust their institutions. Jobs are not secure. Violence is random and capricious. Elected officials are suspected and scorned. Heroes are fodder for tabloid stories about adultery, sex, and murder. People face a confusing set of choices and few solid answers. Society as a whole seems to have lost its moorings and no one is sure what the future will look like.

These events, attitudes, uncertainties, and sense of chaos, have not been lost on the generation of Postmoderns. In fact, they have been profoundly influenced by them. Witness, for example, the following interview:

As I was walking on the campus of Stanford University I came upon two students—Sean, age twenty-six, and Alex, age twenty-one. They helped me to identify a perspective on life shared by many in their generation.

Q: **Where do you see yourselves ten years from now?**

ALEX: I don't know. It's too hard to think about.

Q: **Well, what's your goal? What are you shooting for?**

SEAN: Money. Living comfortably. (He laughs and shrugs.) I guess what it comes down to is that I don't believe in the American Dream—I believe in the American Me.

Q: **So you don't believe in the American Dream?**

ALEX: I don't think too many people do anymore. The American Dream is a pretty hard thing to achieve these days.

Q: **So you don't see yourselves doing better than your parents?**

ALEX: That's not the point. They did their thing, now we have to do ours. The facts are this—nothing is really evolving and everything is recycling. In the seventies there was the back-to-fifties craze. In the eighties there was a back-to-sixties craze, and in the nineties there is a back-to-seventies craze, which was based on the back-to-fifties craze. Everything's just recycling.

SEAN: Faster, and faster, and faster. Soon it will be everything at the same time. Then there will be just nothing.

Sean and Alex are the members of a generation who were born into a world that seems to have reached some kind of end-point. This twilight time is a place of no return, where persons settle for the best they can do in the midst of the situation in which they find themselves. Instead of being a generation united by a single idea or dream, persons are free to pursue, at their own risk, their own dream—whether it betters society or not, whether it makes a difference or not, whether anyone else cares or not.

"We are basically just here and unheard."
Melissa, 17,
Tarkio, Missouri

Sean's and Alex's world is part of an emerging perspective known as postmodernism. It is a different way of thinking about and understanding the world in which we live. It is not as pessimistic or as negative as one might at first think. In many ways this view is more realistic than the scientific, rationalistic perspective of the modern era. It has a human dimension to it. It asks: How does progress affect people? It wonders who really benefits when a new invention is offered. It muses about whether it is time to step back from the future and to ask what this all means to us, today.

The postmodern perspective is one that questions every tenet of the modern era. It is a view of the world that is adroit at asking questions, while not necessarily providing the answers. "Why" is a big word in the postmodern vocabulary, because it forces people to look at the underlying reasons that govern a particular action. Results are not enough. Below the bottom line is another rule of measure: How does this affect people and their relationships to one another?

This attitude of constant questioning is one that rattles the sensibilities of older generations. To Baby Boomer bosses and parents, the why's of life are not so important when a production schedule needs to be met, or when bread needs to be put on the table. But Postmoderns do not see it in the same way. As ones who have been run over by the priorities of others, they want to know the underlying reasons for what people do. They are not content to do something just to get it

"According to my parents my generation is supposed to change the world. But how is that supposed to happen when we were taught by the generation who messed it up?"

Michelle, 17,
Nashville, Tennessee

done. They want to know what is in it for them. They want to know how much it is going to cost.

Postmoderns relentlessly question the underlying moral values, the assumptions, and the principles and world views, that drive the business industry, the technology, and the sociopolitical and religious structures of the world they have inherited. Needless to say, the Postmodern Generation's constant questioning of their rapidly changing world has given rise to attitudes, actions, and reactions on their part that have not always been understood or positively received by older generations.

Slackers?

One name that has been used to describe the Postmodern Generation is "slackers." The term is used to describe what appears to be the young dropouts who spend their time living in their parents' homes, idling their time away watching MTV, and flipping hamburgers in a McJob. Older generations, especially their parents, look at them and say, "Grow up."

But what appears to be slacking by some might in fact be a reasonable way to approach the future. They have watched their parents going for it all—careers, kids, and houses—all in an attempt to keep up with the Joneses. But they also see the price they have paid. Divorce. Stress. Anger. Escapism. A loss of purpose.

Kelsey, age twenty-five, of Burbank, California put it this way:

"I feel like members of my generation are causalities from the 1970's 'Me Generation'—divorce, serial monogamy, parents who used drugs, and so forth. We're the first of the 'Disposable Family' trend. I've seen it happen to too many close friends and family members."

In *Career Crash: The New Crisis—and Who Survives*, Barry Glassner points to the increasing number of Baby Boomers who find themselves crashing in their careers. The crash may come as the result of being fired from a corporation that is downsizing. For example, in 1993, five hundred thousand Boomer managers and professionals were out of work. Drake Bean Morin, the nation's largest outplacement firm, estimates that a typical forty-year-old white collar worker will change jobs two or three times before retirement.[3]

Even those Boomers who have escaped being fired question what they are doing. Many Boomers who gave up on families, the government, and society as a whole in the 1960's and 1970's focused on their careers as the ultimate accomplishment in life. Now, fifteen to twenty years into their careers, they find that their work has lost its meaning or there are so many people in their career field, or ahead of them at work, they see little room for advancement. So they quit to find something else that better meets their personal needs.

The contrast with previous generations is quite remarkable. The work life and expectations of those born before 1946 and those after are quite different. Those of the GI Generation and the Silent Generation, whether in blue-collar or white-collar work, had a sense that once

they got a job with a particular company they were set for life. They were on a career path. Those with union jobs had their pension and health benefits, and those in management had the corner office to look forward to.

But as Boomers reached their thirties and forties (the first Boomer hit fifty years of age on January 1, 1996) many found themselves in companies that were downsizing and they lost their jobs. Those who

"For my great-grandparents, change was slow. They invented the car. For my grandparents, change was a little faster. They invented the television. For my parents, change has been rapid. They invented the computer. But for my generation, change is constant. We don't have time to think about it. Who knows what we are going to invent? We are operating without a manual and we do not know where we are going. It is scary."

Greg, 19,
Newberg, Oregon

kept their jobs questioned their purpose.

Even younger members of the Silent Generation who were born from 1927-1945, have found themselves at the age of fifty-five being offered early retirement while they are still in their prime earning years. Many are lifelong employees whose loyalty makes little difference to the corporation whose main focus is the bottom line. As a sign of the times one TV commercial advertises job placement and training for those who have "retired" in their fifties.

But what about the Postmoderns? What can they expect in a career? Their career prospects are far from the upward movement of the GI Generation and the Silent Generation, for there are no set rules, guidelines, or expectations. Some say members of this generation will have six or seven careers, let alone jobs, in their lifetime.

Maybe those who are taking a wait-and-see approach have it right—maybe they don't. Talk to members of this generation and you will hear some say their greatest hope for financial security lies in winning the lottery.

Anger or Hope?

For Postmoderns the world has shifted from a well-ordered society in which you can have a dependable future to one that is chaotic and filled with too many choices, many of which are unpalatable. Many are angry at previous generations, and wonder if they are being left to pay the bill for the changes that are going on. Bryan, age eighteen, of Lake Forest, California, put it this way:

"There is a lot of junk we have to clean up from the Baby Boom Generation and generations before them. They've saddled us with debt, hate, drugs, pollution, sexism, and ignorance."

Bryan is not alone. Listen to the airwaves and you will hear people of all generations railing against the govern-

ment, complaining about education, fed up over illegal immigration, and aghast at the increase and nature of crime. Across the country there is a general welling up of discontent over the rapid changes that are affecting us all. People are fearful that change equals the destruction of our American way of life. Jobs, religion, family, government, and education are all affected by the accelerating pace of change in our world. For Postmoderns, the question that faces them is who will survive and who won't.

But not all Postmoderns are so negative. In the Los Angeles region people have been upset over the declining prices of houses. One Baby Boomer couple has seen the value of their house drop from $240,000 to $190,000 in the past five years. If they were to sell their house they would lose $50,000. For them the housing market is a disaster. But for those who have never been able to afford a house, it is a blessing. Dan, age twenty-nine, of Riverside, California, remarked, "For me the declining prices of houses is great. I might be able to actually buy one."

Change also equals opportunity for those who can take advantage of the need for computer savvy, quick learners who can lead those who are less technologically gifted. As we head into the next century, computer companies and media-related businesses will spur the economy. Postmoderns who have been surrounded by computers and electronic devices like Nintendo and VCRs find themselves in demand as the economy shifts to the digital age. Change and chaos are not necessarily bad for all.

The question facing Postmoderns and the American culture as a whole is what kind of change are we heading into and can we see a light at the end of the tunnel? Are we doomed to failure and despair or are we on the edge of a new day filled with hope and opportunity?

An Anxious Society

In a thought-provoking article entitled "America's Anxiety Attack",[4] Ronald Brownstein points to four trends that are converging in American life as we head into the 21st century. The first trend is the restructuring of the economy that is caused by the combination of the advancement of information-age technology and the emergence of a global economy. The second is the global migration of workers from poorer to richer countries. This brings into the United States more than a million new workers each year, made up of both legal and illegal immigrants. The third is the erosion of the traditional family. The number of single-parent families has tripled in the past thirty years. The fourth is the end of the cold war, which has obliterated the foundation of our foreign policy and is causing the United States to ask questions about how it will relate to other nations in the future. Brownstein comments:

These trends intertwine and reinforce each other. The Cold War's end has meant a shrinking of the defense industries, intensifying the pressure on the economy. Workers facing declining living standards have resisted immigration. The technological advances that have diminished the demand for low-skill labor have combined with the enormous rise in the number of children born to unwed mothers to drastically worsen conditions in poor urban neighborhoods.[5]

These trends, interwoven together, have affected all of us in one way or another. Those who feel most harshly the brunt of these trends are the ones who have been born into the midst of change.

"Human nature and society have totally corrupted the minds of our generation. Political corruption, media, and pushover parents were the preconditions to this corruption of society. What we need is complete and unquestioned change. Our society makes me sick."

Derrick, 16,
Houston, Texas

It's not just that things are changing. The problem is that change in the past took time, it had a pace of its own. Today change is accelerating at an ever increasing speed that either forces us to try to stay with it or puts us on the sidelines to wait to see what is going to happen.

How Simple Actions Result in Change

Murray Gell-Mann, winner of the Nobel Prize in physics, states that those of us who are alive today live in a complex adaptive system that is the result of four billion or so years of biological evolution on earth and a hundred thousand years of cultural evolution in the human species. One of the rules governing physics and the understanding of complex adaptive systems is that each system at any one time includes contributions from its entire history. As these systems develop they become more complex, leading to a new system that allows it to operate in its new context.[6]

One of the factors that moves a complex system to generate a new way to deal with objective reality is chaos. Gell-Mann states that, rather than the popularized expression relating to any real or apparent complexity or uncertainty, chaos theory is really quite simple to understand. In the past physicists believed that by understanding the laws of motion and the configuration of the universe at any one moment in time a person could predict the complete history of the universe from that moment on. But today's practitioners of physics see it differently. Even when you have all the facts and figures right, "there remains the widespread phenomenon of chaos, in which the outcome of a dynamical process is so sensitive to initial conditions that a miniscule change in the situation at the beginning of the process results in a large difference at the end."[7]

How does this relate to American society as it heads into the 21st century? Gell-Mann's insights give us two important clues about ourselves and the state in which we find ourselves today. First, our society and culture have been passed down to us from generation to generation. Each generation adapts what has been given to it, so it can live successfully in the current situation. Everything we have—from the food we eat and the clothes we wear, from the music we hear to our beliefs about God—has been passed down to us.

When we come into the world we do not simply show up and create a whole new society by ourselves. Instead we are inculturated by the society in which we find ourselves. Our language, dress, and customs are taught to us by the family system in which we live. The family system in turn adapts itself to the wider cultural and societal norms in which it finds itself. In a real sense we are the end-product of all the generations that have lived before. As we face the future, we as a society continue to add on to or tear down what has been given to us from the past.

When someone put two wheels on an axle and put a box on it, that person created a cart—a new means by which to transport things. By putting two sets of wheels together and connecting them with a plank of wood, another person created a wagon. Now they could carry more things. Years later someone put horses in front of the cart, and they suddenly had a stagecoach. As a result they could travel longer distances at a faster speed. Later someone got rid of the horses and added an engine, creating the automobile, which would go at faster speeds and longer distances. Each inventor took what had been given and added to it, making the system more complex while at the same time making it more productive and simpler to use.

Gell-Mann says that something else happens as well—the second clue to what affects us today. This process of adapting is not so orderly. In fact, more often than not it is the unexpected result that causes the most change. The resulting chaos is something that surprises us. Chaos means that even the smallest change at the beginning of an experiment can cause great variations at the end. Thus while the invention of the automobile made it easier for people to move around, no one anticipated that the pollution resulting from the burning of gasoline would dam-

How would you describe the Baby Boom Generation?

Getting all they can before it's too late	24%
Hypocritical	24
Greedy	23
Motivated by deeply felt beliefs and values	15
Self-righteous	12
Matured by experience and ready to lead	9
Giving and caring	7

Spring Break Surveys 1993 & 1995; 600 Responses; more than one answer accepted.

age the health of large populations.

Chaos dictates that when we introduce what seems to be miniscule change into an adaptive complex system, widespread variations ensue that lead to even greater changes down the line. Each introduction of a new idea adds complexity and change to the whole society.

Even the innovation of that most important youth hangout, the mall, has introduced significant changes into our society. Years ago people would go downtown to shop in family-owned businesses. Each business had its own clientele, and the family business run by Mom and Pop thrived.

But with the arrival of the mall things changed. Instead of going downtown to shop or going to the neighborhood shoe store, you went to the mall, where you had a variety of choices. Malls were built in the suburbs, where large developers could buy enough land for their huge complexes. In order to afford to be in business in the mall you had to buy into a franchise, enabling you to sell products in the competitive environment of the mall. Mom and Pop stores could no longer compete because they were not able to offer the variety of options that a mall gives the customer. They were also hurt because they were not able to buy their merchandise at the wholesale prices the franchise was able to receive.

As a result many downtown businesses closed up, hurting the economy of the city. Many people who owned their own businesses got swallowed up by the franchises. As jobs left the city, unemployment increased, and poverty increased along with the crime rate and drug problem. All because someone thought up the idea of the mall, and individual consumers decided to shop there.

Why Are Things So Chaotic?

What makes this so complex is that as technology increases the diversity of choices available to individuals, it creates more chaos down the line for the whole of society. Think for a moment of the inventions that have affected everyday life since 1980. CDs, microwave ovens, cellular phones, personal computers, fax machines, laser printers, satellite dishes for television, and the like have changed our lives tremendously.

Look at what VCRs have done to our way of living. Today more money is made on the release of a movie on videotape than in its theatrical release. Instead of watching TV programs according to the networks schedule, you can choose to see what you want to see when you want to see it. If you are not home, you can tape a program for viewing at your leisure. Instead of going out on a date to see a movie, you stay in and watch a video. The accessibility of videos has caused many families to develop their own rating system. Either the movie is "we've got to see it now" in the movie theater or it's a "we can wait" to see it on video.

The Hinge Generation

What makes this of utmost importance to all of us is that the Postmodern Generation finds itself in a unique place in our society. On a flight from Chicago to Nashville, I had a conversation with Blake, age twenty-nine, which sheds light on what role Postmoderns find themselves in.

> BLAKE: My generation finds itself in a tricky position.

Q: What do you mean?

> BLAKE: We are caught between the large number of older Baby Boomers and the even larger number of younger Millennials who are following us.

Q: That's right. Your generation is smaller in numbers than the generations who are in front of you and behind you.

BLAKE: In many ways that's a plus. As Boomers move on to retirement, our skills will be in demand. But I wonder what the next generation is going to do? What kinds of jobs will they need?

Q: So you're saying the lower numbers of your generation is a plus?

BLAKE: And a minus. It might be easy to overlook us but to do so would be a mistake. We are the generation that is at the hinge, and how we move will affect both those who are older than us and those who are younger. The choices we make will either make things better or worse. It is an important position to be in.

Blake's point is well taken. As a generation, Postmoderns find themselves in a unique position. Although lower in numbers, they act as a hinge between the older Boomers and the younger Millennials born from 1982 to 1999. As a pivot point their role is vital. Their choices and decisions, insights and ideas, will be key to the kind of future to which all Americans are moving.

As the rapid changes now buffeting our society bring us to a point of hyperchaos, where it's not simply one thing but a multiplicity of variations that affect us, Postmoderns are the ones asking the nec-

Generica

A term used to describe same, look-alike stores and franchises that dot the American landscape. Is there a place where there is not a McDonalds? Even malls have the same stores. After entering a mall you could be in anyplace U.S.A. The only difference is the weather when you go outside.

Source: "Jargon Watch," *Wired*, August 1995, p. 50.

essary questions that will clarify what we are moving toward. The culture-shifts propelling us into the future not only challenge our beliefs about God, the church, government, education, and the family but also they increasingly call us to question everything that comes our way.

"I think people should stop looking at teenagers as trouble. They should remember we are the future!"

Carlos, 16,
National City, California

Nothing is sacred. Everything and everyone is fair game.

Maybe at this point in history that is the best place to be. Rather than assuming we are all on the same page, now is a time to push the buttons of all our assumptions before we go into directions that imperil our ability to have a sustainable lifestyle in a world with an exploding population and an unclear sense of direction. As the Postmodern Generation asks "Why?" American society as a whole has an opportunity to wrestle with the answers. Rather than fearing the chaos, chaos provides us with the chance to test the waters, to look for a new vision of hope, and to seek in new directions for the answers that will guide us into the 21st century.

From the Atom to the Bit

We are riding the crest of a wave of technological change as dramatic as any in history. This movement will change virtually every aspect of our lives. If you think this is an overstatement, think again. In 1980 the average American was content to have a color television, a stereo, and a radio. The daily routine of life included scanning the TV guide to see what was on that night. The guide listed anywhere from three to ten channels, depending on where you lived in the country. Your entertainment and information was dependent on the number of local stations that broadcast signals to the receiver in your television. Choice meant deciding whether to watch ABC, NBC, CBS, PBS, or reruns on other independent channels. If this didn't interest you, you could turn on the record player and listen to the latest album.

The only other information-rich device in your home was the telephone. This enabled you to talk to people on telephone headsets—which could go only as far as the wire that extended from the headset to the telephone box.

The hottest gadget on the market was the microwave oven, which enabled you to cook your food in a matter of seconds. Stores still sold a wide variety of foods wrapped in foil, which you could warm up in the oven. (Anybody hungry for a three-piece chicken dinner—the one with mashed potatoes that has to be licked off the aluminum foil that you peel off the top?) It wasn't until 1987 that microwave ovens sales reached levels high enough to make it economically viable to produce the wide range of microwave meals now available.

But in 1980 something new began to happen—something called the personal computer. I remember my first—a Commodore 64—which cost me about one thousand dollars. The computer was so named because its microprocessor had 64,000 bytes of RAM. The computer had to be hooked up to a television. Information

1976 - Apple Computer founded

1977 - Apple II personal computer produced

1980 - CNN broadcasts twenty-four-hour news on cable TV

1981 - MTV broadcasts music videos on cable TV

1982 - Fax machines introduced in limited quantities

1982 - *USA Today* becomes nation's first newspaper to be downloaded from one site and printed in a variety of locations

1983 - First cellular phone network set up in Chicago

1984 - Macintosh computer produced

was saved by using a cassette tape player that came with the computer. The printer outputted its information in a dot matrix form barely readable by today's standards.

Sixteen years later I wrote this paragraph using a laptop computer with a color screen, eight megabytes of RAM (equal to 8,388,608 bytes, or 67,108,864 bits), a 3½ inch disk drive, and a hard drive on which to save information. As I inputed the words, my view was through the window of an airplane some thirty thousand feet above the Arizona desert as I traveled from Nashville to Los Angeles. Within arm's reach was a telephone that enabled me to call anyone in the world within reach of a fixed or cellular phone.

I have one friend in Seattle who always seems to be in his car when I call him. If I were to call him from a plane he could be traveling sixty miles an hour on the freeway while talking to me on his cellular phone, while I fly at who-knows-what speed over the face of the earth. His voice would be as clear as if we were in the same room. This, in essence, is the beginning of the radical change we are undergoing.

Sometime in the next few years all our communication devices will converge. The computer and the television, the CD and the radio, the telephone and the cable system—these will be one and the same thing. Instead of scanning the TV guide to find what you want to watch, you will be able to tell your agent (a software program) to select the program you wish to watch at that particular time. Your agent will be able to scan news services to custom design your evening news, and you will output it on your color printer to produce your own tailor-made newspaper to carry with you.

Instead of television shows scheduled by the day, shows will be scheduled by the week. If you want to watch *ER*, *Star Trek Voyager*, and *X-Files* on the same evening, you will download the programs to your entertainment unit. The only programs that will need to be broadcast in real time will be sports programs such as basketball or football games. In your own home you will be the program director.

Just off Harvard Square in Cambridge, Massachusetts, is a computer-based coffee house called Cybersmith, the motto of which is "Building Community through Technology." I had the opportunity to meet Carl S. Rosendorf, president of the company, during the debut of a new CD-ROM-based software game. As I talked with him I began to get a wider picture of just how all this new technology is coming together.

Q: Who are you trying to reach at the store?

ROSENDORF: Originally I was joking when I said we were interested in getting people between the ages of eighteen and eighty-eight. Quite frankly, now I tell people we are getting them from the ages of two to ninety-two. It's a tremendous cross-section of people, from the youngest kids in elementary school to many senior citizens. The average is probably twenty-five to thirty-four, but there is tremendous interest across all socioeconomic groups and age brackets.

Q: Your vision statement is "Building Community through Technology." What are you trying to say with that?

ROSENDORF: We are bringing people together in an environment that is supportive of the technology while interactively allowing them to learn and enjoy themselves at the same time. As we have more Cybersmith locations, they will be networked so people in Boston's Cybersmith can talk via the Internet or through other video conferenc-

ing technologies. People will be able to play games and learn together regardless of their location. We are not limited by geography with the network we hope to create.

Q: Which one of these technologies excites you the most?

ROSENDORF: They are all so exciting and they all offer so many types of benefits. For example, the World Wide Web. The information that is available through the Internet is phenomenal. The ability to click a button to visit museums in Paris, schools in London, and libraries in California—it's just tremendous volumes of information. That is fascinating and educational. We have many people here who actually look for jobs anywhere in the country via the Internet. It's a tremendous resource. On the other hand, if you're here to enjoy yourself, there's virtual reality. It's a 360-degree experience where people can really get into whatever game or whatever program they happen to be using. The CD-ROM multimedia offers a different experience. It's the video, the sound, the text, the action, bright colors, and feature titles that change on a monthly basis. People can try out the latest CD-ROM titles.

Q: What do you think is the next generation of virtual reality?

ROSENDORF: Virtual reality is going to continue to evolve, and it's going to play a significant role in the whole educational process, enabling people to learn, literally—virtually—through the use of this equipment and technology. Of course, it happens in the military right now, where pilots sit down in a cockpit and go through the rigors of flight activation experience. It's happening in medicine, where medical students learn how to operate using virtual reality. Soon car mechanics are going to learn it the same way, and on and on.

Q: **What is your vision of where this business is going to go?**

ROSENDORF: We are very excited about it. To say any more than that would be premature. We have obviously captured the imagination of many people. We have been featured in news magazines from coast to coast, newspapers, and TV. People enjoy themselves here. It's rare nowadays to be able to go into a store and learn and have a good time and leave with a smile. That happens at Cybersmith.

Rosendorf gives us just a hint of the changes that lie ahead of us. But before we get too far ahead of the game, let's look at how we got here—how current technology is affecting society, and what opportunities and dangers lie ahead.

What Is a Bit?

As an atom is to matter, so a bit is to information. But unlike an atom, a bit has no color, weight, or size. As Nicholas Negroponte, founding director of the Media Lab at MIT says, "It is the smallest atomic element in the DNA of information. It is a state of being: on or off, true or false, up or down, black or white."[1]

Bits are rendered as a 1 or a 0. One means on. Zero means off. A string of eight bits is used to make a code for specific letters and numbers. Programmers use a code of numbers that uses only 1's and 0's. Think of it this way. In spy movies, the spy will make up a code to fool the enemy in case her message is intercepted. So she might write a message that says: 66, 67, 68. Her contact, who receives her message, knows the code. He transcribes the numbers to letters: 66 = A, 67 = B, 68 = C, and so forth.

Computer designers took the same idea; only instead of using numbers they used a series of bits (1's and 0's) to make a code for the alphabet. So, in the binary code, the letter A is represented by 01000001, and B is represented by 01000010. The binary code uses eight bits to make up a number or letter. This is called a byte. To produce one character takes eight bits, which make up one byte. If your computer has 1 megabyte of RAM you can process 1,048,576 bytes, or characters, at a time.

Why all the detail? Because of this: What makes computers work is the microprocessor at the heart of the computer. Perhaps you have seen the Intel commercial that takes the viewer into the heart of a computer and shows you a chip. It's this chip that is transforming the world as we know it.

In 1965, Gordon Moore—who would later cofound Intel—predicted that the capacity of a computer chip would double every year. He proved to be almost correct—he was off by only six months. Since 1965 the capacity of the computer chip has doubled every eighteen months. This capability to double will continue into the foreseeable future.[2] Thus you discover that when you buy a computer today, its chip will be outdated in two years in terms of its capacity.

Negroponte explains exponential growth this way:

> Did you ever know the childhood conundrum of working for a penny a day for a month, but doubling your salary each day? If you started this wonderful pay scheme on New Year's Day, you would be earning more than $10 million per day on the last day of January. This is the part most people remember. What we do not realize is that, using the same scheme, we would earn only about $1.3 million if January were three days shorter (i.e., February). Put another way, your cumulative income for that whole month of February would be roughly $2.6 million, instead of the $21 million you earned in total during January. When an effect is exponential, those last three days mean a lot! We are approaching those last three days in the spread of computing and digital telecommunications.[3]

Today these little computer chips are in almost every electronic device, from the coffee machine to the car, from the digital wrist watch to the VCR. Probably the only electronic device that doesn't have one is your television. The TV is just a machine that receives information, but does nothing to compute it. As these chips increase in their capacity they are able to do more and more things. Each increase in capacity enables the computer to process information faster and to handle more information at the same time.

As a result we are no longer simply retrieving information as it is given to us.

Instead the coming digital revolution will be far more profound. We will control and shape information in the ways we want to use it. The information highway will be a pipeline of bits and bytes that will bring us information from every nook and cranny of the world.

What Do You Mean by Digital Age?

What makes the coming digital age even more powerful than the information age is that the transcription of all sorts of media—print, audio, and visual—into bits and bytes enables their transmission into your home or office through the same line. By digitizing all forms of media they can be mixed and matched at will.

In the future you may want to do a report on the greenhouse effect. Through your computerized information unit you will be able to scan other reports on the topic. As you download the information you can decide if you want to read the material, watch it on video, hear it, or interact with all three at the same time.

What makes this unique is that through a combination of information-rich technologies you can explore a world of information that has been put into a single format. The digital age means that all media can be transmitted to you in the same way, through one conduit. Instead of going to a music store to find the latest Garth Brooks album, you will have it downloaded through the fiberoptic line that comes into your home. There you will store it on a floppy disk or CD-ROM that you can take with you. That's why telephone and cable companies are competing with each other or merging so they can be the source in your home for the coming digital age. AT&T and Viacom want to be your information provider, because whoever is there first will stay in business.

A conversation with Jake, age nineteen, a computer science major at Harvard, reveals how some Postmoderns are using the new technology.

Q: What's exciting about the Internet?

JAKE: The way you can communicate with people. For example, my roommate is a Christian, just like me. He regularly goes onto the suicide line to counsel people.

Q: Suicide line?

JAKE: Sure. There's all kinds of stuff there. Anyway, this girl typed in a message that she was thinking of killing herself, and he witnessed to her about his faith in Jesus. Then he invited her to go onto the Jesus line.

Q: So what happened?

JAKE: She listened some more to him and she gave her life to Christ. Right there on-line. It was great! But that isn't all. About a week later he e-mailed her and she sent an e-mail back. Since becoming a Christian she has received about one hundred e-mails welcoming her into the faith.

Q: That's really something!

JAKE: What's really great is that she is part of a community that is worldwide. Her messages came from people all over. In the past there is no way she could have met all these people, but now she has a hundred new friends. She's not alone anymore.

Some Ruminations on the Digital Age

Before we become overwhelmed or enraptured by the possibilities of the blossoming of the digital age we should focus on the impact of the overabundance of information that surrounds us like an electronic atmosphere. Many people like to talk about being on the "cutting edge," but the cutting edge can cut more than one way.

The Postmodern Generation is the first generation to be raised in the information-rich age of television. Although Postmoderns rate the media dead last as an influence on their core values, media today look very different than even twenty years ago. It is not uncommon for a high school-aged Postmodern to have a cable TV and a VCR in his or her own bedroom. Electronic media for Postmoderns are omnipresent.

While Baby Boomers can lay claim to having been the first generation to see itself come on-line, virtually every Postmodern was raised in an electronically media-enriched environment. It wasn't until 1962 that 90% of American households owned a television. In 1964 only 3.1% of American households owned a color television. But by 1978 78% of American households owned a color set.

Global communications as we know them didn't begin until the first birth year of the Postmoderns. In 1965 one of the biggest steps forward in global communication took place when the first commercial satellite was propelled into orbit. Called the "Early Bird," it relayed telephone messages and television programs between Europe and the United States.[4]

Today global information technology is so common that virtually any person can own a satellite dish. On a recent trip to Louisiana I witnessed a remarkable sight. Driving next to a bayou, I saw a

From whom have you learned your core values?

Family	70%
Church	13
Friends	10
School	5
Media	2

Spring Break Surveys 1993 & 1995; 600 Responses.

whole crop of satellite dishes. These sat in front of ramshackle houses that teetered on top of cinder blocks that kept the houses safe from floods.

A colleague of mine, Tim Bias, tells a similar story. Recently when going into the Appalachian Mountains in Kentucky, Tim had to travel up a hollow on a dirt road for twenty miles. When he arrived at his destination he was greeted by the sight of a satellite dish in front of the house.

The newest version of the satellite, an eighteen-inch dish marketed by RCA and Sony, hit sales of one million units in its first year. Consumers are able to beam into their homes hundreds of channels, and can tailor their programming depending on whether they want to watch movies, news, or sports. A person on the west coast can watch *The Tonight Show* at 7:30 p.m. instead of having to stay up until 11:30 p.m. You can receive two versions of the Disney Channel, or you can see all the baseball games of your favorite team even if the team is based in another state.

Technological availability is not just regulated to the United States. I recently saw a videotape from a new United Methodist church in Cambodia. Using a hand-held video camera a traveler from the United States was able to record a worship service in which over two hundred Cambodians were baptized. The videotape recorded the choir as it sang to music that was played through a large boom box, complete with drums, guitars, and keyboard. So much for listening to native Cambodian music!

Information at What Price?

As exciting as it is to be on the cutting edge of the technological revolution, it must be said that there is a price to pay for all this availability. A trip to the local video store is instructive. As I walk through the aisles of videos I come upon a display of Disney's *Pochahontas*, placed in the new releases section. A number of copies are placed on the top three racks of the section. As I look below this children's movie, what I see at the eye level of children disturbs me. Here I find, each with its own captivating cover (usually a woman either disrobing or in some kind of distress): *Raging Angel, Seduce Me, Red Shoe Diaries, Another Woman's Lipstick, Auto Erotica,*

Return of the Living Dead 3, Replicator: Cloned to Kill, Radio Land Murders, and *Red Scorpion 2.*

What disturbs me might not make a dent in the consciousness of the eighteen-year-old who probably stocked the shelves. Mary Pipher, in her captivating and discerning bestseller, *Reviving Ophelia: Saving the Selves of Adolescent Girls,* says that these images are part of the "wallpaper" of young people's lives. In reference to one of her teenage clients she comments, "Sexist lyrics and the marketing of products with young women's naked bodies are part of the wallpaper of her life."[5]

In the video store the scenes depicting sexuality and violence are part of the environment. In a forest you have trees and flowers, in a video store you have graphic depictions of hate, anger, and sex, mixed in with children's cartoons. It's all one and the same.

Pipher's insights about what adorns the background of young people's lives is important to consider. What other wallpaper surrounds us—material so omnipresent and ordinary that we have ceased to see it? Take for instance a trip to the supermarket checkstand. Invariably there will be a collection of tabloid magazines with their blatant pictures and words, each trying to outdo the rest. Favorite movie stars and celebrities are displayed in embarrassing poses, with headlines to match. Every week during the O. J. Simpson trial there was one picture after another of the deceased Nicole Brown Simpson, pictured either in bathing suits or in close ups of her badly bruised face and body. Once while going down the gauntlet of tabloids with my then four-year-old daughter, I turned the covers around so she would not see them. One day she remarked, "O. J. won't get me. He's too far away." For her, the wallpaper had begun to speak.

Mass Media News

In the 1995 Spring Break Survey, Postmoderns were asked which two events had most impacted their lives. The top four answers prove interesting, as they illustrate the place media and technology played in each event. At the top of the list, at 27%, was Rodney King and the L.A. Riots.

The Rodney King beating was a media event from the beginning because of the nature of the evidence. How many times do you think you have seen the video tape of that beating? Once? Twice? Twenty times? One hundred? Through video tape you were able to see the same event played over and over again. After innocent verdicts were read by the jury in Simi Valley you were shown live pictures of the crowd outside the courthouse, the beating of innocent bystanders on the streets, and the burning of buildings across Los Angeles. It was a national feeding frenzy.

Second, at 26.3%, was the Gulf War, the first real time war. Who can forget

What two events have had the most impact on your life?

Rodney King and the L.A. riots	27.0%
The Gulf War	26.3
Magic Johnson getting HIV	21.7
The O. J. Simpson trial	18.3
The fall of the Berlin Wall	15.0
The birth of MTV	13.0
The Challenger disaster	12.3
The election of the Republican Congress	11.7
The breakup of Russia	10.0
The suicide of Kurt Cobain	4.7
The Anita Hill/Clarence Thomas Hearings	3.3
Watergate	0.7

Spring Break Survey 1995; 300 Responses.

reporters in Saudi Arabia reporting live as scud missiles came their way? You felt as if you were there. Or what about getting a live feed of the first wave of the bombing of Baghdad as CNN gave you a front row seat?

Third, at 21.7%, was Magic Johnson's televised announcement that he had HIV. Suddenly one of the most popular sports and media stars was on the endangered list. Now no one was safe.

Fourth, at 18.3%, was the O. J. Simpson trial and the events that surrounded it. Although the murder wasn't video-taped, everything that followed it was broadcast—from the freeway chase to the final day of the trial. Almost 150 million Americans were tuned in to the courtroom scene on their television sets while the verdict was read.[6] And this was not enough. After the trial, books had to be sold and interviews given. Even O. J. came up with his own video to defend

"Serving in the military, and experiencing the Gulf War, puts a whole new perspective on war and its costs. I feel war should be avoided at all costs."

Rick, 25,
Houston, Texas

himself and to pay his legal fees.

Each of these events would have had a much different impact if it hadn't been for the amount of information made available to the public. What is different today is that one story or event becomes magnified when placed in the media spotlight. On any given day the newspaper, the radio, the local TV newscast, the national nightly newscast, the prime time television news show, and the various independent tabloid news-based shows, can give their own versions and spin on a given story. If this is not enough you can let Letterman or Leno cap your day with jokes about the before-mentioned event. Much of Jay Leno's rise in popularity during the O. J. Simpson trial had to do with "the Dancing Itos" and his spoofs of the lawyers involved.

The Celebrity Culture

The information-rich, hyper media world brings another result: people become instant celebrities in the most unusual ways. Take the talk show phenomenon that swept into television land in the early 1990's. Started earlier by Donahue and Oprah, by the mid-nineties a whole troup of people had their own shows. The stars of the shows are "real" people with a wide variety of problems. Rather than highlight positive role models, most of the shows go out of their way to cater to the bizarre and unusual.

What fuels these shows are the twentysomethings who populate them, or teens who are having problems with their parents. In one show, *True Confessions,* a young man came on stage to confess his secret to his fiancée. He told her that he had been having sex with her best friend. In a moment of "reconciliation" the host asked if she forgave him. The young woman was visibly upset and muttered that she would think about it. The host asked, "What would you say to your friend?" The young woman stared back at him. He responded, "You're not sure? Well here is your chance." Whereupon her girlfriend emerged and sat down so that the young man was in the middle. He now looked quite pleased with himself. When he got home he would be a hero. Not only had he had more than one partner, he had been featured on television with both of them fighting over him.

The main problem with the celebrity culture is that it needs its victims to survive. In the glare of the media, a hero can become a villain or a victim in an instant.

Athletes who are adored become bums to be busted. Just the mention of Tanya Harding and Nancy Kerrigan puts us in mind of the ridiculous maneuvers of the media as they covered the story of Tanya's planned assault on Nancy before an ice skating competition.

Politicians are caught in the same limelight and many qualified people choose not to run because the pressure is so intense. Even worse, people who engage in strictly criminal behavior can become stars in their own right. Did we really need three network prime time movies of the Amy Fisher story? She was the teenage girl in New Jersey who shot her "lover's" wife.

The Danger of Information Without Boundaries

The availability of information does not necessarily make us smarter or wiser. Neil Postman, in his book *Technopoly: The Surrender of Culture to Technology,* contends that what we believe to be an advance is in actuality a danger. In the past, technology provided tools that enhanced the culture. In the Roman Empire such technologies as roads, bridges, aqueducts, tunnels, and sewers enhanced the lifestyle but left unchanged the beliefs of the society. Postman says, "The name 'tool using culture' derives from the relationship in a given culture between tools and the belief system or ideology. The tools are not intruders. They are integrated into the culture in

A conversation with the local manager at Blockbuster Video

Q: How many videos do you have in the store?
A: We have about 10,000 titles.
Q: So how many movies is that?
A: I don't know. We just keep track of the titles. For example we might have twenty copies of a new release that is popular.
Q: How many do you rent in a week?
A: We rent about 500 a day. So that makes it about 3,500 a week.

Reflection: If we multiply 3,500 by 52, we get 182,000 rentals a year. Multiply this by $3.00 per rental, and this gives us $546,000 gross income per year. Not bad for an information-based business!

ways that do not pose significant contradictions to its world-view."[7]

Postman contends that we have moved from a society in which technology is a tool to be used for the betterment of people, to a society in which technological progress is the goal of society. In other words, the means have become the ends. Postman writes:

> The milieu in which Technopoly flourishes is one in which the tie between information and human purpose has been severed, i.e., information appears indiscriminately, directed at no one in particular, in enormous volume and at high speeds, and disconnected from theory, meaning, or purpose. . . . We are a culture consuming itself with information, and many of us do not even wonder how to

control the process. We proceed under the assumption that information is our friend, believing that cultures may suffer grievously from a lack of information, which of course, they do. It is only now beginning to be understood that cultures may also suffer grievously from the information glut, information without meaning, information without control mechanisms.[8]

It is this overload of information, indiscriminate and without boundaries, that so affects the lives of the plugged-in. We live in an world so information-rich that silence is almost an unknown commodity. Alarm clocks wake us up with music, shower radios play while we bathe, TV fills us in during breakfast, talk radio accompanies us to work, computers glare at us from cluttered desks, on our belts or in our purses we carry beepers or cellular phones, during exercise we listen to our favorite artists on our walkmans, and at night we fall asleep to TV. For entertainment we go to movie theaters with THX sound systems so we can be even more plugged-in. We watch endless hours of television, rent videos, play video games, and listen to music. Rare are the times we are unplugged or disconnected. And when we are, we don't know what to do with ourselves. Maybe we will regress and read a book or talk to a living human being.

Sex and the Digital Age

It is not just the amount of information that is confusing, it is also the content of this information that proves to be perplexing. Take for instance the most American of topics—sex. Postmoderns have grown up in a world in which anything goes. Mary Pipher, who as a professional psychologist in Lincoln, Nebraska, has counseled countless young women, points to the barrage of mixed messages relating to sex. She reports:

Our culture has changed from one in which it was hard to get information about sexuality, to one in which it's impossible to escape information about sexuality. Inhibition has quit the scene. In the 1950s a married couple on TV had to be shown sleeping in twin beds because a double bed was too suggestive. Now anything—incest, menstruation, crotch itch, or vaginal odors—can be discussed on TV. Television shows invite couples to sell their most private moments for a dishwasher. The plot for romance movies is different. In the fifties people met, argued, fell in love, then kissed. By the seventies, people met, argued, fell in love, and then had sex. In the nineties people meet, have sex, argue, and then, maybe, fall in love. Hollywood lovers don't discuss birth control, past sexual encounters, or how a sexual experience will affect the involved parties; they just do it. The Hollywood model of sexual behavior couldn't be more harmful and misleading if it were trying to be.[9]

For young people, sexuality is a minefield of mixed messages and expectations. To each encounter they bring their own beliefs, the attitude of their parents, their religious values, the code of conduct of their peers, the images of Hollywood, and the expectations of their partner. The following true story illustrates how confusing this can become.

The youth director at one church presented to his youth group the "Love Can Wait" program started by the Southern Baptists. Youth who get involved make a pledge to wait until they are married before they have sex. The youth were captivated by the message, and thirty-five made the pledge. But when they returned home from the meeting, guess who got upset? The parents were angry, claiming that the youth director was making unreasonable demands on their children.

Imagine being one of those youth. Here she makes a pledge that would seem to be healthy, hopeful, and in line with the beliefs of her faith. But her parents think that this is too great a burden to place on her, that it is too high a standard for her to uphold. So what is the alternative? Does this mean that her parents want her to have sex now so she can experience it? If not now, when? If she doesn't need to wait, why not do it now? How many partners should she have before she gets married? One? Two? Ten? How many is enough in order to know when it is right? Is it important to have a relationship with a person before having sex? Should she have sex on the first date or on the second? Should she even worry about marriage at all?

Or what about birth control? Will her parents allow her to use it? Will they talk to her about the best kind to use? And if she gets pregnant during the experimental stage should she have an abortion or have the baby? If she gets pregnant will her parents be happy or angry? When there is no expected code of behavior everyone becomes his or her own chaperone, priest, and policeman wrapped into one.

A conversation with a group of youth from a church in Florida is instructive at this point.

Q: You have brought up another issue-sex among people your age. Do you think AIDS has any effect on people? Are they waiting to have sex until they get married?

ALLEN (sixteen): People definitely aren't waiting until they are married. I would say the average age for someone to lose their virginity is about fifteen.

Q: Why do you think this is?

ALLEN: Curiosity. Peer pressure—especially among the guys. I don't think people are taught early enough the consequences, like STDs or emotional consequences. They're just taught how to do it and how to be careful, but I don't think they are taught what will happen if you're not careful enough.

SHARON (fifteen): People think that it can't happen to somebody our age.

Q: You mean something like AIDS?

Those reporting having lost their virginity

	Males	Females
Ages 12-16	29%	33%
Ages 17-22	54	46
Ages 23-28	72	75

Spring Break Survey 1993; 300 Responses.

SHARON: That worries me all the time. My friends don't think there is any chance that it will happen to them.

Q: So do they practice "safe sex"?

ALLEN: Most of my friends do, but I have talked with some kids in other schools, and they feel like it's no big deal. People aren't using condoms.

JEFF (sixteen): I think one of the reasons for all of this sex at an early age is because they teach us too much. They really try to put it in your head not to have sex, and what that does is drive people to want to find out what it is like and what they are missing. The reason you drink is not because it tastes good, but because you are not allowed.

Q: Does all of this impact you or doesn't it?

ALLEN: It has an impact for me. I think that you can basically tell— the kids that usually get drunk all the time are the ones that aren't involved in religious life, and the kids that are more promiscuous are not usually involved in religious life. The kids that go to church or that are involved in a youth group maybe drink a little or have sex with one person.

For these youth and their friends, information does not equal abstaining or waiting. When reporting the experience of losing their virginity, women and men shared different views concerning the experience. Notice the contrast between Tony and Ashley concerning their experiences.

Tony, age twenty-one, Tempe, Arizona:

"Losing my virginity was the experience that has most affected me. I felt like a man, and knew I would enjoy that for the rest of my life."

Ashley, age twenty-one, Atlanta, Georgia:

"Losing my virginity affected my life a lot. The feeling of doing something so final and wrong in the eyes of those you love is devastating. Also, the kind of permanent partner (marriage) I am looking for probably will not approve of that part of my past."

Thirty years after the sexual revolution, men and women seem to still have different goals when it comes to sex. For men it is to become a man, to prove their masculinity. For women it is an expression of love and part of building relationship. In the fifties there was an agreed-upon code of behavior: Boys wanted it, and girls said no. Today there is no code of behavior. The girl who says no is almost alone in a world in which the media, friends, and her peers say yes.

In the 1993 Spring Break Survey 33% of girls ages 12–16 said they had lost their virginity. Forty-six percent of women ages 17–22 said they had had sex for the first time, and 75% of those ages 23–28 said they had.

Other studies show higher figures. A study in the 1996 May edition of *Seventeen* magazine reported that 50% of boys and 50% of girls ages 15–16 said they have had sex. Eighty-six percent of the girls and 68% of the boys said they wish they had waited.[10]

Pipher reports that over 50% of girls ages 15–19 have lost their virginity, which is double the rates of 1970. Even more troubling, five times as many fifteen-year-olds are sexually active in the nineties as were during the seventies, and many sexually active girls have had multiple partners.[11]

The Great Educator

U.S. News & World Report conducted a survey in which it looked at sex on television. It found that those who produce material for television, and those who

Why do most girls have sex?

	Boys	Girls
Girls want to	38%	23%
Boyfriends want them to	53	73
Don't know	9	5

DeDe Lahman, "How Are You Dealing?" *Seventeen*, May 1996, p. 148.

watch, have widely differing views on its content and impact on society. When asked if TV contributes to the problem of teen pregnancy, 76% of Americans said yes, while only 37% of Hollywood leaders agreed. When asked if TV contributes to the decline of family values, 81% of Americans said yes, while 46% of Hollywood leaders agreed.

The report also included a survey of content on TV. They studied the content of the four major networks—ABC, CBS, FOX, and NBC—to monitor material. Of the fifty-eight shows monitored, almost half contained sexual acts or references to sex. The article referenced another study that showed that a sexual act or reference to sex occurs every four minutes on prime time.

A report by the Media Research Center found that premarital sex was portrayed eight to one over sex between husband and wife. The consequences of sex, however, are rarely treated. Only one in eighty-five references to sex on TV refers to birth control, abortion, or sexually transmitted diseases.[12]

Of even more concern, the time period that formerly was considered the "family hour" is now littered with shows filled with sex and violence. At the beginning of the 1995–1996 television season, shows such as *Roseanne*, *Cybil*, and *Friends*, were moved up in the schedule to the 8:00 p.m. Eastern time slot. These shows all deal with adult themes. In the Central time zone, this translates to 7:00 p.m. for a large part of the country. In April of 1996 FOX added to its family hour *Kindred: The Embraced,* which portrays a family of vampires. These are just a few examples of the new programming priority among the networks.

It doesn't stop here. Recently I had a conversation with some of my colleagues about whether or not "hell" was still a swear word. We decided it had to do with context. I know if I had used it out of context as a child my father would not have approved. (Soap never tastes good!) But if TV-land is any indicator of what is appropriate, just about every word considered indecent twenty years ago has now found a home. Even MTV's ongoing cartoon about two sarcastic youth, Beavis and his friend, would not have been aired. TV producers now go out of their way to come up with offbeat themes that focus on sex.

If the National Institute for Mental Health is correct, then what we watch does have a profound effect on us. They recently stated that television is an important sex educator in our society. If it is not such an influence, why would advertisers spend billions of dollars a year on television and other media to get us to buy their products?

A Cold-hearted Decision

Take the introduction of ice beer a couple of years ago. Before ice beer, lite beers were the rage. But with new production techniques, beer companies promoted ice beer with an advertising campaign aimed at young adults. It described it as a purer form of beer. Commercial after commercial showed young men and women discovering the delights of ice. Jeff, a twenty-nine-year-old beer distributor, tells us the difference between ice beer and the other beers you find in the grocery store.

Q: **What is the difference between ice beer, regular beer, and lite beer?**

JEFF: Ice beer has a higher alcohol content. Its content is 5.5, while the others are 3.8.

Q: **Who drinks the ice beer?**

JEFF: It's primarily for those twenty-one to twenty-eight years old.

Q: **Why are they the main customers?**

JEFF: Because the younger group likes to get more bang for their buck.

Q: **How long has ice beer been on the market?**

JEFF: About two years.

Q: **Any other trends you see?**

JEFF: A lot of young people are going to microbreweries and imports. Like ice beer, micros tend to have a higher alcohol content. Plus people like to have many different choices. What also sells is beers with weird names. You'll be seeing more like that in the future.

Ice beer is not only purer—it also gets you drunk twice as fast. A couple of years ago some entrepreneurs decided that what young adults needed was a beer higher in alcohol. They embarked on an advertising campaign to introduce this wonderful new product, portraying young adults enjoying the good life with ice beer in hand. So successful were they that now virtually all beer companies produce their own versions of ice beer. All at a time when report after report states that consumption of alcohol and alcoholism is increasing among the young.

Cross-marketing Is the Goal

As the mass media transitions from the information age to the digital age, marketers find the best way to get the attention of the customer is through cross-marketing. The marketing of the movie *Pocahontas* by Disney is a case in point. After the success of their animated features, *The Little Mermaid, Beauty and the Beast, Aladdin,* and *The Lion King,* Disney turned up the notch with its marketing of *Pocahontas.* People were first introduced to *Pocahontas* by a trailer on

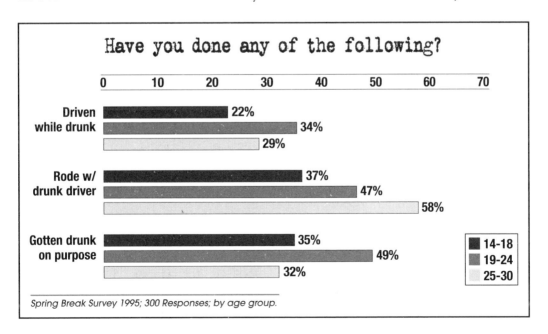

Have you done any of the following?

	Driven while drunk	Rode w/ drunk driver	Gotten drunk on purpose
14-18	22%	37%	35%
19-24	34%	47%	49%
25-30	29%	58%	32%

Spring Break Survey 1995; 300 Responses; by age group.

the video of the hit movie, *The Lion King*. When they produced *The Lion King* video, Disney added a scene from their new movie which featured the song "The Colors of the Wind."

Next kids met *Pocahontas* in the toy store, as more than fifty products pro-

> *"The death of my cousin has affected me the most. It impacted me because of the way he died. He was killed in a drunk driving accident. Because of what happened I know that I will never drink."*
>
> Lissa, 19,
> Glendora, California

duced by toy manufacturer Mattel hit the stores. Once the movie came out, kids could get *Pocahontas* prizes in boxes of Cheerios, or get one of the more than fifty million *Pocahontas* figurines distributed with kids' meals at Burger King. They could buy athletic shoes and moccasins featuring *Pocahontas* characters at Payless Shoe Source. They could buy *Pocahontas* books, clothes, or CDs at stores around the nation. They could see scenes from the movie played at Disney Stores in malls around the country. Or, if they had cable, during Disney's free preview week just before the movie came out they could see the half-hour program, *The Making of Pocahontas*.

Over $125 million was spent on cross-marketing this movie about the Indian maiden who saved the life of Joseph Smith. As a result every child in America knew about the movie, and just about every one went to see it at least once. Even though the movie was based on historical accounts, it was widely panned by historians for turning the relationship between Smith and Pocahontas into some kind of Romeo and Juliet. In this instance the Disney version turns fact into fiction. The goal of the movie was not to inform children about history as much as it was to turn an historical event into "edutainment." Truth and untruth are mixed together to give us a good story.

Although not as successful as some of their earlier animated features, the marketing of *Pocahontas* gave Disney an almost sure bet that it would generate profits from a number of sources. So successful has Disney been in marketing their products that when they became owners of a new national league hockey team in Anaheim, California, the team was named "The Mighty Ducks" after one of their earlier movies about a children's hockey team. Their logo is the best selling logo in the NHL. And the name of the arena is "The Pond."

In the digital age a book is no longer a book and a movie is no longer a movie. In an interview, Steve Brallier, an agent for The William Morris Agency, told me that "a book or a script is not seen as something that is used once. People are looking for stories. One story can become a book, a video, a video game, a TV show, a song, a music video, a computer game, a toy, and a spot on the Internet. Once a company produces something in one format, it looks for ways to maximize the impact by marketing it in as many different venues and as many different products as it can."

The Postmodern Experience Is Interactive

Karen Ritchie, author of *Marketing to Generation X*, points out that the generation raised in the digital age is one who sees technology as a way to stay in touch.

> *Any product or service that feeds the need of young, single Xers to stay in touch and in control at the same time will do well. The future is bright for carphones, beepers and pagers, answering machines, computer mails, and fax machines. These are necessities—not luxuries—to Generation X.*[13]

This need to stay in touch translates into another aspect of media that Postmoderns expect. For Postmoderns, the medium needs to be interactive. While the common picture of a Baby Boomer male is one of the couch potato who randomly surfs cable TV, the picture of the Postmodern is of one who exerts some control and choice over the medium itself.

At the forefront of this change was the video game. In the late seventies and early eighties teenagers mobbed video arcades to play the newest video games. Using the latest computer technology and graphics, games such as *Pac Man* and *Joust* pitted players against the computer. Early versions of video game machines hooked up to television sets. Parents complained of all the beep-beeps emanating from the games, and wondered if this was permanently damaging their kids' brains. Today the video game industry has grown up. Video games now make over $5.3 billion a year just in the United States. Globally, game revenues exceed $10 billion each year. Americans now spend $400 million more per year on video games than they do on going to the movies.[14]

What makes the games so powerful is that they require the active participation of the user. Unlike the passive watching of a television show, video games challenge the user to interact in order to move the character from one level of difficulty to the next.

When people think of media they normally think of movies, television, and newspapers. These were the media of the modern era. Modern media were static. The consumer waited until the medium was "pushed" and "received." You had no control except when deciding whether to watch or listen.

In the postmodern age, people "pull" in the information they wish to receive, and tailor it to their own needs. Postmodern media are made up of interactive media such as video games, personal computers, pagers, videos, cellular phones, e-mail, fax machines, and the Internet. The individual watches or creates or interacts according to his or her own timetable and needs. The consumer can videotape a television show, watch it at his own convenience, and fast forward through the commercials. Consumers now manipulate the information to suit their own desires.

Unlike the mass market of the modern era, the media of the postmodern era are individualized. How will this work in the future? If people are choosing what they want for their own individualized purposes, how will entertainment companies deliver the goods? How will they know what people want? Won't this create chaos?

Don't Forget the Book

Think for a moment of the most basic unit of media that we have, the book. Invented some five hundred years ago, the book is an easily carried media device that delivers to the user information that is highly individualized. In a given year over fifty thousand titles are published in the United States. While we might hear of twelve million copies of a bestseller, it is much more common for a publisher to print five to ten thousand copies of a given title. Most titles are aimed at a very specific group of readers. In the book market, publishers can make a living by providing for the needs of individuals.[15]

The future of media is much more like the production of a book than the offering of ongoing shows on broadcast television. As the modern era mass market disintegrates, the postmodern perspective will center on narrowcasting—focusing on a specific group of end users in order to meet their needs. Nothing summarizes the postmodern worldview better than the Internet and the World Wide Web.

Surfing the Net

The newest medium on the block is the Internet. Created more than twenty years ago as a Defense Department experiment to enable communication in the case of a nuclear attack, the Internet is a collection of computers and providers that allows users the freedom to browse through cyberspace. In 1984, the experiment escaped from the Pentagon and has been doubling in size every year. By the spring of 1995 thirty to forty million people in more than 160 countries had at least e-mail access.[16] In August of 1995, Nielson Media Research determined that some twenty-four million Americans had accessed the Internet in the previous three months.[17]

What makes the Internet remarkable is its grass roots lineage. Anyone with a computer and a modem can log-on through a variety of providers such as *America Online*, *CompuServe*, and *Prodigy*. Most colleges and universities have their own provider services that allow professors and students free access to the Internet. As a result college students are the ones most likely to have experienced the Internet firsthand.

In *Road Warriors*, Daniel Burstein and David Kline describe the interactivity of the Internet:

> Since Gutenberg, printed media (and later radio and television) descended to us on high. We sat and read (or listened and watched). Now, however, we can interact from the ground up: we can search and access planet-wide libraries of media according to our individual level of interest and sophistication. We can manipulate, store, clip, skip, fast-forward, reverse, send, order, buy, connect, annotate, question, or criticize media as we choose and in the way we choose. . . . Internet and other interactive networks allow us to shape the media to a far greater degree than ever before and to use them in accordance with our own individual vision.[18]

The Internet allows users to enter chat rooms to talk about the most recent showing of *Melrose Place* or to look up recent articles listed by major magazines such as *Atlantic Monthly* and *Time*. It allows you to interact with famous authors and celebrities in forums where you can ask a question of the speaker and at the same time talk with a row of listeners. It gives you the ability to send a letter by e-mail to twenty or two hundred of your closest friends, with just one click of your mouse.

Users can also check out the newest serials—on-line shows that are updated daily or weekly, depending on the program. The first interactive soap opera, *The Spot*, was launched from Los Angeles

Yahoo!

America's newest multimillionaires are Jerry Yang and David Filo, both age twenty-seven. In 1994, after graduating in computer science from Stanford University, they created *Yahoo!*—a web site that lists over 200,000 web sites under 20,000 categories. Because of its usability almost 800,000 people a day use *Yahoo!* to find almost anything in the known universe. When their company went public early in 1996, the value of their stock shares went from zero to 800 million dollars in one day.

Source: Steve G. Steinberg, "Seek and Ye Shall Find (Maybe)," *Wired*, May 1996, p. 110.

on June 7, 1995. Styled as an "episodic web site," the site chronicles the lives of five Southern California twentysomethings. The program allows users to communicate with the characters via e-mail, and to suggest plot lines for the show. By November 1995 *The Spot* averaged 62,000 hits (a hit is when someone logs onto a web site) and received 300 e-mails per day from over thirty countries.[19]

Most information about the Internet focuses on its appeal as an entertainment and educational medium. But the greatest impact it will have in the future concerns the way we do business. Steve, age thirty-one, from Signal Hill, California, is making the transition from being an engineer at TRW to becoming part owner of a service that helps businesses advertise on the Internet. While we have heard of large companies such as Pepsi and IBM opening their own web sites, Steve works with engineering companies and manufacturers of items such as airplane parts.

Q: **What do you think about the future of the Internet?**

STEVE: It's going to blow everyone's mind. The overwhelming knowledge available is amazing.

Q: **Do you think it will be a viable medium for business?**

STEVE: Within five years every business will want to be there. Within seven, if you're not, you're out of business.

Q: **Why is that?**

STEVE: When computers first came out, older engineers were using sliderules. Some still are, but they are completely out of it. For my generation the Internet is our computer, our chance to get ahead.

Q: **So you're saying the Bill Gates and Steven Jobs of your generation are the ones who will make the Internet work?**

STEVE: Exactly. People my age are more willing to look at it and try it out. Older people are still trying to figure out how to run a computer. Students below thirty have used the Internet at college, so they are used to it already. It doesn't intimidate them.

Q: **What has your company been able to do?**

STEVE: I'll give you one example. We recently worked with a company based in Arizona and New York that manufactures parts for airplanes. After setting them up on the World Wide Web they received orders for parts from Canada and other parts of the world. Their investment has already paid off and they are now becoming an international provider of parts.

Q: **How do people contact them?**

STEVE: Say for instance someone needs an eight-sided lugnut of a certain size. The person types in "lugnut" on their search engine, and they will find a list of companies that make them. If they are looking for a lugnut for an airplane, they come to the company we have set up on-line. Instead of sending out catalogues, people come directly to the company on the Internet.

Q: **So instead of wide band advertising such as you see on TV, the Internet helps people find specific items they need, when they need them.**

STEVE: You got it. What makes the Internet work is that it is tailored to the needs of the individual.

As the Internet develops and grows it will soon rival the attention other media receive, and will become an essential part of doing business. Different than television, books, and movies, its appeal is the user's ability to interact within the environment of cyberspace, the place in which you meet when you talk to someone on the phone, or the place where e-mail messages wait to be read. It's a place made up of bits of information created out of the genius of the human mind. It is a place that is in the process of connecting the world in a worldwide web of dialogue and sharing, information and ideas.

Clueless?

Postmoderns have grown up in a world in which electronic media are the ocean in which they swim. In the classic Postmodern movie *Clueless*, Alicia Silverstone plays a fifteen-year-old who tries to find her way in the rough and tumble world of Beverly Hills. Hers is a world filled with media and technology. In one scene she uses a computer to choose her clothes for the day. When her beeper goes off in class, all of the students check to see if they are being paged. Her friends are constantly talking on cellular phones as they walk down the halls of the school. The technology of this culture has brought the world of information to her hand.

But even with all her technological sophistication and popularity as the girl who has it all, she still feels lonely. She

At twenty-one, Jewel Kilcher is a Postmodern success story. Reared on an eight-hundred-acre Alaskan homestead where she had no running water and no indoor plumbing, she is celebrating the release of her debut record, *Pieces of You*. Her musical career started when she realized she had to do something or die. She was living out of her van in San Diego when one day she picked up her guitar and went looking for work. After being discovered in a coffee house she went on to play Dorothy in a production of the *Wizard of Oz* at the Lincoln Center in New York City. The production was broadcast on TNT. Of her philosophy Kilcher says, "I'm not an obvious radio hit, much less an obvious alternative MTV thing. My music is really honest and it touches people's hearts, and that's all I care about. I don't have any big delusions of fame or fortune. I just want to eat everyday, doing what I love. And as long as I eat everyday—and sing—I'm okay. And I know that hard wood grows slowly."

"Jewel," *POLLSTAR Magazine*, March 25, 1996, p. 5.

still wonders if anyone will like her. She still feels clueless as to what is most important in life. She discovers that access to information, that being "in the know," is no substitute for real relationships.

This is the dilemma we all face in a world that is becoming digital. As the world becomes smaller, as information becomes even more available, as we double our capacity to manipulate bits and bytes, does our world become a better place? In many ways the Postmodern Generation will be the ones who find out the end result of this grand human experiment. Older generations may have created the technology, but Postmoderns are the ones who live in the midst of what has been created. Their challenge will be to bring meaning to the glut of information that surrounds us. Information and technology without a code of behavior brings society to the brink of breakdown. As the 21st century dawns, the generation who programmed VCRs and, as kids, solved puzzles on Nintendos, will face the greatest challenge of all—to make some kind of sense out of a world awash in information while at the same time wondering what its future is going to be.

From One Truth to Many Truths

s a card-carrying channel surfer I invite you to join me on an excursion of cable TV to see what each channel promotes as truth.

NBC - Singles are good.

HBO - Swearing is good for the soul.

FOX - Sex and the supernatural are cool.

TNN - (Country Music) Boys and girls still need each other.

MTV - The world is messed up— let's party.

AMC - (American Movie Classics) The good old days were better.

CNN - Without the news you lose.

SciFi - Something is out there.

ESPN - Hit a ball, get rich.

PSYCHIC FRIENDS - The future is in your karma.

QVC - If you want it, we've got it.

TV TALK SHOWS - We love you even if you're weird.

These are just some of the messages you can get during a day of television.

This does not include the messages a person receives from commercials, each of which has its own "truth." For example, without a Barbie a girl will never be a girl. Without a Bud you can't have fun. If you have a headache, pop a pill. Don't work, play the lottery. Want a babe, buy a new car. Want a hunk, eat Special K. And on and on it goes.

This endless stream of mixed messages, many of which are opposites, brings one to a point of information overload. Add other media such as radios, CDs, videotapes, multimedia computers, and video games, and you wonder when persons are allowed to think for themselves. With so many messages you have to wonder what filter a person uses to decide what is of value and what is worthless. In an electronic age where a computer artist can make anything look as he or she wants it to look, the question of what is real comes to mind.

Almost immediately, George Lucas gives notice that we have abandoned conventional film making and entered the realm of Digital Hollywood.

"This is not your father's editing session," he jokes. And it's not. The changes Lucas keeps suggesting—and there are lots of them—seem outlandishly complicated and, since much of the shoot was done on location, hugely expensive. A beautiful panorama of Prague unfolds on one of the monitors. There's no real clue as to what time of day it is.

"Sunrise?" asks Lucas tentatively, sizing up the shot.

"You want a sun in there?" the editor answers cheerfully. "That's easy—we have some great suns."

Is Seeing Believing?

Take for instance the common-place concept of a photograph. Since its inception in the nineteenth century it has been assumed that a photo is an accurate visual record of an actual place and time. A photograph of a Civil War soldier is assumed to be a "true" picture because it is a visual record of the soldier's facial expression and manner of dress. When the shutter opened and imprinted his image on the photographic film it made an unalterable historical visual record to be passed down from generation to generation.

Even with photographic wizardry, the well-trained eye—equipped with a magnifying glass or microscope—could still figure out if a picture had been spliced with another to give a false image of what was actually photographed. Until now. Through the use of digital electronics a photograph can be scanned into a computer, adjusted, and changed however the user wants, and outputted as a seamless entity. The changes are virtually impossible to find. Movie makers take this one step further by placing actors in digitally designed backdrops. Thus dinosaurs come alive in *Jurassic Park,* and Arnold Schwarzenegger is chased by a computer-designed enemy who melts into pools of metal, then comes back to life in the blockbuster hit *Terminator 2.* The digital director's goal is photorealism—to create a movie in which there is no appearance of cheating. It gives a seamless vision of a new reality—created out of the imagination of the movie director and assisted by the maverick magic of the computer.[1]

Parents as Filters of Information

Contrast the information stream a child receives today with the amount of information a child received a hundred years ago. Place that child on a farm where 90% of the population lived, and ask yourself from whom he or she received information. The main source and conduit of information was parents. The only information children received came from the immediate community. Church and school supplemented the knowledge of the parent. The only other outside frame of reference came from books. The only books available were those provided by the parent, school, or church. Parents and adults were respected because they were the ones who controlled access to information about the world. They were in authority because they possessed more knowledge than the child. The child adopted the parents' world-view largely because it was the only world-view available. Your choice was to believe as your parents did or to rebel against their beliefs. In both cases you accepted the basic assumptions of the community concerning what is true and false. Your decision was whether you wanted to follow the norms or not.

In the past the parent served as the filter of all outside information that came to the child. The parent acted as a buffer between the world at large and the child. Parents and the immediate community decided when children should know certain kinds of information as they were raised into adulthood. Sex, violence, smoking, drugs, and drinking were the prerogative of adults. Knowledge of these behaviors came when the young person was deemed ready to learn about the dangers and opportunities of the adult world.

Today's young people have no barriers—no filter except themselves. In the PG-13 world of children and youth, sex, violence, smoking, drugs, drinking, and all the varieties thereof are readily apparent. Only the most controlling parent can filter out the adult world that is vividly exposed on the wide variety of media. Even something as mundane as a cartoon can be tampered with to provide messages beyond the parents' scope. A movie commercial inserted in the middle of a children's program can offer fifteen seconds of gunshots, murder, and death. Even more challenging to the authority of parents is that in many instances they know as little as the child about some subjects. Not only

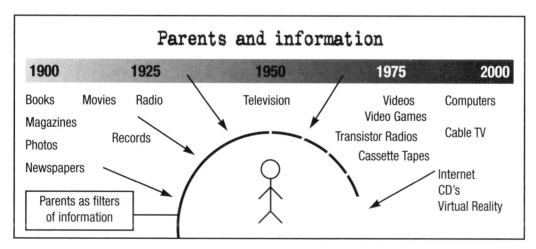

Parents and information

| 1900 | 1925 | 1950 | 1975 | 2000 |

Books   Movies   Radio   Television   Videos   Computers
                                                      Video Games
Magazines   Cable TV
                     Records   Transistor Radios
Photos   Cassette Tapes

Newspapers

Parents as filters
of information

Internet
CD's
Virtual Reality

are they no longer the source of information, but they too are its devotees.

Premoderns Lived in a Different Cultural Context

This point becomes even clearer when we contrast today's situation with the premodern world. In isolated tribes, villages, and early city-states, most people lived within the context of a single cultural package. As a result there was no such thing as coming into contact with another group of people with a different worldview. The individual lived within one cultural context that included language, belief, religion, social norms, and political structure. In any urban environment today, you can come into contact with numerous world-views in a single hour.

Walter Truett Anderson, editor of *The Truth About the Truth: De-confusing and Re-constructing the Postmodern World*, notes that the long march out of premodernity was accompanied by a series of culture shocks, as humanity discovered there was more than one worldview or perspective on life. Throughout history people have tried to deal with this dilemma in various ways. Conquerors killed people who thought the wrong way. Religious groups tried to convert people to their way of believing. Philosophers tried to create a system of understanding that would include all the different world-views.[2]

In contrast to the premodern era,

moderns lived in a time of battles between various belief-systems. The great religions had their distinct doctrines, science clung to reason, and political systems came into conflict. World War II was a contest between political and religious belief-systems. It consumed the lives of over fourteen million soldiers and over thirteen million civilians, not counting the millions killed in China and parts of eastern Asia. It was punctuated by the ultimate technological achievement—the atom bomb—which killed 140,000 in one shot. So great were the differences between the adversaries, it took fifty years for Japan and Germany to apologize for starting that war.

From 1945 to 1989 another kind of war, an ideological war, was waged between the democracies of the West and the communists of the East. The Berlin Wall, which divided East and West Germany in Berlin, was the symbol of this division. When it came tumbling down in 1989 suddenly there was no "other" to fight. The Cold War did not end in a bang, it ended in an eruption of discontent that had eaten away at the inside of the communist block. In the West another kind of cancer has been eating away—a lack of trust in the institutions of society, and the question of what kind of future we are moving toward. Anderson puts this dilemma into historical perspective:

I'd sum it all up this way: People in premodern, traditional societies had an experience of universality but no concept

Are You Postmodern?

Take the following test to see if you are modern or postmodern.

1. If you know more about *Gilligan's Island* than Einstein's theory of relativity give yourself 10 points. ....

2. If you'd rather watch *ER* than *Murder She Wrote*, give yourself 10 points. ....

3. If you believe that values are "whatever works for you," give yourself 10 points. ....

4. If you'd rather have ten options than one when purchasing a product (TV, car, dishwasher) give yourself 10 points. ....

5. If you think that African history, Asian history, and Native American history are as important as Western European/ American history give yourself 10 points. ....

6. If you have to experience it before you believe something is true, give yourself 10 points. ....

7. If you are plugged in to electronic media (radio, TV, VCR, CD, computer) 75% of the time you are awake, give yourself 10 points. ....

8. If you have surfed the Net, give yourself 10 points. ....

9. If you are more interested in spirituality than in religion, give yourself 10 points. ....

10. If you can watch TV, listen to radio, and read, all at the same time, give yourself 10 points. ....

TOTAL

Results: **0 - 10:** Cave Man/Cave Woman; **20 - 40:** Thoroughly Modern Millie or Milton; **50 - 70:** Homo Nervosa; **80 - 90:** Plugged In; **100:** Postmodern Mutant

Craig Kennet Miller, *Postmoderns: The Beliefs, Hopes, and Fears of Young Americans (1965 –1981)* (Nashville: Discipleship Resources, 1996).

Are You Postmodern?

1. If you know more about *Gilligan's Island* than Einstein's theory of relativity give yourself 10 points.

For the Postmodern, meaning is found in the messages seen in popular culture rather than through scientific inquiry. Scientific inquiry always leads to new "truths" as one study updates or overturns another. Popular culture is immortalized through reruns that reinforce one's own life view. "There's no place like home" is much more powerful to the individual than knowing how many elements make up oxygen.

2. If you'd rather watch *ER* than *Murder She Wrote* give yourself 10 points.

In the early 1980's *Hill Street Blues* introduced a new nonlinear format that wove three or four story lines into one show. *MTV* took it one step further by introducing the rock video that communicates through a series of discordant images flashing before your eyes to the beat of the music. *ER* builds on this format by bombarding the viewer with a series of images imbedded in the multiple story line. *Murder She Wrote* follows a plot that builds on one clue leading to the next. It uses linear thinking. The Postmodern relishes the opportunity to make connections between dissimilar objects and ideas. The Modern wants things to build on each other, one step at a time.

3. If you believe that values are "whatever works for you," give yourself 10 points.

The modern person believes that there is one set of values to which all people should adhere. These values might be listed in the Ten Commandments or in the Constitution of the United States. Society must have order and rules to which all agree in order to function. The Postmodern sees rules as being good for the rule giver but not for the one who has to follow them. Each person has the right to create his or her own value system by which to live.

4. If you'd rather have ten options than one when purchasing a product (TV, car, dishwasher) give yourself 10 points.

The epitome of the modern era was the Model-T Ford. Everyone could be happy with the same model. The Postmodern wants options by which he or she can personalize a car to meet his or her needs. Choice and personalization is everything.

5. If you think that African history, Asian history, and Native American history are as important as Western European/American history give yourself 10 points.

The Postmodern is multicultural. All the wisdom and knowledge of the world, gleaned from all cultures, places, and time, is available to the curious mind. No one culture is superior to another. Each has contributed to the development of the human race.

6. If you have to experience it before you believe something is true, give yourself 10 points.

The modern person builds his or her life on logic. Spock, in *Star Trek* personifies the modern pursuit of truth. It must be rational to be true. Data, in *Star Trek: The Next Generation,* personifies the Postmodern who sees the discovery of emotions and human experience as being paramount. Postmoderns must experience something in the soul before they believe it.

7. If you are plugged in to electronic media (radio, TV, VCR, CD, computer) 75% of the time you are awake, give yourself 10 points.

The Postmodern is connected to the world through a wide variety of electronic communication devices never seen before in history. A constant stream of information, both positive and negative, keeps the Postmodern plugged in to the beat of humanity. The modern era had the radio and then the TV; the Postmodern added everything from personal computers to fax machines to the eighteen-inch satellite dish.

8. If you have surfed the Net, give yourself 10 points.

The Internet is the ultimate postmodern tool. It enables a person to send electronic mail in the flash of a second to any place in the world. With a few points and clicks you can access the latest articles from *Time* magazine, see the latest displays from the Smithsonian Museum, or download the newest electronic pinup of Lois Lane from *Lois and Clark.* The world of information is at a person's fingertips.

9. If you are more interested in spirituality than in religion, give yourself 10 points.

The Postmodern has no desire to be churched, to be boxed in by one set of rules or rituals. He or she does not want life to be set in stone. Spirituality for Postmoderns is tied to deeply held beliefs that give meaning to life lived in the midst of adversity. God is not to be pursued like a commodity. God is the one who gives depth and meaning to life.

10. If you can watch TV, listen to radio, and read, all at the same time, give yourself 10 points.

The modern person can only process one stream of information at a time. Postmoderns can process many different streams of information at the same time, enabling them to make unexpected connections.

of it. They could get through their days and lives without encountering other people with entirely different world views— and, consequently, they didn't have to worry a lot about how to deal with pluralism. People in modern civilization have had a concept of universality—based on the hope (or fear) that some genius, messiah, or tyrant would figure out how to get everybody on the same page—but no experience of it. Instead, every war, every trade mission, every migration brought more culture shocks. Now, in the postmodern era, the very concept of universality is, as the deconstructionists say, "put into question." The old strategies of conquest, repression, and conversion are still being strenuously applied in many places—labeled now by nifty euphemisms like "ethnic cleansing"—but they aren't very effective. It begins to look like we're all going to have to get used to a world of multiple realities.[3]

Living in Postmodern Times Means Living in a Sea of "Truths"

Postmodernity is the condition of living in a sea of "truths," each with its own reality and set of beliefs. The individual is left with a decision to believe in something or to drift aimlessly in a sea of information. Rather than the culture or the society dictating the truth, the person in the midst of the postmodern condition has to decide what is the truth for him or her. Thus truth is not something that is found. Instead, truth is something that you create for yourself. As one young woman in Mobile, Alabama expressed it, "I have had to build my own character and to choose my own values. I am luckier than my friends because I have made positive choices. If you never decide, then you will always be lost."

This idea cannot be overlooked. The idea that you create your own truth turns previous assumptions about the world and the state of humanity on their collective head. This is not a New Age Shirley MacLaine saying: "You are God." It runs much deeper. For centuries humanity has bought into the idea that there is one great truth that explains the human condition and our place in the world. Over the years each culture has put forth its own set of beliefs, rules, and practices. The question is this: Did each culture discover the truth, or did it create its own truth? Is there one universal truth that explains it all or, in our attempt to make sense of the world, has each society created the "truth" that gives its members a sense of security, hope, and—most important—a future? Anderson observes:

> *We are beginning to see all manner of things—values and beliefs, rituals, ideas about childhood and death, traditions, interpretations of history, rituals, ethnicity, even the idea of culture—as inventions. This discovery itself, now being made by people all over the world, becomes a part of our common ground. It is central to an emerging understanding of the human condition, and is also a central part of a new global culture which is, in a sense, a culture about cultures. . . . The familiar*

pieces of our cultural furniture don't go away when we see them as inventions. We don't need them less or love them less. Whether they are invented or not, we could not live without them, because these are the kinds of animals we are. That does not change—but something has changed. The world around us has become a more human world.[4]

If culture is an invention of a very active human mind, what about truth? Are not truths also a matter of invention whose purpose is to bind together a group of people? Or is truth that which keeps some in power and some oppressed? If truth is not a given, but something that humanity creates to suit its own ends, then do we have the freedom to create a new and better truth for us all?

The history of Western civilization has been littered with attempts to find the one great truth. From Plato onward, people have sought to discover unifying principles that make sense of this world. The modern mind, imbued with the rationalistic, linear perspective of the Enlightenment, has sought to codify and to delineate the truth that all should live by. But the modern perspective has collapsed under the weight of a thousand voices, each of which says, "I know it all, I've got it and you have to believe." Everyday living in a progressive, modern environment is seeded with contradictory "truths" that bring one to say, "What's the point? I'll do it my way."

At this point we can begin to under-

stand the perspective of the Postmodern Generation. What some would call pluralism or diversity, is nothing of the sort. Instead we find among Postmoderns a fundamental change in the perception of truth. Life is not an endless search for a truth that is out there to be discovered. Truth lives on its own. Truth is "what works for you."

One episode of the hit television show *Friends* shows two of the characters debating about evolution. One of them seeks to prove that evolution is a fact by bringing in a box full of fossils to impress his friend. He tells her that years of scientific discovery and research show that without a doubt evolution is a fact. He asks her how she could disbelieve in the face of all the evidence. She replies that lately she hasn't believed in gravity, either. It seemed like she was being pulled forward rather than down.

When the advocate of evolution goes into hysterics, seriously doubting her sanity, she comes back with something like this: "OK, tell me this. Don't you have the tiniest little doubt that you could be wrong? After all, scientists used to believe the world was flat and they were wrong. Scientists used to believe the atom was the smallest thing in the universe until someone cracked it open. What makes you think that someone won't come along with another theory that will prove that evolution is wrong?" A long silence ensues. He replies: "Maybe you're right." She explodes: "Is that all it takes? You've allowed me to crush your whole belief system? I thought you were stronger than that!"

For the Postmodern, truth is always open to debate. There is no solid foundation. Each truth is dependent on your ability to defend it. Each truth can evaporate in the face of another discovery, another theory, or another perspective never before considered.

Along with constant questioning about the truth comes another troubling question about the future. Because there is no future as envisioned by past utopian visionaries, planning for the future seems to be a fruitless exercise. As technology speeds change, who knows what life will really be like by the time the oldest of the Postmoderns retires in 2030, and the youngest in 2046? Can any of us accurately predict what the world will be like near the half-way mark of the next century?

Contrast this uncertainty with the expectations of the GI Generation, whose oldest members started retiring in 1973. The ultimate goal of the GI Generation was to have a golden retirement. Society as a whole supported this view. Social security was a given for hard working GIs. Powerful labor unions fought to win fringe benefits such as medical insurance and pension programs. The image of the destitute senior has given way to the senior on the golf course playing eighteen holes behind a ten foot wall that offers protection from those on the outside. Millions of seniors now live in huge

W hen a visitor to Japan went into a Tokyo department store, he was surprised to see the Japanese celebrating the Christmas season. And what symbol of the Christmas season did the visitor discover prominently on display in the Tokyo department store? Santa Claus nailed to a cross!

Richard Sweder, "Santa Claus on the Cross," *The Truth About the Truth*, edited by Walter Truett Anderson, p. 73.

retirement communities spread across Florida and the Sunbelt. As they see it, they have earned this through hard work and forward thinking.

But along the way they have been greatly assisted by a government that has provided for them throughout their lives. In their early years they received New Deal jobs. After World War II they got GI bill college degrees. As they bought houses they received subsidized mortgages. Now in retirement they receive social security. As Michael D' Antonio, in an article in the *Los Angeles Times Magazine* entitled "The New Generation Gap" points out, today's elderly—who make up about 12.5% of the population—receive 60% of federal social spending. This is four times more than is spent on American children. America leads the world in its spending for those over sixty-five. The total amount disbursed each year to provide for social security and medical care is over 500 billion dollars.

All that money has created a special

group of citizens. The elderly are the only age group with universal government health insurance and the only one that receives income assistance, up to $24,500 a year for couples, whether they need it or not.[5]

Trey, age twenty-five, a first-year law student at Stanford University shares his perspective on his generation's place among the other generations.

Q: What is the most important issue facing your generation?

TREY: Trying to achieve the same level of success as the previous generation. I don't see myself being able to achieve that status no matter how hard I work. Because of the way the economy is now and the fact that we are going to be supporting a larger number of older people, I don't know how our generation can do better. I have pretty much convinced myself that's what is going to happen. If something better comes out, that's great, but I would be surprised if we could do as well as the Baby Boomers did.

Q: What do you mean by saying you will have to support the older generation?

TREY: Because the Baby Boomers will soon be collecting social security, and Generation X is a smaller group of people, we will be working to support them.

Q: So what is your biggest hope?

TREY: I don't know, I don't think there is one. An individual hope is that I will do what I want to get done and find something in my life that I enjoy doing.

Trey is not alone. Few of his generation believe that the government or any other institution will be able to ensure a reliable future that they can count on. The viewpoint that sustained the GI Generation in the modern era is no longer viable in the postmodern era in which faith in the future or in progress is dead. The GIs benefited by a universal cultural understanding that united them. Faith in God and country has been their motto, and it has paid off. The institutions of society—government, church, family, and work—were secure for them. Their sacrifices in World War II have been rewarded by a longer life span than any previous generation, by greater financial security than any group in the world, and lifelong relationships with family and friends that sustain them in their old age.

Postmoderns on the other hand seem to have little to sacrifice for, have seen faith in the institutions of society decline, and see the future as a blank wall. There seems to be nothing out there to reach for or to look forward to. Since the day they came into the world they have experienced a steady erosion of the ideals that sustained the modern era. John Katz, in his article "Guilty" in the September 1995 edition of *Wired*, points out that Vietnam discredited the military, Watergate discredited the Presidency, the Rodney King beating discredited the police, and the O.J. Simpson trial has discredited the courts and the media.[6]

The perspective of Postmoderns is colored by being raised in a society that seems to be taking a free fall into disorder. Unlike some Boomers, who nostalgically look back to a golden age of childhood in the 1950's, Postmoderns have seen only a steady breakdown of social norms and values since they came into the world in 1965. The result of all this can be summed up in three basic "truths" by which Postmoderns abide.

Truth #1:
We Have No Values

As I was talking with two students on the campus of Syracuse University in upstate New York, I asked them what was the most important value of their generation. They both chimed in at the same time: "We have no values." I responded by saying: "Then having no values is a value." They both laughed and said: "That's right—if there are no values, than having no values becomes a value." In talking further I discovered what they meant by their response. For them, having no values is not having an absence of morality or belief. Rather it is believing that there is no one value that unites them as a generation. Each person sees the world through his or her perspective, and determines

what is a value for himself or herself.

Two weeks before graduation at Hillsboro High School in Nashville, Tennessee, a class of seniors discussed their values:

Q: What does your generation care about?

Nothing, really. Ourselves. We care about our individuality.

Q: In comparison to other generations, what would be the other things that you really care about?

Other generations cared about money, just as we do, so how can we say that we are totally different from them?

But can you name a whole lot of other things we have agreed on?

We want easy money.

We don't have the work ethic.

I think it's going to get a lot worse.

Q: What is going to get a lot worse?

If the population keeps on growing and people keep on not caring and not being responsible for their actions—until people start taking responsibility for themselves, nothing is going to get better.

I think it will change in our generation, once we grow up.

Q: As other generations listen to you, what do you want them to know about you that is

positive and hopeful? What characteristics do you think are very positive about your generation?

Very diverse.

More religious.

Pretty laid back.

Our values have changed.

Q: What values have changed?

Just about marriage, sex, family structure, drugs, rock and roll.

Q: Do you say these are positive changes?

According to my parents I should never live with someone before getting married, have no sex before marriage. I don't agree with that.

For them it was okay.

Gay or lesbian couples adopting children can have a positive effect. My dad would go ballistic over that.

I think what is right for them is not necessarily right for us. That's not wrong.

Q: What are your lives going to look like twenty years from now? Any ideas? Have you ever thought about that? Is that too far off to think about?

My main goal right now is that I don't end up in a little office cubicle.

I don't think there is any use in

my worrying about what is going to happen.

Q: Do you think your generation is going to be more successful than the previous generation?

No.

Yes. Not like money. I think personal satisfaction, definitely.

Our parents wanted to satisfy their parents and their bosses. We are just not like that. We want to satisfy ourselves.

Q: Do all of you think your generation is more laid back than previous generations?

We just don't care what people think about us.

Q: I hear individuality, diversity, and so forth as values. What other values would you say are in your generation that might be different from other generations?

I don't think there are many values that our generation has. What your generation would consider having no values is to us a value, in that we are going to personally satisfy ourselves rather than deal with everybody else's crap.

I can do stuff for other people. There are things that I do that is not self-satisfying that is satisfying to my parents. I may do these because I love them. But it's a value for me to always be able to make myself happy.

I can see what she is saying, but I don't really see how that is a value. Of course, I want to make myself happy, but that's not really a value.

A value is like a moral standard.

This conversation brings to light the Postmodern's definition of a value. For Postmoderns values are what brings to them personal satisfaction. While this might sound a lot like adolescents of previous generations, what is different is that, unlike older American generations, the society at large provides little in the way of a value system to which Postmoderns can move toward. For society as a whole values are not tied to a specific code of ethics such as the Ten Commandments. Increasingly values are relative to the individual. A conversation with Jennifer, a student at Harvard University, brings this perspective into sharper focus.

Q: **What is the most important value of your generation?**

JENNIFER (age seventeen): Integrity toward other kids your age. Keeping your word. Even kids who are not necessarily doing the most legit things are going to college trying to make sure they have security. Integrity is real important to them. You can

even be honorable and have integrity when you are drug dealing. How? You're still going to be judged on your character.

Again values are related exclusively to the individual. According to Jennifer, even drug dealers can have integrity if they are honorable in their relationships with their friends. Here values are tied to a wider circle than just the individual. Values are also what are agreed upon by a circle of friends. The old adage "Honor among thieves" is evident here. But there is no sense that values are tied to some universal truth or belief-system shared by the society at large. Values are good as long as they do not judge another person's lifestyle or get in the way of another person's pursuit of happiness.

Truth #2: Happiness First

In the conversations related above, the personal pursuit of happiness is cited repeatedly as a truth for all to follow. Listen again to what Trey said. "An individual hope is that I will do what I want to get done and find something in my life that I enjoy doing."

Trey is not alone. Repeatedly across the country, being personally happy was constantly stated as the number one goal of this generation. In virtually every conversation I had with Postmoderns, personal happiness was brought up. Dee, a twenty-year-old at Harvard, in response to Jennifer's statement about integrity, replied: "Not only integrity to others but to yourself. Figuring out what you want to do. It's really important to be true to yourself." Her friend Joely, age seventeen, was even more to the point concerning her most important value: "The most important thing is to be happy. Not worrying about pleasing others."

For Postmoderns the slogan of Baby Boomers, "Do your own thing," is taken to a new level. In many ways this is to be expected. After all, since birth Postmoderns have been groomed to be the most selective consumers. How many commercials and advertisements have Postmoderns viewed in their lifetimes? If the average postmodern child watched four to six hours of television a day, and if there are eight to ten commercials in an hour, that gives us thirty-two to sixty commercials a day. Multiply this by 365, and you get 15,330 to 21,900 per year. Multiply this by sixteen years, and you get 245,280 to 350,400 commercials by the age of sixteen. These are rough figures, but you get the idea. One commentator has said that the only universal music of this generation are the jingles played in commercials.

Commercials constantly bombard us with the message that personal happiness is the ultimate goal of life. Underlying that message is another one, equally important to the advertiser: "And we have what you want." A consumer society operates on the idea that personal happiness is something that needs to be ful-

filled. Even our most cherished national document states that "the pursuit of happiness" is a God-given right.

This pursuit of happiness does not mean buying into what your parents consider to be happiness, nor does it mean buying into what society says will make you happy. Happiness is an individual pursuit. It is something that we find or create on our own.

Truth #3:
Time Is Wide, Not Long

Time can be looked at in two ways. First, it is wide. It is tied to the here-and-now of this day and this week. Or, second, it is long. It is seen in centuries. The wide view focuses on the now, what is happening along a narrow spectrum of time. The long views includes the past as it prepares for the future.

In a time of escalating technological and cultural change, the wide view becomes dominant because it is all a person can do just to keep up. Tim, a twenty-year-old student at the University of Florida, delineates the wide view in the dilemmas that his generation faces: "I don't think a lot of people have direction because the job market is really bad and it's always changing. One minute this career seems to be doing really well, and by the time you spend four years or however long it takes to get some kind of degree, the job market has completely changed because it's so radically changing as it tries to improve itself. We are really struggling to try and find some kind of niche in society. Once college life is over, what then?"

Asked if rapid change explains why people his age seem to lack direction, he replied: "Right. People search for direction, but every time they get pointed in a direction that seems stable, the wind blows in a different way and you have to adjust your sail or your ship's going to sink. I firmly believe that. I think that if you are talking about a gap between generations, I think the world is a much more complicated place today, and it's going to be so for my children. I pity them if things continue on the path that they have gone so far. When my parents grew up, the concerns were a lot simpler. Now, today, are we going to find a job? If we hook up with a girl at a party, are we going to wind up with some disease that will kill us? The concerns are much greater. They are life-threatening—everything from economic to sexual and social. For my kids, Jesus, I'm going to keep them in a bubble, I think. Hide them in a box in the basement so they can go on social security."

Tim's view goes to the heart of the matter. Wide thinking focuses on the present and staying even with change as it happens. The long view looks to the past for answers that will prepare us for the future.

Another way of seeing this among Postmoderns is to listen to their frame of reference, which is tied mostly to the pop culture of the past forty years. Movies, rock songs, and television shows form the body of cultural reference for most Postmoderns. The movie *Wayne's World*, a parody of this generation, is littered with references to old movies and TV shows. In one scene Garth puts together an electronic stun gun to protect his honor, while the music from *Mission Impossible* plays in the background. In another scene he whistles the theme music from *Star Trek* as he and Wayne look up at the stars and talk about their future.

In an episode of the TV show *Chicago Hope* as one character faces his divorce he says something like: "Now I know how the witch felt when Dorothy's house fell down." If you are not familiar with the movie *The Wizard of Oz*, then you would be clueless as to what he is talking about. But the scriptwriter assumes that the vast majority will get the point. After Dorothy is caught up in a tornado her house falls right on top of a witch when it lands in Munchkin land. It is from this witch that Dorothy gets her ruby red shoes. The character's reference to the witch tells the audience that he feels like the weight of the world has fallen on him. His reference is not a joke, but rather a way to express a deep emotional moment in his life.

Very few TV shows refer to Shakespeare or to the Bible or to Homer's *Iliad* as a frame of reference as to how people are dealing with issues and problems in their lives. In the world of the Postmoderns, dialogues from movies and snippets of music bring to the viewer a more immediate level of meaning, tied to other movies and songs. Time is wide. Life is seen from the very narrow band of the past forty years. Life is lived in the now.

In a world that seems to have diminishing returns, it's hard to have a long view. When a people has a well-defined belief in the future, they are pulled ahead by a vision of hope that unites and gives them meaning. When the future is unknowable and frightening, a people will collapse within themselves, with each person forced to make it on his or her own.

Stewart Brand in an article, "Two Questions" in *Wired* wonders whether people act better or worse when they think society is declining. If you think things are getting better you will prepare and plan for the future. If things appear to be going down, you will grab for everything you can get before it is too late.[7]

Harmony, of Glendora, California, had this to say: "I feel like our generation is becoming more and more careless. Hardly anyone thinks about success as in their future; they just think about the present and self-satisfaction. Such as partying with drugs, alcohol, and sex. I believe everyone has a right to live the way they want to, but there is also a limit. I feel that morality is becoming real liberal and should be taken more seriously. The attitudes need to change."

To say that Postmoderns have no hope for the future would be misleading.

Rolanda, a twenty-two-year-old from Duarte, California, says her greatest hope for the future is "for our world to be a better place to live. To be able to treat everyone equally without racism." Curtis, age twenty, of Seattle, Washington, says his greatest goal is to "hopefully get a job after college and find someone to love."

But those who have hope for the future seem to temper it with hard-edged realism. Brody, age twenty-one, of Chandler, Arizona, says: "My generation has a job to do. It is an important job in that it will secure a foundation for our children and grandchildren on which to stand. I am often fearful of what the future holds. There is way too much anger, hatred, prejudice, and neglect—all these elements lead to violence and harmful substances. I certainly don't know the answer but I will do my best to work toward finding it."

The question that Postmoderns face is not whether they want to have a better future, it's how to create a better world when everything seems to be working against it. As we will see in the following three chapters, the increase in violence, the breakdown of the family, and the changing economy have put most Postmoderns behind the proverbial eight ball. The challenges they face are greater than those their elders faced, and the choices before them are often confusing and contradictory. Not only are the challenges greater, the risks are higher.

The story is told about the oak beams

in the ceiling of College Hall at New College, Oxford. About a hundred years ago they needed to be replaced. To find the right wood, carpenters used oak trees that had been planted in 1386 when the dining hall was first built. The fourteenth-century builder had a long view. In anticipation of the time when the beams would need to be replaced hundreds of years in the future, he planted the trees.[8]

Today one wonders if anyone is planting new trees for future generations. For Postmoderns the question of whether there will be a future is at issue. Whether

"Mothers and fathers need to be the heroes in the lives of their children. Through service to others one will find himself/ herself. God bless the USA."

Soloman, age 24,
Mesa, Arizona

you are a hard-edged realist or a God-fearing mystic, the future is cloudy and uncertain. Rather than try to predict the future, perhaps the better option is to ask what kind of future you want to be a part of. If small changes in the present make huge differences in the future, what seeds of life are we planting today?

From the War Out There to the War Right Here

Do you remember witnessing your first killing? Perhaps it was during a showing of *Bonanza*. A gunslinger challenges Hoss to a duel in the street. Hoss reluctantly agrees. He has to defend the honor of the Cartright family. They pace off. Twenty steps each. They turn and fire. Hoss flinches as a bullet grazes his shoulder, but his enemy takes one in the belly. He staggers and falls. The crowd rushes in to get a closer look. Hoss saunters over to hear the man's dying words to a young woman who holds him in her arms: "Betsy, I didn't mean to do it." He shudders and dies. You turned to your mom, who sat on the couch behind you: "Mommy. He died."

She replied: "Don't worry, honey, it's just pretend."

You looked back at the television and contemplated her words. It's just pretend. No one was really hurt. It's a game.

Unfortunately the game is now out of control. To say that we live in a violent society is almost like saying the sun is going to shine today. It is so commonplace that we go into neutral at the sound of the word. We ignore the stiletto aimed at the heart of our public conscience and go on with business as usual. Instead of facing it head on, we buy car alarms, or build bigger walls around our houses, or purchase a forty-five magnum for our protection. But in doing so we ignore the larger consequences and forget that there are people getting killed out there; that our young people are caught in the firestorm. After all, who is going to build a memorial wall for the over 325,000 people murdered in the United States since 1980?

How do you begin to talk about something that is so insane and commonplace at the same time? Do you start with a quotation from someone who was shot? Or a statistic that shows a thirty year rise in violent crime? Do you talk about the vast segments of our society who are behind bars? Do you list the crimes of the week—each incident a chilling sign of our inability to come to grips with what is going on? Or what about an interview with the victim's mother, complete with tears and an outburst of anger? Better yet, how about a video of the latest execution? A hanging? That will do. Or how about a firing squad? Perhaps that will get our attention.

The truth is that we are so inundated with violent scenes, whether in a movie, on the local news, or in our neighborhood, that we have almost become anesthetized. We are numb. We are overwhelmed. We have become paralyzed; but we stay so at our own peril. For if we think it's bad now, if we do nothing about it, what will it be like for the next generation of kids that are following the Postmoderns?

Postmoderns are a generation oppressed by the fear of violence. Since World War II we have been experiencing a culture-shift that can best be summed up by saying we have gone from the war out there to the war right here. For earlier generations war was something experienced in a foreign land. For the GI Generation war happened in Germany or Japan. For the Silent Generation war happened in Korea. For Baby Boomers war was experienced in Vietnam. But for Postmoderns war has been experienced in downtown Los Angeles, or in the suburbs of Chicago, or in Walla Walla, Washington, or in Oklahoma City.

From 1980 to 1990, 222,678 Americans were murdered. In over 60% of these cases a gun was used.[1] From 1991 to 1995, an additional 110,772 people were murdered.[2] The total number of 333,450 murdered since 1980 is over six times the number of soldiers killed in the Vietnam War, which lasted a comparable number of years, from 1961 to 1975.

If the 1993 statistics are any indication, a large percentage of these are among the young. Of the 23,271 murders reported in 1993, 12,196—or 52%—of the victims were twenty-nine years or younger. The highest number of murders, 19%, were among those twenty to twenty-four years of age.

The 1993 figures tell us something else. Murder is primarily a male endeavor. Among the twenty to twenty-four-year-olds, 3,667 were men while 684 were women. Murder is also higher among blacks. Of the 4,355 people ages twenty to twenty-four who were murdered in 1993, 2,656—or 60%—were black.[3]

In their 1991 book *The Day America Told the Truth*, James Patterson and Peter Kim reach a startling conclusion concerning young men in our society. They write: "Young American males are our biggest national tragedy. Males between the ages of eighteen and twenty-five are the real cause of our crime problem. They are responsible for most child abuse. They are a violent, untrustworthy, and undependable group."[4] While this is a harsh statement, it is one worth listening to. A number of statistics back up this claim. Take a look, for example, at the leading causes of death in 1992 of Americans fifteen to twenty-four years of age.

As we look at the chart we see that the top three causes are preventable. Motor vehicle accidents lead the pack. For males the rate in 1992 was 40.3 compared to 16.2 for females. A large percentage of these are related to drunk driving. Next comes the homicide rate, which for males was 37.3 per 100,000, compared to that for women at 6.4. Suicide rates from all causes are higher as well for males. The suicide rate for males ages fifteen to twenty-four in 1992 was

Jason:	Guns need to be taken off the streets. There are just too many of them.
Terrence:	Nobody is going to get rid of them.
Jason:	Okay. If we can't get rid of them, then we all should have one.
Terrence:	Yeah, it's like nuclear deterrence. If you've got the bomb, I won't use mine.
Jason:	You got it. It's MAD all right. It's Mutual Assured Destruction for us all if we don't get a grip on it.

Two students from Brooklyn, New York, attending Syracuse University.

21.9, compared to 3.7 for women.[5]

While much has been made of the declining rates of overall crime in 1995, for juveniles and young adults the figures are unacceptibly high. From 1960 to 1992 the homicide rates for black and white males ages fifteen to twenty-four more than tripled. (Note: In all of the available statis-

Deaths by leading causes: 1992 - ages 15-24

	Number of Deaths		Death Rate Per 100,000	
	Male	**Female**	**Male**	**Female**
Accidents (includes motor vehicle)	10,253	3,409	55.5	19.3
Motor Vehicle Accidents	7,438	2,867	40.3	16.2
Homicide and Legal Intervention	6,891	1,128	37.3	6.4
Suicide	4,044	649	21.9	3.7
Cancer	1,084	725	5.9	4.1
Heart Disease	626	342	3.4	1.9
HIV Infection	419	159	2.3	0.9

Source: Deaths, by Age and Leading Cause: 1992. *U.S National Center for Health Statistics, Vital Statistics of the United States*, annual; and unpublished data, *The American Almanac*, p. 94.

The latest FBI report for 1995 has a good news/bad news storyline. The good news: Overall crime dropped 4% in 1995 and juvenile violent crime dropped 2.9% The bad news: The rate for violent crime for juveniles ages ten to seventeen jumped from 300 per 100,000 in 1985 to 511.9 in 1995. In the same time the murder rate jumped from 5.8 in 1985 to 11.2 in 1995.

Source: "Youth Crime Takes a Dip," *The Tennessean,* August 9, 1996, p. A1.

tics, Hispanics are not separated out of the data, and races other than black and white are not distinguished.) For whites the rate went from 5.0 to 16.0 per 100,000, and for blacks, it went from 50.0 to 160.0.[6] Most of these homicides are related to the availability of firearms. The rate of death caused by firearms for white males was 11.8 for those fifteen to nineteen years of age, and 14.9 for those ages twenty to twenty-four. For blacks, it was 123.6 for those fifteen to nineteen years of age, and 164.4 for those twenty to twenty-four.[7]

Adding fuel to the problem is the huge growth of the prison population in our country. The number of persons in state and federal prisons has risen from 196,429 in 1970 to 910,080 in 1993. In 1991, it was reported that 66% of those in state prisons were under the age of thirty-four.[8]

Another set of figures fills in the picture even more. The number of Americans on probation, in jail or prison, or on parole has more than doubled since 1980, from 1,840,400 in 1980 to 4,763,200 in 1992.[9] One national study stated that one in three black American males in their twenties is in the criminal justice system.[10]

Ken Waters, a pastor at Vermont Square United Methodist Church in Los Angeles, California, says that this translates into a pernicious problem. In some inner city communities, young women outnumber young men ten to one. As a result many women remain unmarried because there are no men to marry. Homicides and imprisonment have deprived many young women of the opportunity to have a stable relationship, let alone a marriage. In this environment a person's family is oneself and one's children. If you have that, you are lucky.

But even this doesn't tell the whole story. Violence is no longer the province of urban centers. In February 1996 alone, the following incidents took place. In St. Louis a teenager was shot to death by another student on a school bus. In Los Angeles a teacher was critically wounded in the head by a stray bullet fired in a gang dispute. In a junior high school in Moses Lake, Washington, a student shot and killed a teacher and two other students. Earlier in the same school year, a student killed a fellow student and a teacher in a high school in Giles County, Tennessee. In October 1995 in Blackville, South Carolina, a sixteen-year-old student shot two teachers, killing one, before he shot and killed himself.[11]

This rate of violence does not go unnoticed by members of the Postmodern Generation. I remember asking one high school student how school went that day. She replied: "It was great. I didn't get shot today."

When asked about their greatest concern for the future, 38% of Postmoderns in the 1993 Spring Break Survey said that ending the violence of crime and drugs was at the top of the list. Second, at 21.5%, was fighting racism and sexism. In the 1995 Spring Break Survey, 61% reported that there was more violence in their communities.

The question that comes to mind is how this affects Postmoderns in their perception of life. The short-lived teen drama, *My So-Called Life* centered around the life and times of fifteen-year-old Angela Chase and her high school friends. This was no *Happy Days* sitcom with the Fonz and friends living it up in the 1950's. Instead, Angela, played by fifteen-year-old Claire Danes, faced the problems most teens face in the 1990's— sex, drugs, and violence—with an often teary-eyed semiacceptance of her fate. Part of the problem with the show was that it was too close to life. After watching it you felt as if you had just endured the cancer operation of a close relative, and were not too sure of the results.

In one memorable scene Angela comes to school after a shooting has taken place on campus. Parents have demanded that the school board take action to protect their kids. The school board devises a most modern solution— they install a metal detector on the door leading into the school.

As Angela approaches the door, she spots the metal detector welded to the door frame. There is no escaping it, nor is there any way to avoid its meaning: School is war. Angela reacts to this sudden intrusion into her everyday life like a deer caught in the lights of an approaching car. She stoops. She pauses. She blinks, and walks through the door. Her expression reads like a book: "My life will never be the same."

Which of the following is of the greatest concern as you look to the future?

Stopping the violence of crime and drugs	38.0%
Fighting racism and sexism	21.5
Finding our own identity as a generation	19.0
Paying the bills of previous generations	17.5
Taking care of the environment	17.0
Overcoming the stress of change	7.0

Spring Break Survey 1993; 300 Responses; more than one answer accepted.

The Death of a Close Friend Is Common Among Postmoderns

Although Angela is a fictional character, her story is quite reflective of reality.

When asked if they had experienced the death of a close friend, 45% of Postmoderns said yes. When asked how they died, 11% said they had a close friend die of a gunshot. Nine percent said they had a close friend die of suicide. Three percent had a friend die of an overdose. And 20% had a friend who died in an accident. As people live longer we expect the number of those who have experienced the death of friends to increase. In the survey, this proved true with the exception of one figure. Eleven percent of Postmoderns ages fourteen to eighteen said they had a close friend die of a gunshot, in comparison to 8% of twenty-five to thirty-year-olds.

Although I have no numbers to back it up, when talking to Baby Boomers, very few seem to remember having a close friend die when they were in their teens. If they did it usually had to do with an accident or with sickness, not suicide or gunshots. Baby Boomers can point to the Vietnam War and can talk about persons they knew who were casualties. But knowing someone who was murdered down the street, or shot at school, or who committed suicide—that is a different matter.

Postmoderns, on the other hand, have experienced these things firsthand. Listen to some of their voices. When asked what experience has had the most impact on their lives the following replies were given:

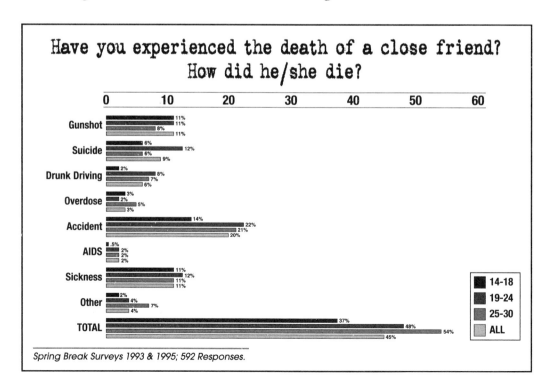

Have you experienced the death of a close friend? How did he/she die?

	Gunshot	Suicide	Drunk Driving	Overdose	Accident	AIDS	Sickness	Other	TOTAL
14-18	11%	6%	2%	3%	14%	.5%	11%	2%	37%
19-24	11%	12%	8%	2%	22%	2%	12%	4%	48%
25-30	8%	6%	7%	5%	21%	2%	11%	7%	54%
ALL	11%	9%	6%	3%	20%	2%	11%	4%	45%

Spring Break Surveys 1993 & 1995; 592 Responses.

Phoebe, age twenty-one, Huntington Park, California:

"A friend getting shot because of drugs. This impacted me most because I lost a friend. The guilty person was never found and I have a lot of anger because they took away something very special to many of us. I also began to think a lot about my own life and my own death."

LeAnn, age twenty-eight, Boston, Massachusetts:

"Being shot in 1982 while I was walking down the street in my neighborhood. I was bedridden for almost a year while I was studying to be a paralegal in college. As a result of the shooting I had to stop my education process."

Craiton, age twenty-one, Altadena, California:

"Death of a friend. When you see it on TV or read about gang violence, it really doesn't affect you. You can always say 'I didn't know the person so I don't have to care.' It's only when you see your homeboy on a Monday and hear about his death on Thursday that you really give a damn."

For some it is not only having one friend die, it's having several friends die.

Suzanne, age seventeen, Arlington, Texas:

"The deaths of classmates by drowning, overdose, accidental shooting, and sicknesses have all affected me. To see so many die so young is hard to take. You wonder if you are next."

Juan, age sixteen, National City, California:

"Many of my friends and family have been in danger from gunshots. Three of my friends have died in drive-bys."

Kevin, age seventeen, San Dimas, California:

"I would say so many people I know or have known have been dying lately and it hurts—two suicides, another friend hit by a car, another killed by a drunk driver."

As we listen to these remarks, it is important to consider how this affects a person's attitude toward life. For Postmoderns the effects of violence lie barely under the surface. There is almost a sense of casual acceptance tempered by an unanswered question: "Is anyone going to do something about this?"

Postmoderns deal with the violence around them in three basic ways. First, there is a combination of fear and acceptance, that it is just part of life. Violent death is just something you have to handle. Second, the question of whether or not you're next is always present. The issue is not just safety, it's survival. Third, violence seems to affect a person's perception of the future. Some Postmoderns who were questioned even wondered whether or not they would be alive ten years from now. Listen to the comments of two groups from widely divergent educational opportunities and backgrounds to see if you can find these threads running through the conversation. First, here are the comments from three students on the campus of Harvard University.

Q: What is the most important value of your generation?

JAMIE (nineteen): That depends. Certain people are just motivated by education. Somebody else will tell you to basically have fun.

DARIUS (seventeen): One person might say money, and another education.

DAN (seventeen): I think a lot of people are worried about making the same mistakes of past generations—the environment, government. That's going to be really important to us.

Q: What is the biggest problem your generation is facing?

DARIUS: I think there are so many things. When we retire, there is not going to be any social security. A lot of things like that, that we have to worry about.

DAN: The job market when we get out of school. Even with the degrees of our choice we're still going to have a hard time.

JAMIE: Meeting our personal needs as well as the needs of society.

Q: What is the most positive thing your generation has to offer?

DAN: Every generation has to offer new ideas and a lot of good leaders. You can't really generalize that our generation is going to save the world. Life goes on, basically.

Q: You don't see your generation aspiring to save the world?

DAN: Your generation, for example—you tried to save the world, but look around you. For us, probably one of the goals will be to help the environment, and I guess to try to end hunger and war—stuff that has always gone on.

Q: What's your biggest hope for the future?

JAMIE: I personally just hope that when I have kids, they can have a fairly decent quality of life. I am fairly skeptical about that right now.

Q: How would you define "fairly decent quality of life"?

JAMIE: Just issues like safety. I have a friend who was twenty who was murdered on Saturday just driving by a place. Just safety—a decent education, parks, places to go, just a normal childhood. I'm not sure how feasible that is going to be in the future.

DARIUS: I am just hoping that crime won't get out of control and that order will still be maintained—that government doesn't have to take away some of our freedom. I am just hoping anarchy doesn't rise up on us.

Two youth from Texarkana, Texas—a

world apart from Harvard—share similar concerns.

Q: **What is the most important thing to you?**

DARNELL (seventeen): My car and money.

Q: **What do you see yourself doing ten years from now?**

LANCE (seventeen): I see myself as a doctor in some hospital in New Orleans.

DARNELL: I don't know. Working, having a family.

Q: **What's your biggest concern?**

DARNELL: It's got to be drugs and alcohol. It's all over the place.

Q: **Is this problem growing or diminishing?**

DARNELL: It's growing.

Q: **What is your biggest hope for the future?**

LANCE: Accomplishing my dreams. My short-term goal is to win the state championship in football. For the long term, to succeed as a doctor.

Q: **You sound like you're into sports, what do you think about the NBA going on strike?**

LANCE: All they do is go out there and shoot ball all day. The teacher, she goes to class and puts up with two hundred and something kids every day. She should

Homicide is now the leading cause of death for black men ages fifteen to twenty-four.

Source: Cheryl Russell, "True Crime," *American Demographics*, August 1995, p. 30.

be paid the million and they should be paid the $30,000 a year.

Q: **So there should be a change in the value system?**

LANCE: Yeah.

Q: **What do we need to know about your generation?**

DARNELL: We're more laid back and carefree, and don't worry as much.

LANCE: Not everybody can afford to be laid back. You've got to really watch yourself.

Q: **What's your biggest fear?**

DARNELL: Somebody running up on me, jumping on me, shooting, stabbing, crossfire, whatever.

Q: **Do you have friends who have been shot?**

DARNELL: My cousin was killed.

Q: **How do you deal with that?**

DARNELL: You have to learn from what he did and not follow his example.

LANCE: You can't deal with it. Being an innocent bystander and getting in harm's way, that's what scares me. You haven't done anything to anybody, but something winds up happening to you. That's the problem.

Suicide and Suicide Attempts

Random violence is not the only thing that comes up for Postmoderns. Equally troubling is the prevalence of suicide among Postmoderns. Nine percent of those surveyed said they had a close friend who had killed himself or herself. Of those surveyed, 10% said themselves had attempted suicide. Surprisingly, the youngest group had a much higher response to this question. Eleven percent of those ages fourteen to eighteen said

they had attempted suicide, 10% of those ages nineteen to twenty-four said they had, and only 2% of those ages twenty-five to thirty answered in the affirmative.

Concerning the issue of teenage suicide Harry F. Water makes the following observation:

Suicide already ranks as the third leading killer of 15–24-year-olds. While the rates have leveled out, they're still up an astonishing 200 percent over the last four decades. What makes teens especially vulnerable is the tendency—by the healthy and troubled alike—to view life as an all-or-nothing proposition. Unlike adults, they haven't the ability or experience to see that every defeat isn't permanent. The young also tend to view suicide itself as impermanent, glamorizing how pain-free their existence may be afterward.[12]

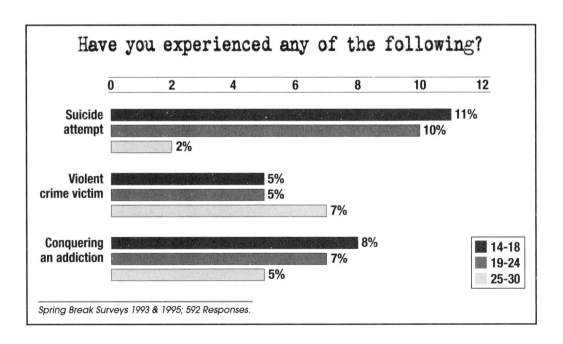

Have you experienced any of the following?

	0	2	4	6	8	10	12

Suicide attempt
- 11%
- 10%
- 2%

Violent crime victim
- 5%
- 5%
- 7%

Conquering an addiction
- 8%
- 7%
- 5%

Legend: 14-18, 19-24, 25-30

Spring Break Surveys 1993 & 1995; 592 Responses.

I remember getting a frantic call from some parents back in 1989. Their sixteen-year-old daughter's boyfriend had taken a gun out into the middle of a field and killed himself. They were afraid she would be next. I immediately went to talk to her and found that he had left a note inviting her to join him. He had written: "We can be together forever, you and me." In talking to the young woman I found that he had been abandoned by his parents at a young age and was being raised in an orphanage. He had just tried contacting his mother and she did not want to see him. Normally a happy, outgoing individual he had fallen into despair. Suicide became his way out. Fortunately the girlfriend did not join him. Through prayer and counseling she worked her way through the grief.

As I reflected on her experience I thought that she was too young to be facing such anguish. She was the last one to speak to him. She wondered if she could have stopped him. She had too many life and death questions running in her head. At sixteen a person should be ready to embrace life, to look forward to a great future, to begin dreaming about life as an adult, to begin thinking about college or a career, to experience the joy of finding a relationship that will last a lifetime. Instead, far too many sixteen-year-olds are going to their friends' funerals, and wondering for themselves if life is worth living.

In a discussion with me, some teenagers made the following remarks.

One young women said: "Suicide is a way to release the stress and the pain that's inside you, that you can't let out." Next to her a young man said: "It's a way to get out of a hard situation. A person says, 'If I do it, I will never have to face that again.' " Another young man said: "I think it's too easy to do. There are books out there that tell you how to do it in a clean way. They tell you the types of drugs to use."

What appears to be happening is that suicide—once considered to be the last, desperate act of a person whose life choices are at an end—is now seen as a reasonable option. The first movie in which I remember seeing a suicide was *The Deerhunter*, a movie about Vietnam veterans and their trauma following the war. In some way the action of the character made some kind of sense. Lately, however, suicide is thrown in as a ready-made plot device, added to action flicks like a car chase. In movie after movie the bad guy gets it in the end by his own hand. Michael Douglas, in *Falling Down*, makes his dramatic exit by blowing his head off with a shotgun as he flips backwards off a pier into the Pacific Ocean. How much more romantic can you get?

In the movie *The Web*, before you take your first handful of popcorn, a senator calls his son, tells him to have a nice day, hangs up the phone, and then blows his head off. What a way to begin.

Need I say more? The way I see it, suicide is now the way poor screenwriters get rid of characters in their movies. Criminals no longer get arrested. They kill themselves.

I remember listening to the radio the day after O. J. Simpson's low speed "chase" on the Los Angeles freeway system. One young man called in to say: "O. J. blew it. If it was me I would have jumped out of the jeep with my gun blazing. That way the police would have blown me away. Who wants to go to jail? He took the chicken way out. He should have gone out in a blaze of glory." Who says Hollywood doesn't make an impression?

Kurt Cobain: Voice of a Generation?

Suicide is not romantic, nor is it the easy way out. It is a devastating way to thumb your nose at society or to say life is worthless. This message came home to many fans of the rock group Nirvana in April of 1994. Their lead singer, Kurt Cobain, had captured the angst of his generation. Many said he was their spokesperson. Born in Aberdeen, Washington, in 1967, his parents divorced when he was eight years old. For one period of time he didn't see his father for eight years.

In 1989 Nirvana recorded their first album *Bleach* for $606.17. They released it on the independent label Sub Op. The music was supposed to be an updated version of punk rock—angry, confrontational, and antiestablishment. But some-

thing went wrong. It found an audience. Soon Nirvana was the leading edge of grunge music. They defined something called the Seattle Scene. They made a video for MTV, and their next album *Nevermind*, with its megahit "Smells Like Teen Spirit," sold over ten million copies worldwide.

Cobain's lyrics focused on the crumbling vision of the American dream. He called himself stupid and mocked the values of family, work, and commitment. Unfortunately for him he became an overnight sensation—rich and famous—everything he spoke out against.[13]

In April of 1994 he locked himself in his house and killed himself with a shotgun. With his death he became even more famous. He suddenly was front page news. People who had never heard of him paid attention to what he said. His wife, Courtney Love, derided and deified him as she sang in her own group, Hole. In death he became even more powerful. For months MTV played his "Unplugged" concert during primetime in an never-ending stream of Cobain images. Grief was hard to come by.

In January of 1995 I talked to Todd, age twenty-seven, a Seattle rock musician in a group that has no name. As one who has been around the music scene in Seattle he seemed to have a pretty good take on what has happened to Cobain and the bands who have followed in his wake.

Q: What can you tell me about the Seattle Scene?

TODD: It died in 1991.

Q: What happened?

TODD: It got commercialized. Every record producer in the country showed up and signed up any kid in a flannel shirt. It didn't matter if they could sing or play. They just wanted the look.

Q: The look?

TODD: You know. Unwashed. Unkempt. Dirty. Grunge. Now kids come into my music store all the time with a goatee and torn up pants to be like Kurt Cobain. And you know how he ended up.

Q: So you're saying the record companies ruined it.

TODD: Yeah. They wanted to make money off of anything that moved.

Q: Tell me about grunge rock.

TODD: Well, that's different than the Seattle Scene. Really there isn't a Seattle Scene. People just wanted to make music. Grunge is all that's left. If you can sing bad and play bad you've got a band. Kids think it's cool to sing off-key and make noise.

Q: Are you in a band?

TODD: Yeah, I play. You ever heard of Frank Zappa?

Q: Sure, so you're into retro rock?

TODD: No. I'm not into labels, man. I'm just into music.

Q: What do you make of what happened to Kurt Cobain?

TODD: First of all he was an idiot. He never washed himself. He was always high. Couldn't really sing. He just wrote great songs.

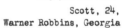

"Attempting suicide—it forever changed my perception of life and my place in it. It made me realize that I do not want to die. Suicide was only the easiest, most sure way of ending all my problems."

Scott, 24,
Warner Robbins, Georgia

"My parents' nasty divorce led to my 'attempt.' But I didn't have enough guts to go through with it."

Ann, 19,
Nashville, Tennessee

Q: Why did he commit suicide?

TODD: Some say that he was murdered. It really wouldn't surprise me. Actually let me tell you what really happened up here. It all started with a guy by the name of Andrew Wood who was in a group called Mother Love Born. Just before he was to make it in the big time he overdosed on heroin. He was an okay musician

Sub Op, the independent label for Nirvana, parlayed its initial investment of $20,000 to a $20-million-dollar windfall when it sold 49% of its business to the Warner Business Group in December of 1994. Its most lucrative source of income is the 2% royalty it receives off of the sales of Nirvana's *Nevermind.*

"Swingin' on the Flippity Flop with Sub Op," *Spin*, April 1995, p. 155.

but the guy was crazy. He liked sticking things in his arm. One guy that played with him said that he had been clean. The night he overdosed someone showed up at his door with a package. Just one more bag did him in. Some of the members of Mother Love Born became Mucky Vallock, the now famous Pearl Jam. They and Sound Garden did an album called "Temple of the Dog" which was a memorial for Andrew Wood. That just set the stage for the whole thing. Rock. Drugs. Death.

Q: **How does this relate to your generation?**

TODD: It pretty much sums it up, doesn't it? We're a group going nowhere fast. It's sad when you think about it.

Drugs and Violence

Cobain's death brings into focus another aspect of the kind of world some Postmoderns are living in. Preceding his death by about a month, he overdosed on painkillers and champagne while in Rome. Just before his suicide he had checked out of a rehab center in California. His mother filed a missing person's report that read: "Cobain ran away from a California facility and flew back to Seattle. He also bought a shotgun and may be suicidal." For Cobain, who had admitted at one time to being a heroin addict, the mix of drugs and violence, disillusionment and escapism, proved to be deadly.

Some say Cobain's suicide has entitled him to become a member of the real Dead Poets Society, whose members include Jimi Hendrix, Janis Joplin, Elvis Presley, John Lennon, John Belushi, River Phoenix, Selena, and others—all rock and roll and media stars whose lives ended suddenly through drugs or violence.

Following a number of years of decline, drug use has begun a steady increase since 1992. In the eighties drug use declined as society in general echoed the now famous slogan of Nancy Reagan's campaign: "Just Say No." But in the nineties, drug use is taking a different turn.

A National Household Survey on Drug Abuse by the Department of Health and Human Services (HHS) showed a 78% increase in drug use from 1992 to 1995 among teens age twelve to seventeen. Another survey by HHS showed emergency room visits since 1992 had risen as the result of the following drugs: 96% for marijuana, 58% for heroin, and 19% for cocaine.[14]

In the 1995 Spring Break Survey it was surprising to see how the younger age group was just as likely as the older group to have smoked pot, tried other drugs, intentionally gotten drunk, and smoked cigarettes. In two cases—smoking cigarettes and taking other drugs—the numbers were even higher. Nineteen percent of those fourteen to eighteen years of age reported smoking cigarettes, compared to 12% of those twenty-five to thirty. Eleven percent of those fourteen to eighteen years old reported trying other drugs, compared to 7% of those twenty-five to thirty years of age.

Monika Guttman, in a *USA Weekend* article entitled "The New Pot Culture," points to a number of reasons behind the increase in pot use. First, as the pop cul-

ture has glamorized the sixties and seventies, pot use has come back into fashion. In one TV episode of *Roseanne*, Roseanne and Dan are caught smoking marijuana in their bathroom. In music, Yo-Yo's "I.B.W. (Intelligent Black Woman)" is shown making a blunt in one of the hip-hop star's videos, and artists such as Cypress Hill and Black Crowes have contributed songs extolling the merits of pot use on the *Hempilation* CD—a CD promoting the legalization of pot. In merchandising, *Adidas* recently came out with a shoe called "The Hemp"—a term for marijuana, so named because the shoe is made partly from hemp.

Second, the availability of marijuana has cut down on its cost. In 1992 an ounce cost $200, now it costs around

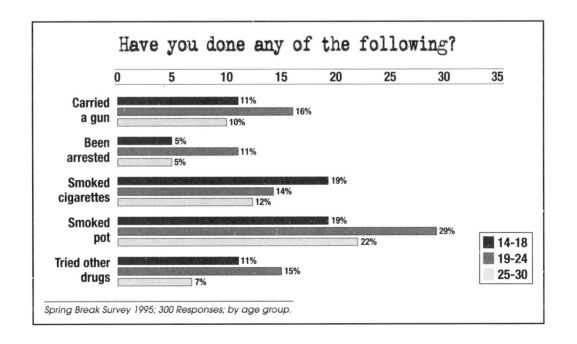

Have you done any of the following?

	14-18	19-24	25-30
Carried a gun	11%	16%	10%
Been arrested	5%	11%	5%
Smoked cigarettes	19%	14%	12%
Smoked pot	19%	29%	22%
Tried other drugs	11%	15%	7%

Spring Break Survey 1995; 300 Responses; by age group.

$125. Joints can be had for three to five dollars. New technology has brought such innovations as the use of hydrophics to allow growers to set up small farms indoors, where they grow the plants in super-nutrient rich solutions. Genetic engineering also is producing plants that have double the potency of the marijuana that was smoked in the sixties. The result is that marijuana is now the number-one cash crop in the United States.

Third, Baby Boomer parents who smoked marijuana in their youth find themselves in the tough position of convincing their children not to do as they did. Elected officials from President Bill Clinton ("I did not inhale") on down have admitted to their own encounters with pot. As a result their credibility among youth and young adults is low. Many

"Len Bias's death had a great impact on me because of what drugs are doing to our community. It made me realize drugs can kill at all levels of income. Not only the poor are dying of drug or alcohol addiction. Magic Johnson's ordeal with HIV opened my eyes to safe sex. I NEVER have sex without a condom."

Grace, 26,
Silverdale, Washington

adults do not realize that the amounts smoked and the potency of the drug have increased, making it more likely that those who smoke marijuana will move on to other drugs or get hooked. A 1994 study by the Center on Addiction and Substance Abuse found that 43% of teens who smoked pot before the age of eighteen moved on to cocaine.[15]

Eric, age twenty-two, from Alexandria, Virginia, echoes many of these themes in his experience of taking marijuana for the first time.

Q: What's the biggest change in your lifetime that has affected you?

ERIC: Drug use is really socially unacceptable. My mom used to be on marijuana and never kept it a secret, and other parents and families never kept it a secret. Now if they are doing it, they are keeping it more of a secret.

Q: You think that's better?

ERIC: Yes, I think it's better to have it socially shut out, to keep it behind closed doors.

Q: Do you want to use it or not use it because your mom did?

ERIC: I waited for twenty-two years until I did it, and I did it about a month ago to try it once so I could see what it was like.

Q: What were the results of your test?

ERIC: Memory loss. Short-term memory loss and attention deficit disorder. It seems like just all of a sudden I had an attention deficit disorder. After about two weeks, it went away, but I could notice my mind wandering. I tried it about three times total and then I told myself I would never do it again. The first time I did it, a girl told me she wouldn't have sex with me unless I did it. It was the only time I ever succumbed to peer pressure.

Q: Are you still seeing her?

ERIC: No, it was just a sexual thing. I had thought about doing it anyway and I didn't want any kind of peer pressure, and when she said that, I decided I might as well do it with someone who really knows what they are doing to make sure I was doing it right.

Eric is not alone. Around the country people are trying drugs. Some are paying unintended consequences for their actions. In the fall of 1995 the following incident took place in Nashville, Tennessee. While at a meet in Memphis, ten members of the varsity wrestling team from a Nashville high school were caught smoking pot in their hotel room. Because of the school district's zero tolerance policy, all ten students were suspended from school for a year.

As the news hit the media, parents of the students went on TV to complain that the policy was too strict. One mother, whose son was pictured with numerous trophies from his sports exploits, exclaimed: "These are good kids who just

A survey of 209 high school students who reside in or near the Ida B. Wells complex in inner city Chicago reported that 45% had seen someone killed, 6% had been shot, 8% had been stabbed, 7% had been raped, and nearly half the students had been shot at.

Source: Scott Minerbrook, "Lives Without Father," *U.S. News & World Report*, February 27, 1995.

made a stupid mistake. Don't penalize them for one bad decision. It's not like they killed someone."

The irony of the situation is that these same parents would be up in arms if one of the "bad kids" were caught on campus selling pot. What they fail to see is that the simple purchase of a joint or a snort for recreational fun leads directly to the inner city where drugs and guns are decimating the lives of the youth and children of that neighborhood. When an upper class person buys drugs they participate in a chain reaction that leads to the poorest neighborhoods where drug use is rampant.

The must-see 1994 documentary *Hoop Dreams*, about two black youths pursuing the dream of playing in the NBA, relates the true story of their lives in high school. Both are recruited by St. John's, a school in the suburbs that is known for its basketball team. To get to St. John's from inner-city Chicago it takes a three-hour round trip by train and bus every day. Late in the ninth grade one player's life becomes disrupted when his father gets hooked on cocaine. The father is arrested for dealing, and as a result the son has no money to pay the nominal fees to go to the school. Because of back unpaid bills he is kicked out of the school. As a result he ends up back in his local public high school. The other player stays at the private school where he becomes a star until he is injured and is never the same player again.

In a story of overcoming difficult odds the young man in public school perseveres and takes his team to the state championship. Just before he leaves for college, he is shown coming to an interview all shaken up. On his way home he had been held at gunpoint by a druggie. In some way he was able to escape being shot. His story shows the great odds many young people face in making something good out of lives lived in the backdrop of drugs, gangs, and violence.

The Other Side of the Coin: Abuse

The story of violence does not stop here. As was said earlier, males are the main perpetrators of violent crime, as well as the ones most successful in killing themselves. But what about females?

As the 1993 and 1995 Spring Break Surveys show, for women, violence equals victimization. Twenty percent of the women surveyed said they had suffered some form of abuse, compared to 12% of the men. They were twice as like-ly to have experienced physical abuse, and ten times more likely to have experienced sexual abuse. Only in verbal abuse were their numbers similar. Additionally, 8% of the Postmodern women surveyed said they had been raped.

Listen to the voices of these Postmodern women when asked which experience in their lives had affected them the most:

Mira, age twenty-one, La Puente, California:

"Being sexually abused and seeing my father beat my mother; while he verbally abused us. Those experiences had the biggest impact on my life. I felt like I could NOT trust men, and I began choosing boyfriends that were abusive to me."

Marie, age twenty-three, Augusta, Georgia:

"I was sexually abused as a child. When I got married I was physically abused by my husband."

Tory, age twenty, Phoenix, Arizona:

"Because of physical abuse I lost my ability to trust the opposite sex. It is still difficult for me even now when I am in a serious relationship that will lead to marriage."

Amy, age twenty, La Puente, California:

"Not telling my mom my grandfather molested me. Attempting suicide and being mentally and verbally abused. It makes you feel bad."

Shamila, age nineteen, West Covina, California:

"My abuse and victimization affected me the most. As a result I was hospitalized for depression and suicide issues."

Molly, age eighteen, Sioux Falls, South Dakota:

"Sexual abuse—you can't trust anyone in any way."

Jamie, age eighteen, Mesa, Arizona:

"After being raped I carried the feeling of guilt for four-and-a-half years until I got involved in my church—I haven't been able to get close to any man."

The testimonies of these women reveal the long-term effects of abuse. Abuse is not a one-time experience. It is something that continues to affect people in their relationships as they grow up. For some, abuse has led to women choosing abusive boyfriends or marrying an abusive husband. For others it has led to depression and suicide attempts.

After telling me about his first-time experiment with pot, Eric, from Alexandria, Virginia, revealed a disturbing pattern that shows how the abused can become the abuser.

Q: Do you think you will get married?

ERIC: If I did, I doubt that I'd stay faithful. I see that a lot with my friends. I work in a nightclub in Washington, D.C., and I get a lot of social diversity. The nightclub is gay, lesbian, and straight. The gay people are more socially oriented, looking for relationships; but the straight people are looking to have a good time more than making relationships. I tend to look for the sexual act more than for a relationship.

Q: Will you be doing the same

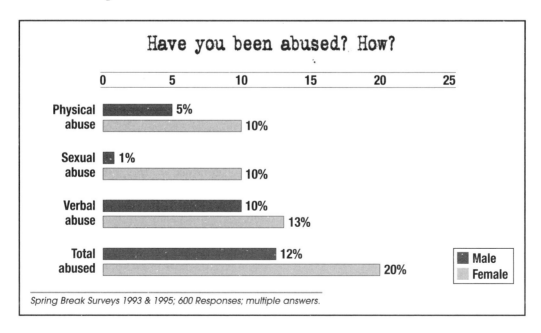

Have you been abused? How?

	Male	Female
Physical abuse	5%	10%
Sexual abuse	1%	10%
Verbal abuse	10%	13%
Total abused	12%	20%

Spring Break Surveys 1993 & 1995; 600 Responses; multiple answers.

thing ten years from now?

ERIC: Yes, I think so. I like to have fun. I'm thinking about moving down to Miami. My grandparents live there and I visited them for the last couple of years. Miami is really liberal down there. The beach on 9th Street is topless. That intrigued me. It's a lot easier for someone who is sexually oriented to party down there.

Q: What are your values?

ERIC: People usually say they have strong family values, but I really don't have any. When my mom makes me mad, I tend to yell at her. I know I don't want to cuss at her, but I do.

Q: Is your dad in the picture?

ERIC: No, he was in the picture until I was abused at three, and then my mother cut off contact with him. When I was ten years old, she wanted me to have a father figure because I had started to go bad at school. I didn't like to listen to women. I was getting bigger. She couldn't control me anymore, so she contacted him and asked him to step in and show me the way. So I went to live with him, and things changed until I found out that he had a girlfriend and he was sexually abusing her. She was sixteen and was consent-

ing. I saw them one evening when I was slipping out. I went to a school counselor and told her about it, and nobody believed me. She said I did not have enough evidence. That I should have taken a picture. I moved out. My mother said that my father's sex life is my father's sex life. She said she loved her freedom, and since she had gotten rid of me, she didn't want me back because I was getting too old. So I moved out on my own, and that's about it. That's my life.

But Eric's story was not complete. His life is not lived in isolation. The pattern of abuse learned from his parents affects his relationships as an adult. As we will see, Eric's story is not just about his abuse, it is also about his abuse of others. Eric is not alone. Study after study shows that those who suffer abuse as children tend to repeat the same actions as adults. I asked him:

Q: Are you following your father's pattern or your mom's?

ERIC: I don't know what it is, and it's not that I want to be attracted to younger girls, but I'm attracted to nothing under fourteen. But if I had my choice between a twenty, a twenty-two year old, or a fourteen-year-old, I would be more attracted to the fourteen-year-old. For some reason the innocence and knowing that she hasn't slept around and knowing that she is experimenting—it's weird, but it's nothing like a child abuser or anything like that. I feel that at fourteen they are confused. Maybe I was just brought into it at a young age. I think I picked up that trait from my father. He liked younger girls, but I would never start a relationship with one—but I would choose a young girl for sex, not a relationship. They play too many mind games. They don't know what they want anyway.

Q: Anything else to add? What would you say to someone of my generation if they said: "I don't want you with my fourteen-year-old daughter"? What answer would you give back?

ERIC: We have been exposed to a lot.

Q: Abuse from your mother or father?

ERIC: My father physically abused me. I used steroids when I was sixteen because I was on the wrestling team and football. I wanted to be big, but I also wanted to kill him—not really kill him, because I loved him. But I wanted to beat him up, to hurt him like he was hurting me. I built myself up until I was big enough, then I kicked his butt, and then he got some respect for me. But then this

Violence and community

	Yes	No
The criminal justice system is just	23.6%	76.5%
There is more violence in my community	60.8	39.2
People should be allowed to carry guns	36.3	63.7
I believe in capital punishment	72.6	27.4
The media is responsible for much of the violence in our society	55.6	44.4

Spring Break Survey 1995; 300 Responses.

sex issue came in with the girl and then that was it.

In Eric's story we find a frightening lack of compassion or concern for the girls he wished to be with. A sense of right and wrong seemed not to be part of the equation in his mind. Instead his goal was to pursue his pleasure regardless of the cost to others and their families. Underlying his lack of compassion lies the raging anger of a son abandoned and abused by his parents. Eric, who looked like the all-American boy when I met him walking in a mall, turned out to be a dangerous man-child who has no conception of what it means to love or to be loved.

After I turned off the tape we talked some more. He said he wasn't alone in his views. His other friends liked fourteen-year-olds also. I wasn't sure I wanted to believe him at this point. His views were appalling to me. But he is one person that stays on my mind. Not only because he frightened me as he revealed his inner self and thoughts, but because his life is one so torn by abuse and neglect. As we left I told him not to forget about God. I wonder how many more Erics are out there, lost and alone, looking for someone who will listen to them before it is too late for them and the women they encounter.

As we reflect on the level of violence and abuse seen among members of this generation a number of questions come to mind. What is the value of a human life? Do we all operate exclusively out of our own desire without thinking about how this affects others? Are we moving toward becoming an armed nation, with each person constantly looking over his or her shoulder for danger? Does anybody believe in a sense of community in which we all work together and help one another out? Have we lost the connection between what we do as individuals and how this affects the society as a whole? Is life precious anymore?

This is not the end of the story. The experience of Postmoderns challenges us to look deep within ourselves and ask if we as a people can afford to ignore what is going on. Report after report says that if we think it is bad now, just wait. For as noted before, Postmoderns are lower in number than the generation that is following them, the Millennials. To get an indication of the size of this younger generation the Department of Education reported in the fall of 1996 that there were twice as many students enrolled in kindergarten as there were seniors in high school.[16] As the Millennial Generation enter their teenage years and young adulthood, chances are that the rate of violence will get worse, not better.

As a nation we have to decide whether we are going to learn from Postmoderns the devastating effect violence has on a person's view of life and their hope for the future. Then we have to decide to turn it around before violence soars among the next generation. We have to decide whether we will invest in children or whether we will ignore the seeds of anger and discontent that rip at the heart of our young people. Depending on what we decide, we will reap the rewards of our own efforts.

From the Traditional Family to the Multifamily

high school administrative assistant in an upper class neighborhood told a story that shows us something about changing values in relationship to family and children. She said: "Last year thirteen young women in our school got pregnant. It was the popular thing to do. One day one of them went into labor and we sent her off to the hospital. After the baby was born she called me and asked if I would announce the birth of her little girl over the school intercom system so every one could hear about the happy news. I refused to do it. Why throw gasoline on the fire? When I was in high school, if a girl got pregnant, she went to visit relatives in another town, and we would never hear about it again. For these girls, having a baby is a status symbol, like having a new car or having the best-looking boyfriend. What they don't realize is that like a kitten that becomes a cat, babies grow into children. She had made a decision that will last her and her child a lifetime."

Everywhere we look we realize the American family is not what it used to be.

Some say that it is better, that people have more freedom to choose the lifestyle they want to live. They say the good old days are a figment of embellished memories, layered with images of watching *Ozzie and Harriet* and *Father*

Knows Best. Others say that the only hope for our society is that we return to traditional family values, where children come first and parents are committed to

"I didn't think it would be so hard, but being a single parent and wanting the best out of life for your child and yourself is not easy. It is a hard struggle financially and emotionally. This is my everyday life—not just an experience. I was just able to go back to school three years ago."

Joely, 28,
Dorchester, Massachusetts

each other for life. Still others point to declining standards of living for youth and children, and wonder if we as a society are forgetting about investing in our most important asset, our young people. Whichever side of the spectrum you are on, the issue of the family is a hot button. Because everyone has a family of some kind, everyone has a point of view.

Many Baby Boomers reared during the golden age of childhood in the 1950's and the early 1960's can remember coming from school to a home where Mom was always there and Dad provided for the family. Most grew up with brothers or sisters. They remember going from elementary school through high school with the same group of friends. They had a sense of security that provided the boundaries within which they were free to experiment. They had a home base

that was always there for them.

But Postmoderns have had a different experience of the family. Their view of the family is different from their parents,' and their experience is clouded by disruptions and pain. Their voice is far from comforting, and in many ways is confrontational. For if you want to know what makes the heart of a Postmodern tick, ask him or her about his or her family. You may get an earful. Both in conversations and in the survey, Postmoderns made it clear that what was done for them or to them has made a big difference in how they view life. I remember getting clued in to this when I overheard a conversation between two high school students. The conversation went something like this:

Anna: "Well, you know, my parents are divorced."

Ellen: "Mine, too."

Anna: "So, I have an older brother who was born before the divorce. His name is Allen."

Ellen: "Right. I have a little sister. Her name is Jamie. She's eleven. She's a good kid."

Anna: "And then my mom got remarried to Ted. And they had two children, my half-sister Page and my half-brother Nicky."

Ellen: "So you have younger siblings?"

Anna: "That's right. One is six and the other is three."

Ellen: "It's like you're part of a new family."

Anna: "Something like that."

Ellen: "Well, Anna, my Mom remarried too. Jack's my stepdad."

Anna: "Then my real dad married Sally and she already had a son, Eric, from her first marriage. So Eric's my stepbrother."

Ellen: "A stepbrother? You've got a big family."

Anna: "I'm not done yet. My father and Sally had a little girl, Annabelle. So she's my half-sister from my father's side."

Ellen: "This sounds confusing."

Anna: "Then Dad got divorced again and he's seeing Sassy."

Ellen: "Divorced again? That's got to be tough."

Anna: "Then I have about five zillion grandparents, which is great for presents at Christmas, but a real pain when it comes to introductions, if you know what I mean."

Ellen: "Yeah, but the presents. You must get a ton of them."

Anna: "You would think so. But actually because I was in the first family I sometimes feel lost. Especially on holidays. It's hard to know whose dinner table I will be sitting at, and who will be with me."

Ellen: "I see what you mean."

Anna: "At first I lived with Mom. But when she got remarried I moved in with Dad. But when he divorced Sally, I went back to Mom's house. So I live with Mom, and see Dad whenever."

Ellen: "I'm lucky. I've stayed with my mom the whole time. I don't know where my dad went to. Somewhere in Montana."

Anna: "You're not missing out on much."

Ellen: "So where's Allen?"

Anna: "Allen? Oh, yeah. My brother Allen. He escaped. He's in college."

This scene is not unique. In fact, quite unlike the Baby Boom generation, 80% of whom were raised with their original parents, Postmoderns were raised in the age of divorce. In 1965, the first birth year of the Postmodern Generation, the divorce rate took off. From 1965 to 1980 the divorce rate more than doubled. William Dunn, in *Baby Bust: A Generation Comes of Age*, notes that in the 1970's the United States had the highest divorce rate in the world, with about 40% of marriages likely to end in divorce.[1]

A report in the January 25, 1996 edition of *USA Today* stated that in 1996 60% of new marriages will end in divorce or separation.[2]

Many explanations have been given for the reasons why divorces began to rise in the late 1960's. The feminist movement encouraged women to go to work. The downturn of the economy and the opening up of new types of work made it possible and for some made it necessary for mothers and fathers both to work outside the home. This breakdown of the traditional roles of men and women meant that men no longer had to wear the provider's hat. They were free to do their own thing.

The sexual revolution encouraged men and women to experiment with many different partners. Free use of drugs broke down traditional ways of living. Marriage was viewed by many as a dying institution. As women's consciousness was raised many were not willing to stay in abusive relationships with which they may have previously tried to live.

The late-sixties culture as a whole seemed to embrace divorce as a new way of living. Books such as *Open Marriage,* written by Nena O'Neil and George O'Neil, promoted the idea of serial monogamy and allowing marriage partners to have sex outside of marriage. One quotation from their book sums up the values of the sexual revolution that were being promoted throughout the culture in movies such as *Bob and Carol and Ted & Alice,* and in books such as *Everything You Always Wanted to Know About Sex.*

> *Fidelity is redefined in open marriage as commitment to your own growth, equal commitment to your partner's growth, and a sharing of the self-discovery accomplished through such growth. It is loyalty and faithfulness to growth, to integrity of self and respect for the other, not to a sexual and psychological bondage to each other.*
>
> *In an open marriage, in which each partner is secure in his own identity and trusts the other, new possibilities for additional relationships exist, and open (as opposed to limited) love can expand to include others. . . . These outside relationships may, of course, include sex.*[3]

Notice here the underlying message of the sexual revolution. Marriage is bondage. Sex and love are best fulfilled outside of duty or obligation; in other words, without long-term commitment. Fidelity is redefined as being true to yourself. The most important priority is commitment to your own self-discovery and personal growth, even if it leads you to enjoy relationships outside of marriage.

Based on the modern notion of evolutionary progress, the sexual revolution promoted the idea that the needs of the individual could best be served by having a wider range of personal involvement than that provided by the two-parent family. Thus the progressive individual was one who could forge a series of relationships, each of which would help him or her become the person he or she was meant to be.

While all divorces cannot be laid at the feet of the sexual revolution, the sexual revolution did create an atmosphere in which divorce became permissible. In the 1950's divorce was rare and many couples stayed together even under the most trying of circumstances. But in the late 1960's and early 1970's men and women were no longer bound by the conventions of society to stick with it no matter what.

The sum total of these changes was the dissolution of families on a wide scale. While the adults who went through divorces can point to many different reasons for the breakup of their families, Postmoderns are the ones who have had to deal most directly with the consequences. Many are not so concerned with the reasons as they are with the results. One Postmodern put it this way:

"If this is what the sexual revolution has wrought, then I'm not so sure it was for the best. Suddenly with our parents' generation it was okay not to work marriages out, to have open marriages, to screw around, etcetera, as though the only people they were hurting were themselves. But we were there too, really young and really emotionally vulnerable. What do you do when everything you believed in is blown to hell? What do you believe in? And then when we started ending up in therapy or on *Prozac* in our twenties they blamed it on us . . . said we're crazy (or lazy)."

Christopher Lasch wrote his book *Haven in a Heartless World: The Family Besieged* as divorce was hitting its peak in the 1970's. He saw the change in the family as a rejection of hope for the future. In contrast to those who promoted the seemingly positive notion of sexual freedom and relationships without boundaries, he regarded this approach as fundamentally pessimistic. He wrote:

> *The fear and the rejection of parenthood, the tendency to view the family as nothing more than marriage, and the perception of marriage as merely one in a series of nonbinding commitments, reflect a growing distrust of the future and a reluctance to make provisions for it to lay up goods and experience for the use of the next generation.[4]*

What Lasch brings into focus is that the causalities of divorce are the children, those who are born into the midst of the chaos. For hand-in-hand with the growing divorce rate is the complex question of what to do with the children.

By 1979 it was becoming clear that children were getting caught in the middle of the divorce wars. The movie *Kramer vs Kramer*, which won the 1979 Oscars for Best Picture, Best Director, Best Actor, and Best Supporting Actress, tells the story of a divorcing couple's battle for the custody of their seven-year-old

"My parents' separation—it changed everything I had grown accustomed to. I had to move in with my father, and for the past four years I've been separated from my three brothers and my sister, and have missed out on being the older sibling in their lives."
Paula, 18,
Warner Robbins, Georgia

boy. When Joanna Kramer walks out, leaving her child with her husband, Ted, he is forced to change his life.

As the story progresses Ted discovers the joy of raising his child, but ends up losing his job because his priorities are not "right." After about eighteen months, Joanna comes back and wants custody of the child. A nasty court case ensues, with each partner exposing the weaknesses of the other. When the boy is told he has to go back to his mother, he breaks the heart of the movie audience when he loses control and cries. He wonders why Mommy and Daddy can't love each other. At the end of movie, Joanna decides that her exhusband is a changed person and that he is best suited to take care of their child.

Kramer vs Kramer refuses to gloss over the cost of breakups, and brings into focus what happens to families as a result of divorce. What *Kramer vs Kramer* did not point out, however, was the role reversal portrayed by the movie. In the vast majority of divorces, children are left with their mothers, and it's the mother who has to make the sacrifices to keep the family going.

One third of America's children go to bed without their father in the next room. Many won't see their father once a week. Forty percent of children who live in fatherless households haven't seen their father for over a year. Although plenty of women are perfectly capable of raising

"My parents' divorce has left me without a father, who I only get to see once a year at the most."
Hope, 18,
Nashville, Tennessee

well-adjusted children on their own, and while children are better off without a dad who is abusive, research shows that children without a father in the home are at a much higher risk of being in poverty, doing poorly in school, and are prone to depression and in some cases violence.

Seventy percent of the minors who are in prison have spent at least part of their lives without a father. Girls who are without a father in the home are much more likely to get pregnant. Boys tend to feel they have been abandoned, and are looking for a male role model to take their father's place. Girls often experience low self-esteem and rocky romantic relationships as they search for the ideal father figure.[5]

Postmoderns Have Felt the Personal Trauma of Their Parents' Divorce

Over 29% of the Postmoderns surveyed had gone through their parents' divorce, and an additional 5% have gone through their parents' separation. *Time* magazine reported in its July 16, 1990 edition that an estimated 40% of twenty-year-olds had gone through their parents' divorce.[6] In raw numbers, 17,915,000 divorces were performed from 1965 to 1985. An estimated twenty million children under the age of eighteen were involved. From 1986 to 1990 another five million divorces took place, with an additional seven million children and young adults involved.[7]

No previous generation has ever had to go through such personal trauma. While it is true that in the past many children lost their parents through death, what makes this different is that one or both parents decided to leave. In the case of the death of a parent, the living parent still cherishes his or her memory. The deceased parent still retains some sense of moral authority: "Your father would have wanted you to go to college."

In the case of divorce, parents end up fighting each other, memories of the past are painful, and in some cases the parent who has left is never mentioned again. In one poignant scene of *Kramer vs. Kramer*, an angry Ted Kramer takes down all the pictures of Joanna in an attempt to erase her memory and history. For the children of divorce, the memories are not so easy to erase.

Across the country, Postmoderns shared with me the painful experiences of their parents' divorce. One conversation sticks in my mind. At a youth convention in Salt Lake City, I asked two fourteen-year-olds what was the biggest issue they were facing in their lives. Amy, from Arizona, responded: "It's my family.

Four years ago my parents got a divorce, and this summer they both got remarried. One day my father came home from overseas and just showed up with his new wife. I went to my mother's wedding but I was very uncomfortable during the whole thing. My biggest problem is that I do not know who I am going to live with. I've lived with four different relatives in the last four years. I think I might end up at my grandma's, but I don't know yet."

Next to her sat Seanda, from Houston, Texas. "What about you?" I asked. She replied: "My family is worse."

In talks around the country I heard the same kind of response from members of the Postmodern Generation. One young woman in Mobile, Alabama said: "It's not the first divorce that's so bad. It's the second one that really hurts."

Another young woman in Pittsburgh

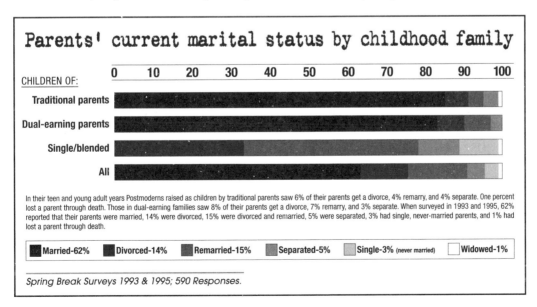

Parents' current marital status by childhood family

CHILDREN OF:

	0	10	20	30	40	50	60	70	80	90	100
Traditional parents											
Dual-earning parents											
Single/blended											
All											

In their teen and young adult years Postmoderns raised as children by traditional parents saw 6% of their parents get a divorce, 4% remarry, and 4% separate. One percent lost a parent through death. Those in dual-earning families saw 8% of their parents get a divorce, 7% remarry, and 3% separate. When surveyed in 1993 and 1995, 62% reported that their parents were married, 14% were divorced, 15% were divorced and remarried, 5% were separated, 3% had single, never-married parents, and 1% had lost a parent through death.

■ Married-62%　■ Divorced-14%　■ Remarried-15%　■ Separated-5%　■ Single-3% (never married)　☐ Widowed-1%

Spring Break Surveys 1993 & 1995; 590 Responses.

said: "Try three. Both my parents have gone through three divorces. My dad's not a Christian and he's just doing his own thing. My mom's a Christian but she never finds the right guy. As for me, I just don't understand it. If I ever get married, it's for life. I'd never want to live the life they have led. It's too messy for everyone."

"My parents' divorce has had a lot of influence on me, but probably not the kind of impact it has for most other kids. Instead, it has showed me that many times divorce can be for the better if two people are unhappy together. This unhappiness affects everyone. So, it seems to be for the better."

Wanda, 17,
Los Altos, California

Even those Postmoderns who have not gone through a divorce have felt its effect on their generation. As I was walking in a mall in Shreveport, Louisiana, I entered into this conversation with Lisa and Kim, both eighteen years old.

Q: What is your most important value in life?

LISA: Friendship.

KIM: Family.

Q: What's your biggest challenge?

LISA: Getting a job and getting through school. Also being a good Christian.

Q: How is that a challenge?

LISA: You're kind of run down if you are a believer. You don't fit in.

Q: When you say a job, what are you looking at?

LISA: Nursing.

KIM: I haven't decided.

Q: Your greatest hope for the future?

LISA: Having a family and finding a Christian spouse.

KIM: Getting out of school in less than five years.

Q: What is your greatest fear?

LISA: Not knowing what is going to happen as a whole in society. I'm afraid society is going to get a lot worse, and I wonder if I am going to be successful myself.

Q: Is society getting better or worse?

LISA: Worse, right now. People are not depending on God anymore. They are depending on themselves. Parents aren't teaching their children morals. Their moral standards aren't as high as they used to be. They are more concerned about their children's popularity than they are about their Christian lives and how it's going to end at the end.

Q: What do you think about the family?

KIM: I have a *Leave It to Beaver* family.

Q: Does that make you different?

KIM: Yes. Most people are liberated. All the women are working. I was the only kid in my class who had a parent who stayed home.

Q: Was that good for you?

KIM: For me it was great. But my friends didn't understand it. They thought I had it made. I always feel sort of strange about it. My life has been different than theirs. I guess it all has to do with your family. If you have a good family you can't go wrong; well, you can. What I'm saying is a good family gives you a better chance to make it.

Q: What about you, Lisa? Are friends or family more important to you?

LISA: To me friends are more important because I don't have a family. My parents are divorced. Some of my family members are dead, and a whole bunch of other stuff. Stress is a big factor. I've gotten ulcers over the whole thing. It's really hard to talk about.

In this interchange between Kim and Lisa, there is one thing that words don't convey. Kim acted as if she felt guilty for having a "good" family, and Lisa had tears in her eyes as she talked about her family situation. Underneath the conversation there was a palatable sense of anxiety and pain when it came to talking about the family.

The Effect of Divorce on Children

Now, thirty years since the divorce rate started to rise, long-range results are beginning to come in. The numbers of broken families, unwed teenage mothers, sexually-transmitted diseases, and children born outside of marriage have skyrocketed. Barbara Dafoe Whitehead, writing in the April 1993 *Atlantic Monthly* under the title, "Dan Quayle Was Right," points to a growing body of social-scientific evidence that shows that children of divorce, and those born out of wedlock, do worse than children in intact families. She states:

> *Children in single-parent families are six times as likely to be poor. They are also likely to stay poor longer. Twenty-two percent of children in one-parent families will experience poverty during childhood for seven years or more, as compared with only two percent of children in two-parent families. A 1988 survey by the National Center for Health Statistics found that children in single-parent families are two to three times as likely as children in two-parent families to have emotional and behavioral problems. They are also more likely to drop out of high school, to get pregnant as teenagers, to abuse drugs, and to be in trouble with the law. Compared with children in intact families, children from disrupted families are at a much higher risk for physical or sexual abuse.*[8]

Whitehead points out that a divorce is not a one-time event in the life of child. In fact it is one of a series of life-changing events. Typically following a divorce is the trial over the custody of the child. This usually entails a new living arrangement in which the child spends part of the time with his or her mother and another part of the time with his or her father. This means having two places to live and two networks of relationships to deal with. As the parents get beyond the period of the divorce, the child faces the prospect of watching one or both parents date. Somewhere down the line this may lead to remarriage and learning to live with a stepparent. It also might mean taking in a new set of stepbrothers and stepsisters.[9]

Ironically, when children have problems adapting to their parents' divorce, many times the children are seen as needing help to deal with "their" problem. *USA Today*'s report, "Children of Broken Homes," states that divorce contributes to as many as three in four teen suicides and to four in five teen psychiatric admissions.[10] A conversation I had with three youth in Fort Lauderdale brings home some of the issues that surround how many members of this generation feel about divorce and their parents.

Q: Do you feel your generation is going to be more successful than your parents' generation?

RYAN (seventeen): Younger generations are getting a lot lazier. Just doing the minimum.

Q: Why is this happening?

RYAN: Parents. A lot of kids in my school have separated parents. In schools where I recently went, about 50% of the parents are split up, and lots of the kids come from homes where parents say, "Get out of my face. I don't want to see you. Do good in school." There's no love or expectations coming from their homes, nothing. The kids are just on their own. There's no motivation there.

MIKE (fifteen): It's got to be the divorce rate. I would say that half of the kids that come out of divorced homes end up on drugs. The other half end up perfectly normal.

JULIA (fourteen): My parents are divorced. I was just listening to that.

Q: Anyone else's parents divorced?

No.

Q: How has this divorce affected you?

JULIA: My parents split up when I was in the second grade, and it took them four years to get the divorce. They fought over who was going to have custody. I have a younger brother and sister. They still go to court every month and fight; my dad doesn't want to pay my mom the money she is supposed to get. I took it pretty well, but my parents didn't think I did, so all through the divorce I must have gone to at least five different psychologists.

Q: Did that help you?

JULIA: No. I would go and just sit there. I wouldn't talk to the people.

Q: Why wasn't it helpful?

JULIA: I was angry. I was just mad at the fact that they got divorced. I don't like the way things are. I like them to live in one house and everything. I thought that everything that I told the psychologist would go straight to them, and I didn't want them to know.

Q: Do you think it's harder to make it in school coming from a divorce?

JULIA: In a way. When my parents were separated, my grades really went down, even though I was younger. I was always frustrated. I got in trouble a lot more in school. I was just so mad at both of them. During the whole divorce, I hated my mother. I thought it was all her fault because she was the one who wanted the divorce. Whatever one said, the other said the opposite. I didn't really know who to believe, but I always really believed my dad. But now we're not friends. I don't ever see him. I talk with him maybe once a week. I live with my mom now. He remarried and I don't like my stepmom.

Q: Why don't you like your stepmother?

JULIA: My dad always wants to please her. When we're together, I always feel left out.

RYAN: I think there is a big problem in a divorce situation when you get stepparents coming into the picture. It causes some problems because you are used to the parents that brought you up, and then having a new person introduced into the picture is hard. It's tough to adjust. In most cases the child doesn't like the new parent or has a problem with them. I have several friends who have stepparents and there is no relationship at all. They hate the person and then they become more attached to their real mother or father they had from birth.

Q: Do you think you want to get married someday? Will it be for life or as long as it works?

JULIA: Life. I want to get married but I certainly don't want to have a divorce because I know what it's like for kids and I know how upset it's made both of my parents.

RYAN: Life, definitely.
MIKE: Yeah, I agree.

The Traditional Family of the 1950's

Divorce and family breakups are not the only things that have shaped this generation's view of the family. In fact, the family most older generations grew up in has greatly diminished in size and influence. Much is said about the "traditional family." What most people have in mind is the middle-class family structure of the post-World War II period that was experienced as the Baby Boom Generation came into the world. Fueled by a growing economy and people moving from rural America to the cities and suburbs, a new family structure came into place.

Unlike the farm economy where both the husband and wife were involved in the family business, industrial and white-collar work separated the spouses, sending one to work while keeping the other one at home to raise the children. This commuter lifestyle kept the father away at work while keeping Mom intimately involved with her children and with community activities. It is no wonder that women's clubs, women's organizations at churches, and other women-based charitable organizations saw their zenith during the fifties and mid-sixties.

This two-tiered system provided family income and child-care in a unique way in history. On the farm, Dad did not commute. The child knew what his father did, and learned the family business out in the fields. Mom was responsible for canning food, making clothes, candles, and quilts, and keeping track of the livestock. Each person had a direct role in the family system. A child of the fifties would have had a hard time explaining the day-to-day work of a commuting parent, but in his or her mind it seemed to be somehow more important than the household work Mom did. Dad built office buildings or was a vice president of planning. Mom washed clothes and made lunch. Rather than a hands-on experience, "real" work was something mysterious that took Dad out of the house in the morning and returned him home with a paycheck.

Although not all people lived this way, over 52% were able to do so, and this was the predominant model of the family portrayed in the culture. The American Dream personified by *The Dick Van Dyke Show* and its clones was one in which harmony was achieved in half an hour, and where the biggest problem was whether or not Richie should get a new bike for Christmas. But over the years this type of family has diminished in size. Of those Postmoderns surveyed, 41% said they were raised in the traditional family model of the 1950's. Those who were born between 1976 and 1981 were even less likely to grow up in this kind of family. Only 31% said their childhood family was traditional. Furthermore, 10% of Postmoderns who came from a traditional family saw their parents get a divorce while in their teen or young adult years. An additional 4% saw their parents separate.

For many Postmoderns the traditional

family is something they see on TV reruns rather than something they have experienced. In fact, if we are to be honest about the whole thing, what we have called the traditional family is a generational experience of mostly Euro-American Baby Boomers and their parents, who benefited from an economy that enabled the majority of Americans to live a unique lifestyle that lasted from 1950 to 1973. For the vast majority of Postmoderns this is not a goal to be obtained, nor is it seen as one that is necessarily better. Instead, two other family systems have emerged since 1965 that are increasing in number while the traditional family system of the fifties is decreasing in number.

Rapid Growth of the Single-parent Family

The family system that has received the most attention in the past two decades is the single-parent family. Twenty-two percent of Postmoderns identified the single-parent family as the family of their childhood. While most were in single families as a result of

"I've never had my dad living in my house, so it never made me feel weird. It's always been just me and my mom."

Tyler, 16,
Glendora, California

divorce, only 3% of those surveyed were raised by single, never married mothers.

Postmoderns are taking a different route; they are having children outside of marriage. This shift is quite dramatic. Most Postmoderns who found themselves in single-parent families as children did so after their parents got a divorce. Today, as parents, a significant number of

Total number of births to unmarried women (1970 & 1992)	1970	1992
Total births to unmarried women:	399,000	1,225,000
White.	175,000 (44%)	722,000 (59%)
Black.	215,000 (54%)	459,000 (37%)
Other.	9,000 (2%)	44,000 (4%)
Under 15 years old.	10,000 (2%)	11,000 (1%)
15 to 19 years old.	190,000 (48%)	354,000 (29%)
20 to 24 years old.	127,000 (32%)	436,000 (36%)
25 to 29 years old.	41,000 (10%)	233,000 (19%)
30 to 34 years old.	19,000 (5%)	128,000 (10%)
35 years and older.	12,000 (3%)	63,000 (5%)

Source: U.S. National Center for Health Statistics, Vital Statistics of the United States, annual; Monthly Vital Statistics Report, and unpublished data, *The American Almanac*, p. 79.

Postmoderns are skipping the marriage and divorce stage; they are having children without the mess. The percentage of children born to unmarried women has increased from 10.7% of all births in 1970, to 30.1% in 1992. For whites it has increased from 5.7% to 22.6%, and for blacks from 37.6% to 68.1%.[11]

While the image of the unmarried mother is one of a poor, black youth in an urban area, by 1992 the average profile of the unmarried mother became that of a white woman in her early twenties. By 1992 more white women were having children outside of marriage than were black women. From 1970 to 1992 another change took place. Women in their early twenties were having children outside of marriage more frequently than teenagers.[12]

In March of 1995 the *U.S. Census* issued a report that showed a surprising profile of the single-parent family. Thirty-five percent of children lived with a never-married parent, while 37% lived with a divorced parent. The other 23% lived with a parent who was separated from his or her spouse. Ten years ago a child living with one parent was twice as likely to be living with divorced parents than with a never-married parent.

This radical shift in parenting and marriage patterns might be explained in a number of ways. It could be because of increased sexuality in the media, the loss of a moral compass in society, the lack of values, or a permissive society that encourages women to be as sexually active as men at an earlier and earlier age.

But another explanation must be added to the mix. Like produces like. If a large percentage of this generation has seen parents get divorced or separated, what model of a healthy relationship do they have to follow? Why get married in the first place? One young man, age thirty, put it this way: "I don't know what it means to be married. My parents divorced when I was about eight, and the only memories I have of my parents marriage are of the arguments and fights. I don't have a positive image of marriage in my head. Marriage scares me. And having children? That is too much to think about."

Ted, age nineteen, commented: "I think it comes down to a question of responsibility. When they got married they made a pledge to their partner, to God, and to their family to stay together for life. But when they get a divorce, they are breaking their promises. When they have a child, they also make a promise to bring them up. When they divorce they are throwing away all their credibility. When they ask their child to be responsible, the child's response is, 'Give me a break; look at you.'"

Postmoderns distrust the double-talk of their elders about marriage and family. It is one thing for politicians and religious leaders to espouse family values. It's quite another when these same leaders resort to divorce and serial marriage in their own lives. Under such conditions,

Postmoderns who have been burned by their parents' divorce have a hard time separating rhetoric from action. When leaders model the values they talk about, they will listen. When a person does the opposite of what he or she is saying, he or she loses credibility.

As a result, Postmoderns approach marriage with some healthy reservations. But waiting for marriage does not necessarily mean delaying getting involved in a relationship. In 1993, the number of unmarried-couple households was 3.5 million, seven times larger than the 523,000 unmarried-couple households in 1970.[13]

This points to another important factor. Postmoderns are delaying marriage in record numbers. In 1994 the *U.S. Census* reported the highest median age for first-time marriages since the census started keeping track of the figures in 1890. In 1994 the median age for first-time marriage was 26.7 for men and 24.5 for women. They also reported that the number of never-married persons doubled from 21.4 million in 1970 to 44.2 million in 1994, and that the number of currently divorced quadrupled from 4.3 million to 17.4 million in the same years. This does not account for those who have been divorced and have remarried.[14]

The implications of these numbers are important to consider. Singlehood is a growing lifestyle in the United States. The most popular shows on television focus on the single lifestyle. *Friends, Seinfeld, Frazier, The Single Guy, Cybil,* and so forth all portray different aspects of this growing American lifestyle. Rather than something to be avoided, singlehood is seen as an option just as valid as marriage.

One important group among singles are single parents. Perhaps the largest factor contributing to the increase in out-of-wedlock births among members of the Postmodern Generation is the lack of positive role models on the part of their parents. As the children of the sexual revolution, many have seen their parents go through a revolving door of relationships. Moms and Dads may have boyfriends and girlfriends just like they do. More than that, families look to many to be a battleground in which children are the ultimate losers. Why go through the hassle? If you want to have a child, why not have one? At least you'll have someone to love without having to worry that they will run out on you. Besides, motherhood has its own rewards. What mother doesn't enjoy holding a newborn in her arms and getting the validation and attention that motherhood brings?

Cheryl Russell points to some other reasons why we have seen an increase in teenage pregnancies. Observing that teenage pregnancy is nothing new in America, she points out that in 1957 the birth rate for fifteen- to nineteen-year-old women both married and unmarried was 59% percent higher than it is today. The difference is that in 1957 teenage mothers got married before the baby arrived.

Today's teens stay single. Seventy percent of Americans under the age of twenty who give birth today are not married. Russell states:

> *One reason for the increase in out-of-wedlock births is the growing economic independence of women. Another is the declining wages of men. When men can't earn enough to support a family, women have no economic incentive to marry them. This helps explain why out-of-wedlock births are higher among teens, young adults, blacks, and Hispanics. In these groups, men's earnings are low and getting lower.[15]*

Russell points to another change. Most of the recent increase in teenage births can be credited to increased births among Hispanic teenagers. From 1987 to 1992, 84% of the increase in teen births can be credited to Hispanic teens. The number of births to teens from 1987 to 1992 jumped 51% for Hispanics, 11% for non-Hispanic whites, and just 6% for blacks. Much of the reason for this growth is due to immigration and to the fertility patterns brought from Latin America. In Latin America families are formed earlier than in the United States, and common-law marriages are more common.[16]

The Multifamily

These figures point to the shift from the traditional family of the fifties to the multifamily of the nineties. In the 1950's, teenagers were much more likely to get married, have children, and start a full-time job. They entered the world of adulthood as they turned twenty-one. Today, the accruements of adulthood, marriage, children, and a steady job, are more likely to be gained by age thirty-one than by age twenty-one. The problem is that in the midst of that ten-year gap, children are being born to parents without the support system that previous generations had available. As a result, many Postmoderns find themselves with children just at the time when they are trying to form relationships that might lead to marriage and at the time when they are making decisions about careers and work.

The end result of having children outside of marriage is the development of a number of family arrangements whereby grandparents, other relatives, daycare workers, and friends take part in raising the children. This leaves single parents with the task of creating a network of shifting relationships and arrangements in order to raise their children. What once seemed simple has become confusing and complex.

For many young persons another question emerges when talking about marriage and the family. What is the positive alternative? What great benefit is there to postpone sex and to wait to have children? What dream is more powerful, what hope is greater than giving in to what comes naturally? In a society that glamorizes sex and offers few alternatives to young women and men, especially those who grow up in poor rural or urbanized neighborhoods, the decision not to have a child and to wait to have sex until they get married would be a huge leap to make from their current reality. The challenge to society as a whole is to offer a more acceptable alternative, one that allows for a longer waiting time before having children, and that gives teenagers and young adults hope for a better and more productive future.

The Rise of the Dual-earning-Parent Family

With changing expectations in the roles of women and with the diminishing earning power of one paycheck, women have been entering into the world of work in increasing numbers. From 1950 to 1985 married women with children ages six to seventeen doubled their participation in the workforce from 28% to 68%, while women with children under six quadrupled their participation rate from 12% to 54%. In February of 1986 women workers became the majority of professional employees in the United States. This reflects two factors. One is the increase of school teachers as the younger Baby Boomlets entered school. The second factor is the growing number of women entering previously male-dominated occupations.[17]

One result of this is the growth of the dual-earning-parent family. In 1993 65% of married-couple families had both spouses working. Even more important, only married-couple families with both spouses working have increased their earnings since 1975. Dual-earning families have increased their income from $44,319 in 1975 to $51,204 in 1993, while married-couple families without the wife working have seen their income go from $32,788 in 1975 to $33,310 in 1980 and back down to $30,218 in 1993. (See table below.) This trend means that in order to stay ahead or to see a growth in income, two paychecks are needed to live out the American Dream.

What makes the dual-earning-parent family unique is that the rearing of chil-

1993 median income of families (in 1993 constant dollars)

	1975	1980	1993
Married Couple Families:			
Wife in paid labor force:	44,319	47,193	51,204
Wife not in paid labor force:	32,788	33,310	30,218
Male Householder, no wife present:	33,412	30,759	26,467
Female Householder, no husband present:	17,597	18,274	17,443

Source: "Median Income of Families, by Type of Family in Current and Constant (1993) Dollars: 1970–1993,"
U. S. Bureau of the Census, Income and Poverty: 1993 Series, CD-INPO-94-03, on compact disc.

dren is an experience shared with those outside of the nuclear family. While some parents have extended family members such as grandparents to take care of the children during the day, most parents have to depend on the services of outsiders who do not necessarily share their values or their deep personal interest in the welfare of the child. The number one issue of dual-earning parents is childcare, an issue that is increasingly acute for infants, toddlers, and preschoolers.

In the 1993 survey, 40% of Postmoderns who were raised by dual-earning parents reported staying with their parents as preschoolers, while 30% were in daycare, 17% were with a babysitter, 8% were with a relative, and 5% were with a neighbor. This is in sharp contrast to those with traditional families, of whom 94% stayed at home with a parent. Even in single-

family and blended-family homes, a higher percentage stayed at home with a parent. Forty-six percent reported that they stayed at home with a parent, while 26% were in daycare, 11% were in the home of a relative, 11% were with a babysitter, and 6% were with a neighbor.

This shift in parenting styles has spawned various opinions about childcare. Many parents express regret that they cannot stay at home with their children. Others say that daycare kids are better socialized and have a wider range of experiences than their stay-at-home counterparts. One thing is clear: Postmoderns are the first generation to be part of this grand experiment. What is fascinating is that those who were raised by dual-earning families were the only ones to say that the family is working well. Fifty-two percent said yes to this

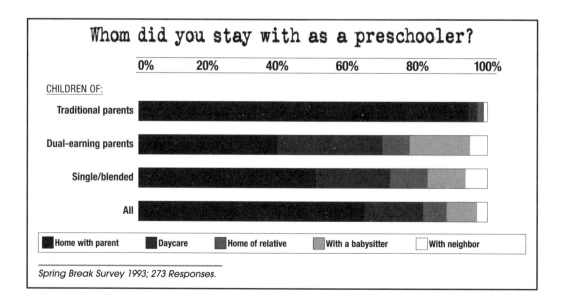

Spring Break Survey 1993; 273 Responses.

question while 48% said no. Only 35% of those raised by single-parent or blended-family parents said yes to this question, while 45% of those raised by traditional families answered in the affirmative.

Because dual-earning parents have higher incomes than other families, children of dual earners will have better economic opportunities and higher educational attainment than their peers. But income does not necessarily translate into marital bliss. Eighteen percent of Postmoderns raised in dual-earning families reported that their parents had since divorced, remarried, or separated after their childhood years.

The Ideal Postmodern Family

As Postmoderns look to the future and to having their own families, the dual-earning family is the one most have in mind. The combination of higher educational attainment by Postmodern women, the example of a greater number of women in the workforce, and an increasing need to have two paychecks to pay the bills leads more and more Postmoderns to envision themselves in the dual-earning family.

Unlike the generations before them, Postmoderns see the family unit as one in which both partners take responsibility for bringing home the bacon and for raising the children. Unlike GI Generation and Silent Generation fathers, Postmodern fathers who are married start out their par-

enting in the delivery room. Most mothers expect their husbands to be on hand to watch the delivery of their child. This shift is more than symbolic. It is a statement of expectations about whose job it is to raise the child. Changing diapers, taking care of the child while the breadwinner is working, cooking meals, and cleaning the house are no longer just women's work. In the dual-earning family both parents share responsibility for all aspects of family life. In many Postmodern households it will be the husband who cooks dinner while the wife pays the bills.

Different Family Experiences Produce Different Expectations

In the 1995 Spring Break Survey, Postmoderns were asked a number of questions dealing with the family. When asked if it was okay to have children outside of marriage, only the children of single parents or those in blended families answered in the affirmative. Fifty-five percent said it was okay to have children outside of marriage, while 45% said it wasn't. In contrast, 75% of children of traditional parents said it was not okay, and 77% of children of dual-earning parents said it was not okay.

Another question received the same kind of response. When asked if it is better to live together before getting married, 58% of children of single parents or blended families said yes, while 57% of children of traditional parents said no, and 61% of children of dual-earning parents said no.

All three groups agreed that it is much harder than it used to be to find someone to marry (82% said yes, 18% said no). This response shows up in the new marriage pattern for Postmoderns. Instead of rushing into marriage, this generation is waiting to get it right.

This brings us to an interesting place from which to view the attitudes of Postmoderns concerning family. In both the survey and in interviews it became clear that there are three basic responses when it comes to the way Postmoderns look at their future family. One response is to say:

"Perhaps the greatest impact on my life was my parents' unyielding efforts to love me and educate me. Because of that I feel that I may have avoided many bad experiences and have had many positive opportunities in my life. As a result, one of my goals for the future is to be a loving and respected husband and father, and to have children who are happy and healthy."

Jeremy, 26,
Mesa, Arizona

"I'll never get married." If marriage does not work, why even try it. Another response is to say: "I'll try it, and if it doesn't work out, I'll try something else." The most common response was: "If I do get married it will be for life." Eighty-one percent of Postmoderns, no matter what their family background, said that they are committed to having a long-term relationship.

While much has been written about the demise of the family, Postmoderns are not ready to give up on it completely. Unlike older generations, many carry with them the bitter experience of their parents' breakup. As a result they are not ones to rush head-over-heels into marriage. Instead they have a realistic attitude when it comes to relationships. This leads them to look for positive models. Some are looking to their grandparents' generation and are asking what they did to make it work. Others are saying that, with or without a spouse, they still want to have children. Others are forging group relationships with friends, and are postponing life-long decisions until they feel they are ready. Still others want to build on the positive experiences of their own families, and are looking to be in a relationship for life.

What is true for most is that the question of family and family background is a complex issue that no longer can be answered in a simple sentence. Family is a mixed bag of pluses and minuses, of hopes and fears, of desire and despair. The word family no longer has one meaning. Each person brings his or her own personal experiences and expectations to the dinner table. The question for many is whether their network of relationships will sustain and nourish them over the long haul. As a society it is to our advantage to foster and encourage relationships that last a lifetime.

From the Job to the Task

hen *P.O.V.* (Point of View), the *Esquire*-type magazine for twentysomething males, came out with its May 1996 "Annual Picks of 10 Career Fields," it showed the economy from the perspective of Postmoderns. At the top of the list of most desirable careers was computer animator. With a current workforce of five thousand, the ten-year job growth expectation is 600%. Second choice was on-line content producer. With a current workforce of five thousand, it anticipates a 500% growth over the next ten years. Third was mutual fund money manager, fourth was industrial environmentalist, and fifth was family doctor.

In contrast, the top of the endangered list included accountants, only expected to grow by 10% in the next ten years; bank tellers, who will see a 27% decrease; and government bureaucrats, who are projected to lose 300,000 jobs in the next ten years. Other jobs predicted to lose big

are telephone operators, whose jobs will be slashed by 70%, and factory workers who are expected to lose more than 700,000 jobs. Eva Pomice observes:

> *Without the proper skills, post-industrial America is a rough place. New technology, cheap foreign labor, and rampant cost-cutting have made the word 'career' sound quaint. Free trade creates new jobs but necessitates a write-off of factory jobs. And, eager to boost stock prices, Fortune 500 firms eliminated 4.7 million jobs (about one quarter of their entire workforce) in the past 15 years. . . . Economic flux will hit the uneducated and low-skilled the hardest.*[1]

Pomice's statements highlight the dilemma Postmoderns face as they enter the workforce. Do they follow in their parents' footsteps or do they blaze new trails on their own? In many ways the decision is not theirs to make. The reality is that the work-world their parents lived in is coming to a close. Rather than a top-down hierarchy of business, the world of work is becoming customized and team-driven. Instead of focusing on mass production, companies strive to meet the needs of the individual.

Companies that once sold products, now sell something else. Nike does not produce shoes. It markets a lifestyle. General Mills does not make cereal. It creates key components of a healthy diet. Coke does not manufacture a drink. It brings the world together to sing in peace and harmony.

The challenge for Postmoderns is that they are entering the workforce in the midst of a change that rivals the introduction of the assembly line back in 1914. When introduced by Henry Ford for the manufacturing of the Model-T, mass production revolutionized the way people worked. People became more productive and created many of the products that we now take for granted, such as the telephone and the car. When first introduced, these were luxury items for the very rich.

With the introduction of computer technology in the 1980's, the information revolution began a process of radically changing the way people work. The movie *Apollo 13* shows a perfect example of this change. As Jim Lovell, commander of the ill-fated April, 1970 Apollo 13 mission, tried to do the calculations that would bring his spacecraft back to earth, he asked mission control in Houston to double check his math. The camera pans a row of technicians as they furiously work the calculations with pencil, paper, and slide rules. As each person finishes

the calculation he gives the thumbs up sign. The figures were correct. Today one ten-year-old with a calculator could do the same equations in less time.

Harry S. Dent Jr., author of *Job Shock*, writes about these changes as they affect the workplace:

> *Jobs in America will change so much that we'll have to stop calling them jobs. People will be getting their own micro-missions rather than a job description, and will be allowed greater latitude than ever to be creative in fulfilling these missions. The work people do will vary from situation to situation, even from day to day in some cases. Rather than complying with some checklist from a job description, workers will exploit that underused organ the brain to help companies and customers solve problems. Individuals will be performing a variety of exciting functions and exercising independent thinking. In many ways, each individual will become a business or a valued member of a team.*[2]

As positive as this sounds to those who are highly educated and have entreprenurial spirit, to the person who just wants a stable job so that he or she can take care of a family, this is frightening. Instead of a job, the worker will be paid for a finished task, and will then have to look for a new one. This brings up a whole host of unanswered questions. If people go from place to place for work, how are they provided benefits such as health care and pensions? Will they be able to stay in one community, or will this necessitate constant movement from one place to another? Where are the safety nets when the worker is looking for his or her next project? You might thrive on change while you are young, but constant change renders it difficult to make commitments such as marriage and having children. How can a person plan for the future, when so much seems to be up in the air?

Job Security? Not!!!

What seems to be most unsettling for Postmoderns and their parents is that Postmoderns do not seem to be making it financially like their parents did at the same age. In the 1993 and 1995 Spring Break Surveys, 40% of those who had gone to college returned home to live with their parents. Unlike Baby Boomers, who got out the door as soon as they could, Postmoderns seem to want to stick around. But what appears to be slacking might actually be surviving. Mike, age twenty-eight, with a B.A. in business, describes his experience finding a job in today's economy:

Q: **What is it like for a person your age to be looking for a job in the current job market?**

MIKE: Very tedious. The only way to make it right now is by having experience—they don't really seem to care about the education. They don't actually care where you have worked. They just basically care

Ten top careers for Postmoderns

1. Computer Animator
2. On-line Content Producer
3. Mutual Fund Money Manager
4. Industrial Environmentalist
5. Family Doctor
6. Management Consultant
7. Intellectual Property Lawyer
8. Priest, Rabbi, Minister
9. Interactive Advertising Executive
10. Physical Therapist

Ten top endangered careers

1. Accountant
2. Bank Teller
3. Government Bureaucrat
4. Telephone Operator
5. Factory Worker
6. Real Estate Agent
7. Bartender
8. College Professor
9. Librarian
10. Corporate Middle Manager

Source: Eva Pomice, "Is your job cool? Or does it suck?" *P.O.V.*, May 1996, pp. 55–62.

about what you can do for the company. If you have the experience, you have a pretty good shot at it. If not, or if you have several different fields of experience, it's very difficult to get a job.

Q: **How long have you been out of college?**

MIKE: Five years.

Q: **What are the different jobs you have had?**

MIKE: I've been in insurance sales, mortgage sales, health insurance sales, and that is basically it.

Q: **Do you see a difference between people of your age group and those who are in management in terms of the way they treat you?**

MIKE: People in management are a lot more stressed out than even the sales force. They are being grinded constantly. In fact, the last company I was with just cut out five hundred more jobs, and a big chunk of that was middle management. They don't stand much of a chance.

Q: **So it's hard for you to look toward what you might be doing in ten years?**

MIKE: I have no idea. Who knows? It changes from year to year. I hope to get out of sales and get into something more stable, but nothing is really stable right now. I'm seeing all my friends go down. This is very difficult. The pressures are intense.

Q: **How do you deal with the pressures?**

MIKE: Not very well. We don't deal with them. I see lots of my friends on the verge of nervous break-

downs. They are having a very difficult time out there. It's tough.

Q: **So the issue is that those who are ahead of you in the job market-say someone who has been in the same company for ten to fifteen years-they are losing their jobs, and your generation is coming into the work force and doesn't have much of an opportunity.**

MIKE: Sure, there is no room for advancement and growth because when everyone gets crunched down you have a lot of people who are demoted instead of promoted. The only way to really get ahead is to own your own business—get into it in your own way.

Q: **How does your experience vary from your dad's? What is the major difference?**

MIKE: My dad got in when the opportunities were good with a big utility company. He is going to be able to stay with the company thirty years. There's no way I am going to be able to stay with a company for thirty years. He has actually come to the realization, finally, that it's not like it used to be, not even close.

Q: **What is the biggest change?**

MIKE: The companies have become so competitive that they need to downsize and cut all their overhead, and that's where all the management and middle management people go. He's lucky to be in senior management and have seniority, that is the only thing that's keeping his job alive.

Q: How does that affect your values? What values do you and your friends have?

MIKE: All our values now pretty much go around survival. It's just a matter of surviving until either the economy gets going or something gets better. That's why a lot of my friends are looking to open up their own businesses. Just trying to break away from the gridlock of working in a big company where there's not much security anymore.

Q: How do you feel when you look at you and your generation compared to the generation before you?

MIKE: The major difference is that the opportunities were a lot better back then. It has become more "dog eat dog" today. No one is really safe. The stability, the old idea of getting a college education—or even a high school education—and going on and working for a company and having security for thirty or forty years, and then retiring nicely, is gone. Anybody in my age group and younger knows that the security is not there.

Q: What is your hope for the future as you look down the line?

MIKE: Getting my own business, being successful that way. Not having to worry about someone else telling me what to do or not to do, how much money I can make, and when I can retire.

Q: What's the biggest thing that you fear?

MIKE: Not being able to provide for a family. It's scary thinking about bringing kids into the world, let alone being able to support them.

Q: One of the stereotypes is that the only jobs that people of your generation get are McJobs-service jobs at fast food restaurants that receive little pay.

MIKE: Not everyone is working at hamburger joints. There are a lot of respectable jobs out there. At least they sound respectable on paper—but you start talking to people and they are not happy. They have to answer to someone, they are working long hours, driving long hours on the freeway, while having to deal with all the bureaucracy in these companies that are trying to scale down. It's tough. It certainly isn't the way it used to be.

Mike's insights bring into focus the dilemma of finding work in a rapidly changing economy fueled by change. As he notes, his world is much different than his father's world. When his father left college he was looking to have a career. For Mike and his friends, they are just happy to get a job.

As Postmoderns look at work and the economy, three keys factors seem to come into play: education, investment in the future, and the definition of success.

Dumb and Dumber?

In the past five years the education system in the United States has increasingly come under attack. Critics point to lower scores on SAT tests, high school students who can't find Japan on maps or write a grammatically correct sentence, and the lowering of academic standards in college.

Educators defend themselves by saying that their job is much harder than it used to be. Children come to school with a variety of social problems that they have to deal with before the child can even begin to think about learning to read and write. Children seem to have shorter attention spans. Parents are less willing to work with kids on homework, and have less time to be involved in the school. Children come with more diverse needs. For more and more students, English is a second language.

Like so many other issues, Postmoderns are the ones who have been caught in the middle. And like the abuser who blames the victim, Postmoderns are the ones who have taken the blame.

A picture in the December 1992 *Atlantic Monthly* that leads into the article

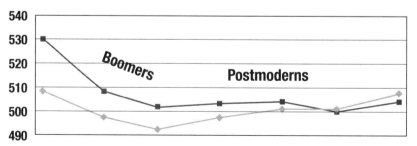

SAT scores adjusted upward by 100 points

In the summer of 1996 the college board readjusted the SAT scores to reflect 100 points higher on combined scores. The new scale is as follows:

	1972	1976	1980	1984	1988	1992	1996
Verbal ■	530	509	502	504	505	500	505
Math ◆	509	497	492	497	501	501	508

Source: College Entrance Examination Board, New York, NY. *National College Bound Senior*, annual.

"The New Generation Gap" typifies the stereotype of the dumb Postmodern. It shows an urban Baby Boomer male at the checkout stand in a grocery store. The clerk is a Postmodern woman who is having problems making change. In her hand is a twenty-dollar bill. On the cash register is the price of the goods—$16.73. Her face conveys her puzzlement as she tries to figure out how much change to give back.

Neil Howe and William Strauss, authors of *Generations* and *13th Gen,* describe in an article in *The Atlantic Monthly* how Boomers view the Thirteeners, so-called because Postmoderns are the thirteenth generation since the birth of the nation:

> Who are they and what are they up to? On the job, thirteeners are the reckless bicycle messengers, pizza drivers, yard workers, Wal-Mart shelf-stockers, healthcare trainees, and miscellaneous scavengers, hustlers, and McJobbers in the low-wage/low-benefit service economy. They're the wandering nomads of the temp world, directionless slackers, habitual nonvoters. In school they're a group of staggering diversity—not just in ethnicity but also in attitude, performance, and rewards. After graduation they're the ones with the big loans who were supposed to graduate into jobs and move out of the house but didn't, and who seem to get poorer the longer they've been away from home—unlike their parents at that age, who seemed to get richer.[3]

Howe and Strauss bring home the point that Postmoderns appear to older generations as a struggling, unsuccessful group who are not making it as did their elders. This common stereotype is echoed in the media through such movies and TV programs as *Bill and Ted's Excellent Adventure, Wayne's World, Dumb and Dumber,* and *Beavis and Butthead.* All of these portray Postmodern males as savvy idiots who know how to make it in their own world but are not successful in comparison with their parents.

Wayne's World is a classic portrayal of this stereotype. The movie begins by showing Wayne, a twentysomething male, walking through his parents' house. He introduces himself by saying he has a nice place to live, even though it is bogus that it's his parents' place. He opens a closet where he shows the audience his collection of hair nets that he received in the various fast-food places in which he has worked. Later his goal in life is seen as getting a new guitar. His greatest hope is that his public access cable television show, called *Wayne's World* will pay off someday. His costar, Garth, is a long-haired blond who is afraid of his own shadow.

Wayne's world is filled with heavy rock music, friends who are not making it in the real world, and Baby Boomer executives who want to rip him off by stealing the rights to his show. While not book smart, he is street smart. When he meets a Chinese rock singer, he purchases an audio tape on how to speak Chinese so he can talk to her in her own language. Later, when he realizes he is being taken advantage of by a television producer, he figures out a way to use technology to win. Wayne's friends are his family. His parents are never shown throughout the whole movie. The theme of the film is "Wayne and his friends against the world."

While it is tempting to label this as a generation of want-to-be's, the reality is that they are obtaining high school and college educations in record numbers. The percentage of blacks, whites, Asians, and Hispanics receiving their high school diplomas has increased. The same is true for those entering college. What is ironic for this generation is that while the economy has been transitioning away from one in which more technical and knowledge-based skills are needed, the cost of education has skyrocketed for those wish-

ing to go on to higher educational levels.

The High Cost of Education

As Postmoderns have sought to increase their educational attainment, they have found themselves facing some daunting obstacles. Take for instance the cost of higher education. From 1985 to 1994 the cost of higher education for students at both private and public universities and colleges doubled. Unlike earlier generations who benefited from government-sponsored programs such as the GI bill, Postmoderns have had to bear the cost on their own. It is not unusual for college graduates to have $15,000 to $30,000 loans to pay off, especially if they have gone on to advanced degrees.

At the same time that costs went up, many colleges initiated cutbacks in staff

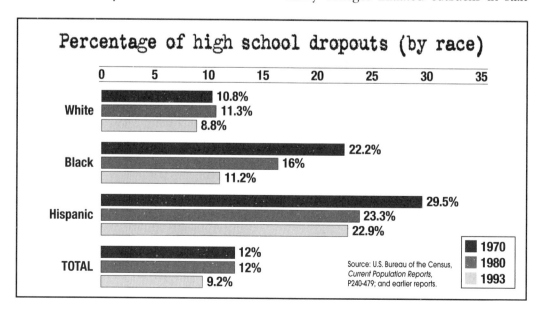

Percentage of high school dropouts (by race)

	1970	1980	1993
White	10.8%	11.3%	8.8%
Black	22.2%	16%	11.2%
Hispanic	29.5%	23.3%	22.9%
TOTAL	12%	12%	9.2%

Source: U.S. Bureau of the Census, *Current Population Reports,* P240-479; and earlier reports.

and salaries. Because of cutbacks in certain fields, many Postmoderns had to stay longer in college in order to fulfill their degree requirements. Having fewer professors required that classes be offered in alternating years.

The public schools found themselves in similar situations. In one of the most cynical ad campaigns of the late 1980's, Californians were encouraged to vote for a state lottery because "your kids win too." Instead of passing bonds at the local and state levels in order to support public schools, Californians opted to play the lottery under the guise that profits would support the "extras" at schools. After the lottery was passed, schools throughout the state cut funds for music, the arts, and sports. Participants would have to pay if they wanted to play.

These problems are not relegated only to the nation's most populous state. The U.S. General Accounting Office esti-

> *"There was a cartoon in the school paper, 'Now that you have graduated, when are you going to Disneyland?'—and we poke fun at it, but it's a very serious concern. We spend thousands of dollars on our education, and once I get out of law school I'm going to be tens of thousands of dollars in debt. Whether or not I can find a job that's going to pay back what I owe in a year, who knows?"*
>
> Nate, 22,
> Florida State University

mates that $112 billion is needed to repair and upgrade the nation's schools. In Tulsa, Oklahoma, the newest school building is twenty years old. The average age of buildings is the same as the

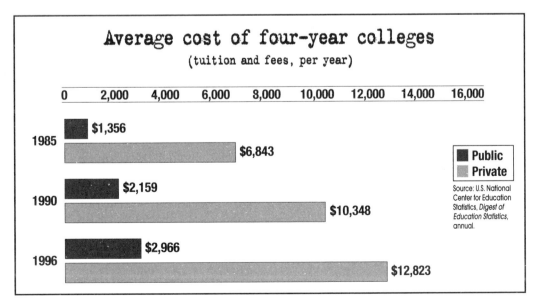

Average cost of four-year colleges
(tuition and fees, per year)

	0	2,000	4,000	6,000	8,000	10,000	12,000	14,000	16,000

1985
Public: $1,356
Private: $6,843

1990
Public: $2,159
Private: $10,348

1996
Public: $2,966
Private: $12,823

Legend:
■ Public
▨ Private

Source: U.S. National Center for Education Statistics, *Digest of Education Statistics*, annual.

Boomers for whom they were built, forty-four years old. Tulsa, like many other school districts across the United States, has deferred building maintenance for years, opting instead to put money into programming. Two recent school construction and technology bonds have failed in the past two years. Antitax sentiment, middle-class flight, and an aging population of which only one in four voters has a child in school almost ensures the defeat of future bills.[4]

This narrow mindset is reflected in many ways throughout the culture. While the poverty rate for those over sixty-five has decreased from 24.6 in 1970 to 11.7 in 1994, the poverty rate for children and youth under the age of eighteen has increased from 14.9 in 1970 to 21.8 in 1994.[5] While programs for seniors, such as Medicare and social security, are sacred cows not to be touched, programs for children and youth are up for grabs. As a nation, Americans are far more willing to cut funding for children than they are to deal with the mushrooming problem of social security.

A Generational Time Bomb

In 2011 the first member of the Baby Boom generation will retire. While this may not seem like a big deal at first sight, it concerns a major issue toward which Americans are in deep denial. Social security, and its cousin, Medicare, have been hallowed programs for the GI Gen-

eration. Created during the depression of the 1930's as a way to ensure a stable retirement, social security is as American as apple pie and the American flag rolled up into one.

But for Postmoderns and Baby Boomers, social security is a time bomb waiting to go off. The problem is this. When the social security system was formulated in 1930 people did not live nearly as long. In the 21st century, with the increase in life expectancy due to improved medical care and technology, the number of those over age sixty-five will mushroom.

By the year 2030 one out every five Americans will be over age sixty-five. Because the Baby Boom generation is the largest demographic block, younger generations will bear a heavy financial burden to support the payments needed to finance social security for the Baby Boomers. One of the common myths is that when you pay into social security it somehow goes into your personal account and is saved for you when you retire. In actuality it is a pay-as-you-go program.

In 1960 there were 5.1 taxpaying workers to support each social security beneficiary. In 1996 it had diminished to 3.3, but by 2030 there will be fewer than two workers per beneficiary. By 2030, when all Boomers will have reached the age of sixty-five, social security will be running an annual deficit of $766 billion. If current laws remain the same, deficit payments for social security and Medicare

Hospital Insurance will run a deficit of $1.7 trillion.

Another way to put this: In order to pay the same benefits in 2030 as those over sixty-five now receive, payroll taxes for individuals would have to rise from the current 11.5% to 35 to 55% of every worker's paycheck. Who would have to pay these taxes? The Postmodern and the Millennial generations. Will they pay these kind of taxes? What generation would be able to afford to?

Peter Peterson, in a must-read article in the May 1996 *Atlantic Monthly* makes these observations:

> Consider how we deny the truth about entitlement programs. In justifying every new benefit increase and every refusal to accept slower growth in expenditures for the elderly, the senior lobby talks as if 'old' meant 'poor.' But elderly Americans now have the highest level of per capita household wealth of any age group, and counting in-kind income such as health benefits, a lower poverty rate than younger adults. Although old-age benefits were originally intended to be a safety net for the truly needy, today's entitlement system more closely resembles a well-padded hammock for middle- and upper-class retirees. One third of Medicare benefits, and nearly two fifths of Social Security benefits, and more than two thirds of federal pension benefits now go to households with incomes above the U.S. median. Back in the early 1960s the typical seventy-year-old consumed about 30 percent less (in dollars) than the typical thirty-year-old; today the typical seventy-year-old consumes 20 percent more.[6]

As the United States heads into the 21st century, the most vital issue for the

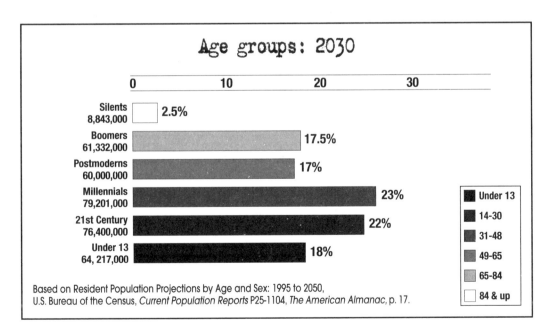

Based on Resident Population Projections by Age and Sex: 1995 to 2050, U.S. Bureau of the Census, *Current Population Reports* P25-1104, *The American Almanac*, p. 17.

future will be how to finance the needs of the elderly. Peterson and others are saying that if Baby Boomers and Postmoderns were to begin saving today for their own retirements, the crushing payments for future social security benefits could be softened. The primary point Peterson makes is this: The longer we wait to deal with the issue the worse it is going to get.

Generation Debt

Ron Nelson and Jon Cowan, cofounders of *Lead . . . or Leave*, a political organization for Postmoderns, point to another major issue for their generation. Along with payments for social security and Medicare, the national debt is a major financial burden for this generation. In 1960 the total national debt since the founding of the country was only $290 billion. From 1960 to 1979 a trillion dollars of debt was added. But from 1980 to 1994 the nation rang up an additional debt of $3.5 trillion. By 1995 the total debt was $4.5 trillion. While older generations have rung up the numbers, it is the younger generations who will have to pay them off. This money was not spent on children or on education or on building up the country's infrastructure—such as roads and bridges, all areas in which investment actually decreased. Instead the money was spent on military endeavors, tax breaks for the rich, and middle-class welfare. For example, in the early 1990's, $120 billion a year in federal benefits went to households making over $50,000.[7]

As a result, many Postmoderns are concerned about their financial future. In the 1995 Spring Break Survey, Postmoderns echoed many of these same concerns. While 63.3% felt that their career options were better than the previous year, 56.3% did not believe they would stay in one career during their working

Do you agree (yes) or disagree (no) with the following:	Yes	No
My career options are better than they were a year ago	63.3%	39.7%
I believe I will stay in one career for my working life.	39.7	56.3
Boomers understand our generation's needs at work	33.7	54.7
I will receive social security benefits when I retire	53.7	39
The government's first priority should be to cut the deficit	48.3	46.3
The generation following us will have more opportunities.	50	44.7
Children will have it better than we when they are over 12	41	53.3

Spring Break Survey 1995; 300 Responses.

years. While 53.7% believed they would receive social security when they retired, 48.3% thought the government's first priority should be to cut the deficit. While 50% thought the generation following them would have more opportunities, 53.3% did not think they would have it better than they when they reached their teens.

While these appear at first to be conflicting responses, they reflect another part of the picture. Individuals see themselves as doing well. But when they look at the culture at large they are not so sure. When you are caught in the middle, it is hard to see how vast changes in the marketplace will affect you as an individual.

What Is Success?

A common statement made about Postmoderns is that they will be less successful than their parents' generation. This judgment is based on evidence that seems to show that Postmoderns are having a hard time achieving the hallmarks of adulthood at the same age as did previous generations. When asked what they hoped to achieve by the age of thirty, Postmoderns were given the choices of owning their own home, having a child, being married, and having a secure job. Seventy-eight percent of the youngest group thought they would meet all four expectations of adulthood. The oldest group, of whom some were just turning thirty, gave a lower response. Fifty-four percent of those twenty-five to thirty saw themselves as achieving all four by age thirty.

In reality Postmoderns are waiting

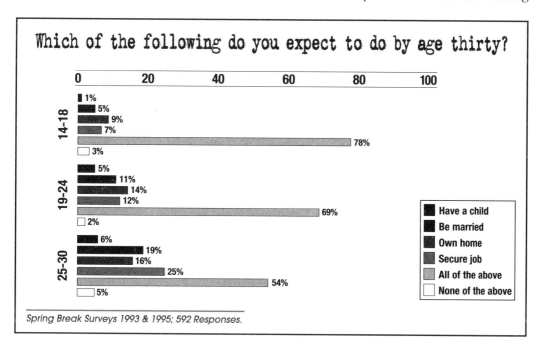

Which of the following do you expect to do by age thirty?

14-18
- Have a child: 1%
- Be married: 5%
- Own home: 9%
- Secure job: 7%
- All of the above: 78%
- None of the above: 3%

19-24
- Be married: 5%
- Own home: 11%
- Secure job: 14%
- All of the above: 12%
- (next): 69%
- None of the above: 2%

25-30
- Be married: 6%
- Own home: 19%
- Secure job: 16%
- All of the above: 25%
- (next): 54%
- None of the above: 5%

Legend:
- Have a child
- Be married
- Own home
- Secure job
- All of the above
- None of the above

Spring Break Surveys 1993 & 1995; 592 Responses.

On a scale of 1 to 4, with (1) highest, how do you define success?

Having fulfilling relationships with other people	2.14
Growing in knowledge and wisdom as you age	2.20
Owning a home and having a family	2.57
Having enough money to meet all your needs	2.60

Spring Break Surveys 1993 & 1995; 592 Responses; average scores.

later to get married, are staying in their parents' house longer, and are having a harder time finding secure employment. All of these factors put together paint the picture of a generation that does not seem to be getting its act together. The funny thing is that Postmoderns do not see it in the same way.

Rather than rushing into marriage at an early age they want to wait until they get it right. Staying at the parents' house is not a failure, it is good planning for the future. When you cannot find a job in your field, you go back to school for more training.

As a result Postmoderns are developing a different definition of success than previous generations. When asked if they would be more successful or less successful than their parents' generation, 68% said they would be more successful,

while 32% said they would be less successful. If based on conventional wisdom it would seem that Postmoderns do not have a realistic view of their future. But Postmoderns have a vision of an American Dream that is not based primarily on owning a home and having a family. Instead, developing fulfilling relationships is seen as a more accurate description of success. Along with this is the importance of growing in knowledge and wisdom as you age.

These two factors show another side of Postmoderns when it comes to work and the economy. If success is based on relationships, rather than owning a home or accumulating money, then what is the purpose of work? Rather than having a job for life with one corporation, many Postmoderns will be paid for work done on a particular project. They will move from task to task as their skills are needed. A task may last one month or two years. When it is finished, it will be time to find a new one.

For Postmoderns, work needs to have a different purpose than just the accumulation of money. It needs to be an avenue through which they grow and develop in professional knowledge and as human beings. Many Baby Boomer managers have had a problem understanding this aspect of the Postmodern generation's attitude toward work. When asked if Boomers understood their generation's needs at work, 54.7% said no. Many a Boomer boss has been heard to complain that when the clock hits five o'clock the Postmoderns head out the door. When Boomers were in the same position they worked overtime to impress the boss so they could get ahead.

But Postmoderns ask: "Get ahead of what?" If they face a job situation that is going to be ever-changing, in which lay-offs and job searches are the norm, in which they will be sought more for their expertise relating to one piece of the corporate puzzle than for their future in the company, what do they really need?

If few Postmoderns expect to stay with one company or even with one career in their life, then climbing the corporate ladder to success is not a feasible option. What they need from work is an atmosphere in which they can contribute to the company while at the same time developing skills and knowledge that will be transferable in the future. If more work will be done in teams rather than as individuals, then mentoring and building relationships become key areas of development for the Postmodern worker.

While this may sound somewhat self-ish, the reality is that in an economy that is fast-forwarding to the 21st century, the ones who survive and thrive will be the ones who keep their options open, who are adaptable, and who are constantly building knowledge.

Rather than learning one set of skills that will last a lifetime, Postmoderns are faced with the daunting task of creating and recreating themselves as the impact of digital-age technology explodes the way work was done in the past. Rather than depending on the paternal love and concern of the corporation, they will more and more have to depend on their network of friends and contacts, and on their own abilities to flex with the world that surrounds them. As the economy moves from the job to the task, Postmoderns who make it will be the ones who stay one step ahead of the competition and who constantly retool themselves for the future.

From One Way to Diversity

One of the great art forms of the 6th century was the mosaic. Taking cubed pieces of colored glass and marble, artists of the Byzantium Empire decorated with mosaics the inside walls of their places of worship and their public buildings. The most beautiful mosaics are those found on ceilings. When you view these from a distance you see the whole picture, as one color blends with and enhances the others.

Almost every day Americans spend a great deal of time looking at modern day versions of the mosaic. If you were to take a magnifying glass and look at a television screen or the monitor of a computer screen you would find small dots called pixels. Each dot has its own color. When combined with other pixels an image is created on the screen. In the fifties almost all screens were black and white. In the nineties almost all screens are in color.

When we talk about diversity we tend to think in terms of black and white, or rich and poor. While these classifications may have served to describe different groups of people in earlier times, the diversity of Postmoderns is much more like the color screen of a television. The Postmodern Generation includes many different perspectives, colors, and mixtures, with hues and patterns intermixing to create new personal and social images. For this generation diversity takes on many different aspects and arrangements. There is no simple classification system into which the members of this group easily fit. Instead each person brings his or her own complex mix to the table.

In the pages that follow we will talk about factors that make Postmoderns more diverse than previous generations. We will see how American culture has shifted from one way of seeing the world to a diversity of viewpoints. We will also look at some different classifications of diversity, in an attempt to build a framework in which we can see the whole picture.

Racial Ethnic Diversity

Our society is becoming more and more racially diverse. In the past much of the United States' racial ethnic mix was created by people from European nations such as England, Germany, Ireland, Italy, and Sweden. In the 1990's, by contrast, the mix is made up of people from around the world. This trend is reflected in many different aspects of our society.

When General Mills celebrated the seventy-fifth birthday of its icon Betty Crocker, it unveiled its eighth updated version. The company took pictures of seventy-five contestants and merged them together to create a new composite picture of the all-American woman. Instead of the blue eyes that were part of previous versions, the nineties version has brown eyes. Instead of a fair skinned European, the new Betty Crocker could be Greek, Hispanic, or Italian. Instead of gray hair, the new version has dark brown hair shaped in a very professional style.[1]

More major league baseball players have the last name Martinez than any other name. The starting rotation of pitchers for the 1996 Los Angeles Dodgers had one pitcher from Japan, one from Korea, one from Mexico, one from the Dominican Republic, and another from the United States. The pitcher from the United States is one of the oldest members of the team. Dubbed the United Nations staff, it is considered to be one of the top rotations in the league. In San Jose, California, there are more Nguyens in the phone book than Joneses.

Racial ethnic diversity of the five American generations - 1994					
	Whites	**Blacks**	**Hispanics**	**Native Americans**	**Asians/ Pacific Islanders**
Gls (1908–1926) 24,901,000	86%	8%	4%	0.4%	1.6%
Silents (1927–1945) 43,316,000	80	10	6.5	0.5	3
Baby Boomers (1946–1964) 78,193,000	74.5	12	9.25	0.75	3.5
Postmoderns (1965–1981) 62,587,000	68	14	13	1	4
Millennials (1982+) 49,868,000	66	15	14	1	4

Based on "Resident Population, by Race, Hispanic Origin, and Single Years of Age - 1994": U.S. Bureau of the Census, *The American Almanac*, p. 22f.

These are just some of the signposts of one of the great demographic shifts taking place in the United States. While we hear a lot about age in reference to different generations, more telling is the difference in racial ethnic diversity. For example, while the GI Generation's population is 86% white, the white population of the Postmodern Generation is 68%. The generation that follows the Postmoderns, the Millennials, has an even smaller white population, 66%. By the year 2050 the *U.S. Census* projects a total population of 392,031,000 with the following ethnic mix: 52.5% white, 22.5% Hispanic, 14.4% black, 9.7% Asian, and .9% Native American.[2] In places such as Los Angeles, Miami, and New York City this level of ethnic diversity has already been reached.

As we look at the racial ethnic make-up of the United States we find four factors that contribute to increasing diversity: The growth in world population, births in the United States, growth of the multiethnic population, and immigration.

Factor #1: Growth in World Population

The population of the world is growing at a rapid rate. It is estimated that from 1975 to 2020 the population of the world will double from four billion to eight billion. By 2025 the United States will have the world's third largest population, at somewhere around 338,300,000. Largest will be China, at 1,504,300,000, and second will be India, at 1,376,100,000.

While population growth in the so-called developing countries will continue at a rapid pace, populations will grow

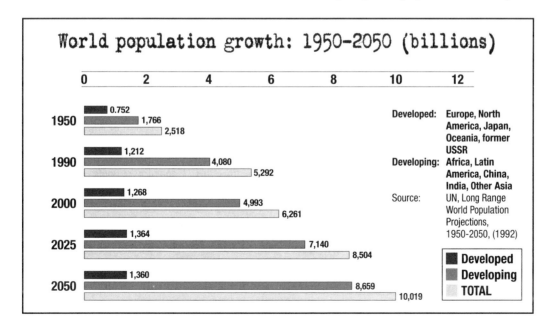

World population growth: 1950-2050 (billions)

1950	Developed: Europe, North America, Japan, Oceania, former USSR
1990	Developing: Africa, Latin America, China, India, Other Asia
2000	Source: UN, Long Range World Population Projections, 1950-2050, (1992)
2025	
2050	

1950: 0.752 / 1,766 / 2,518
1990: 1,212 / 4,080 / 5,292
2000: 1,268 / 4,993 / 6,261
2025: 1,364 / 7,140 / 8,504
2050: 1,360 / 8,659 / 10,019

- Developed
- Developing
- TOTAL

more slowly in developed countries. For example from 1990 to 2025 the developed countries will remain relatively stable, growing from 1,212,000,000 in 1990 to 1,364,000,000 in 2025. In developing countries the population will explode from 4,080,000,000 in 1990 to 7,140,000,000 in 2025. (See chart on page 127.)

A surprising result of this change is that while the age of the population of developed countries such as the United States and Japan grows older, in developing countries such as Egypt, Nigeria, and Thailand the population is getting younger. In Latin America, Africa, and the Far East people under eighteen years old form the majority.

While poverty is a major problem in many parts of the world, another factor that tends to be overlooked is the growing consumer culture among youth worldwide. This consumer culture is fueled by access to television. As Postmoderns hit their teen years in the early 1980's one of their slogans was: "I want my MTV." MTV, the first cable network to offer round-the-clock music videos and programming for teenagers and young adults, now reaches 239 million viewers in sixty-eight countries. Other cable networks such as ESPN, CNN, BBC, and The Discovery Channel have similar numbers of viewers. Today people in over two hundred countries can tune into CNN at the same time to view the same emerging crisis.

The New World Teen Study, conducted among teenagers in twenty-six differ-

ent countries in 1995, asked participants to name the activities they had engaged in on one particular day. Ninety-one percent said they had watched TV, 63% had read a newspaper, 57% had listened to a radio, and 35% had read a magazine.

While most countries produce their own local programming, shows like *ER* and movies such as *Home Alone* are popular with teens around the world. Of even more interest is the fact that television is creating a worldwide teen culture. The New World Study found that viewers of MTV were more likely to wear the teen uniform—blue jeans, running shoes, and denim jackets—than were nonviewers. These same youth are much more likely to own personal electronic gear such as walkmans, and to consume candy, sodas, and fast food in numbers as high as their American counterparts.

Chip Walker, global trend director of The Brain Waves Group in New York City says that in order to communicate with this growing demographic group one has to understand their perspective on life.

Advertisers interested in targeting the planet's future adult consumers must remember to 'stay real.' No matter where they live, teenagers struggle with the opposing forces of worry and optimism. The prevailing result in light of the conflicting forces is a down-to-earth mindset.

Walker further points out that the one statement teenagers worldwide agree with is: "It's up to me to get what I want out of life."[3]

The growth of the worldwide population will affect the United States in a number of ways. Increased population growth worldwide will increase the demand for immigration. Increased need for resources will force the United Stated to be in worldwide competition for natural resources such as oil. Environmental problems and health issues will compete for the world's attention. For example, according to the *World Population Profile: 1994*, deaths from AIDS will increase in many parts of the developing world. Peter Way, who authored the report, states that by the year 2010 the average life expectancy in Haiti will have plummeted to forty-four years, instead of the fifty-nine it would have been without AIDS. In Uganda life expectancy could fall to thirty-two years, whereas without AIDS it would be fifty-nine years.[4]

These issues will confront the United States with a terrible moral dilemma. How should the richest nation in the world respond to the epidemics and food shortages that some nations are sure to face? What will "defense" look like in this more complex world? How will population growth affect the world's environment? How will technology help or hinder our ability to be a leader in the world? Does wealth bring with it responsibility? Do we shelter ourselves against the rest of the world or do we work to make it a better place for all? As the Postmodern Generation takes its place of leadership in the early part of the 21st century it will face great challenges as the world population continues to grow rapidly.

Factor #2: Higher Birth Rate Among Asians/Pacific Islanders and Hispanics

The second factor affecting diversity in the United States is the number of projected births to certain racial ethnic groups. The number of births to non-Hispanic whites, blacks, and American Indians are expected to remain fairly stable from 1990 to 2000. Non-Hispanic whites are expected to go from 2,720,000 births to 2,363,000 births per year, while births among blacks are expected to decrease from 659,000 to 655,000. American Indian births are expected to remain the same at 42,000.

Asians and Hispanics, on the other hand, will continue to see increases in the number of births per year. From 1990 to 2000, births per year to Hispanics are expected to increase from 595,000 to 690,000, and for Asians/Pacific Islanders from 149,000 to 205,000.[5] This suggests yet another element of diversity—whites, blacks, and Native Americans will have higher percentages in the older generations, while Hispanics and Asians/Pacific Islanders will increase in the percentage of younger generations.

Factor #3: Growth in the Multiethnic Population

A 1993 special issue of *Time* dealing with ethnicity reported that over the course of two decades the number of interracial marriages in the United States has tripled. Seventy-two percent of Americans know at least one married couple in which the husband and wife are of different races. The incidence of births of mixed-race babies has multiplied twenty-six times as fast as that of other groups. Sixty-five percent of Japanese Americans marry people who have no Japanese heritage. Native Americans measure even higher in this category at 70%. This diversity is not limited to race. Among Jews, the number of those who have married outside of their faith climbed from 10% to 52% since 1960.[6]

In 1994 the *U.S. Census* reported that there were 1,283,000 interracial couples. Twenty-three percent were black/white couples, 6% were black/other race couples,

and 70% were white/other race couples.[7]

The issue of how to categorize biracial or multiethnic persons is an explosive one. It challenges America's historically simplistic categories of whether a person is black or white. In the 1920's much debate took place over the classification of race and the identification of "desirable" immigrants. In 1924 the Congress severely restricted immigration of the so-called "inferior races" from southern and eastern Europe. In the same year, the state of Virginia determined that a white person could not marry anyone with a single drop of "Negro" blood. Earlier in its history Virginians were more lenient. In the 1800's someone with less than one-fourth "Negro blood" could be classified as white. It wasn't until 1967 that the state of Virginia eliminated its laws

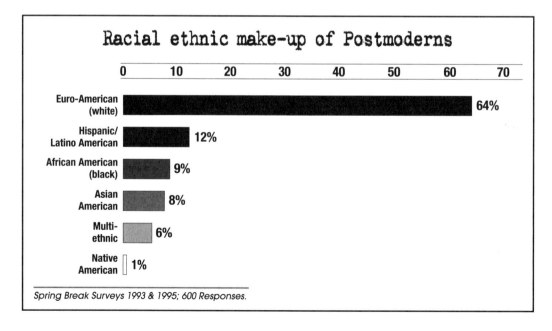

Racial ethnic make-up of Postmoderns

	0	10	20	30	40	50	60	70

Euro-American (white) — 64%
Hispanic/Latino American — 12%
African American (black) — 9%
Asian American — 8%
Multi-ethnic — 6%
Native American — 1%

Spring Break Surveys 1993 & 1995; 600 Responses.

prohibiting interracial marriage.[8]

These classifications are clearly breaking down in the 1990's. While walking in a Springfield, Virginia mall, I was amazed to see the number of interracial couples—black, white, Asians, and Hispanics—who were clearly out on a date. This mixing of cultures gives Postmoderns a kind of built-in resistance to easy stereotypes and classifications. How do you classify someone whose ancestry is Ghanaian-German-Irish-Japanese? Is he or she black? White? Asian?

The 1990 Census shows how racial ethnic categories are breaking down. Americans claimed membership in nearly three hundred races or ethnic groups and six hundred American tribes. Hispanics had seventy categories of their own.[9]

Because the census does not have a place for people to identify themselves as multiethnic persons, numbers for this group are rarely reported. In the Spring Break Survey, 6% of Postmoderns identified themselves as being multiethnic. As a result, when compared to the census figures, the numbers of blacks and Hispanics appear smaller. The number of blacks reported by the census is 14%, while in the Spring Break Survey it was 9%. The number of Hispanics was 12% compared to 11.5%. What explains this difference? The category of multiethnic.

When given a choice of ethnicity, children of black/white couples will more than likely choose black. When given a choice of multiethnic, they will likely choose multiethnic. The same is true for other mixtures of races. In this politically correct era of affirmative action, rarely would persons of biracial parents choose white. Why? Because it is not to their advantage. If the child of a black/white or Asian/white union were applying to college, would it be better to indicate black or white, or Asian or white, as the race? If colleges are looking to increase the ethnic mix of the student body, then choosing a race other than white will increase that person's chances for admission.

This kind of decision exposes the problem of classifying people simply on the basis of race. I recently had a discussion with a couple of colleagues about this issue. My colleague from Puerto Rico does not consider herself to be Hispanic or Latino, even though she speaks Spanish. She pointed out to me that most Spanish-speaking people prefer to be called by their nationality. An African American pointed out that among younger African Americans the preference seems to be black.

At a meeting at my daughter's school two Native Americans from the Postmodern Generation came to give a demonstration of Native American dance. They both said they like to be called American Indians. Asians who come from a wide variety of countries feel much more pride in their nationality than in being lumped together. Korean, Chinese, and Japanese people have different languages, traditions, and relationships with one another

‖**T**he reality is we are one human race. Period. We share a rich heritage of culture and ethnic diversity, but when it gets down to the bottom line we are one."

Douglas Armstrong, associate professor of anthropology, University of Syracuse

that stretch down through history.

Even whites are not too sure what to call themselves. "Anglo" refers mainly to people from England. "White" could refer to all participants in the conflict in Bosnia. Surely they all do not have one mindset. Euro-American encompasses all European countries but is not widely used.

As a result there is much confusion as to how to categorize one another. In a talk, should you refer to blacks as "blacks" or as "African Americans"? Native Americans as "Native Americans" or "Indians" or by a tribal name? Each term brings its own risk of offending someone, all in the attempt not to be offensive.

Scientists are coming to the conclusion that putting people into the three racial categories of black, white, and Asian does not do justice to the immense diversity of the human race. The categorization of people by race started during the age of exploration in the 1600's. When explorers came to Africa and Asia it was simple to label people by racial categories. Today when barriers between

nations are breaking down and with the mixture of different races, these categories lose their appeal.

Today 70% of cultural anthropologists and 50% of physical anthropologists reject race as a biological category. Instead they look to categorize people by genes, traits, or evolution. By analyzing people of particular races, biologist Richard Lewontin of Harvard University found that there is more genetic difference among people of one race than between the members of different races. Only 6.3% of genetic differences could be attributed to racial markers such as skin color.

For example, if you were to pick at random two black people and compare their twenty-three pairs of chromosomes, you would probably find that they have less in common with each other than with a white person picked at random. Most of our differences and commonalities have less to do with race than with how our DNA stacks up against that of another individual, regardless of race.[10] Underneath we are more alike than we ever before believed.

Factor #4: Growth in Immigration Since 1965

The fourth factor that has increased the diversity of the racial ethnic population in the United States is the growth in immigration. Beginning in the first birth year of the Postmoderns, 1965, the United States raised the level of legal immigration. From 1971 to 1993 over 15 million legal immigrants were admitted to the United States. As a result, by 1994, 8.7% of the resident United States population was foreign-born—the highest level since 1940.[11]

Almost 10% of the American labor force is foreign-born. If current immigration rates continue, this could rise to 14% by 2010.[12]

Because many new immigrants are younger than the general United States population, their numbers are higher in the younger age groups. In the Spring Break Survey, 12% of Postmoderns identified themselves as foreign-born.

Surprisingly, while recent immigrants arrive with less schooling than native-born Americans, a larger percentage of foreign-born Postmoderns are going to college. According to a report in the April 29, 1996 *U.S. News & World Report*, 24% of recent immigrants have a college degree, compared to 20% of natives.[13] This shows us that while older immigrants may have a lower level of education than those in their generational group, their own children in the younger generations are focusing on educational attainment. In 1996 the University of California at Davis in northern California reported that 49% of its undergraduate students were nonwhite ethnic students. Additionally, 32% of the students said that English was not their primary language.[14]

Racial ethnic diversity is increasing among Postmoderns because the majority of new immigrants are from non-European

Immigration: 1901 to 1993

Period	Number	Rate Per 1,000 U.S. Population
1901 to 1910	8,795,000	10.4
1911 to 1920	5,736,000	5.7
1921 to 1930	4,107,000	3.5
1931 to 1940	528,000	0.4
1941 to 1950	1,035,000	0.7
1951 to 1960	2,515,000	1.5
1961 to 1970	3,322,000	1.7
1971 to 1980	4,493,000	2.1
1981 to 1990	7,338,000	3.1
1991 to 1993	3,705,000	4.8

Source: U.S. Immigration and Naturalization Service, Statistical Yearbook, annual, *The American Almanac*, p. 10.

countries. In 1993, the top eight countries of origin were Mexico, China, Philippines, Vietnam, the Soviet Union, the Dominican Republic, India, and Poland.[15]

It is estimated that there are three to four million undocumented immigrants in the United States. The majority of these come from our neighbors in North and South America, with Mexico contributing about one third of the total.[16] In 1993, 29% of the legal immigrants lived in California.[17] In 1994 it was estimated that 44% of the undocumented immigrants lived in California as well.[18]

This diversity is not without its problems. At Arcadia High School in California, over 50% of the students are from Asian countries. The rest of the popula-

Grade point average (GPA)

GPA	American-born	Foreign-born
2.0	5%	3%
2.5	17	11
3.0	35	29
3.5	32	36
4.0	11	21

Spring Break Surveys 1993 & 1995; 461 American-born, 66 Foreign-born.

tion are American-born whites, Hispanics, and blacks. While in the past diversity was based on race, diversity is intensified for these students by language differences. American-born students find themselves in the awkward position of being in a school where English is not the primary language of their peers. This leads to mistrust and anger, as those who do not speak Chinese or Korean feel left out, and wonder if these other students are talking about them. Baby Boomers who grew up in multiethnic schools had a common language to help bridge the gap. In places like Arcadia, where a large influx of immigrants has added to the racial ethnic mix, language has become another barrier to cross.

Tribes

In the activities of business, foreign-born Postmoderns are an important asset in the global economy. Joel Kotkin, in his ground-breaking book *Tribes: How Race, Religion and Identity Determine Success in the New Global Economy,* points out that global trade is increasingly done along tribal lines. He details the growth and emergence of five global tribes—the Jews, the British, the Japanese, the Chinese, and the Indians (India). While these groups have roots in their countries of origin, increasingly their home bases are found in the cultural and ethnic traditions they carry with them. A person of Chinese ancestry can be equally at home in Hong Kong or in Monterey Park, California.

With the advent of communications technology such as the fax machine and the Internet, a family business can have instant communication with its members even though one person may be in Canada, one in Australia, one in the United States, and another in Great Britain.

These cultural and family groups have three things in common that enable them to impact the world economy. First, they have a strong ethnic identity and sense of mutual dependence that helps members cope with change without losing their essential unity. Second, they have a global network based on mutual trust. Third, they have a passion for technical and other kinds of knowledge, coupled with an essential open-mindedness that fosters rapid cultural and scientific development.[19]

Kotkin identifies another factor in the growing success of the tribes:

The transition of the Indians, Chinese, and Japanese from the status of 'natives' to that of global tribes stems largely from the fact that, like the Jews and the Anglo-Saxons of earlier times, they have developed a strong, ethnically based, morally anchored form of capitalism. Today, the rationalistic capitalism developed by the Anglo-American diaspora has lost its grip on its ethical moorings, in particular, its intrinsic belief in family and self-help and the need for continuous self-improvement. Instead those virtues seem more evident today among the Asiatic global tribes. Indeed, on one critical measurement of capitalist vitality—investment as a percentage of GDP—East Asia by 1990 led all regions of the world, investing in domestic industry at a rate 25 percent higher than America or Europe.[20]

Experiences - by place of birth

	American-born	Foreign-born
Parents' Divorce	28%	9%
Suicide Attempt	10	1
Lost Virginity	49	25
Victim of Violent Crime	6	1

Spring Break Surveys 1993 & 1995; 514 American-born, 70 Foreign-born.

Kotkin identifies three basic factors that are needed for the continual improvement of a people: first, the belief in family; second the belief in self-help; and third the desire for continuous self-improvement.[21]

According to the combined 1993 and 1995 Spring Break Surveys, foreign-born Postmoderns are doing better in some areas than American-born Postmoderns. By a three-to-one margin, American-born Postmoderns have gone through the divorce of their parents. By a ten-to-one margin, American-born Postmoderns have attempted suicide. Almost twice as many American-born Postmoderns have lost their virginity.

Although it would be simplistic to say that the factors of divorce, suicide, and virginity are the key indicators of future success, they point to two different life experiences when it comes to the family and the role of parents in a child's life. For many American-born Postmoderns parents were somewhat reluctant to make any choices for them. They were told: "You have to choose for yourself." Raised with open boundaries, many American-born Postmoderns have had to choose whether or not to go to church, what kind of education to pursue, the types of relationships they should develop with others, and what, if any, career field to enter with little input from their parents. They were told "to be what they could be" without the guidelines to support their decision. The last thing a parent would want to do is "program" their children. Children need to find themselves.

In contrast, listen to what Victor Quon, youth minister at the San Jose Chinese Alliance Church, has to say about the parenting style of Chinese-American families. He points out that Chinese-American parents have high expectations for their children. These parents see as one of their main tasks in life to do all they can to make sure their children do better than they did. Early in life they work with children to set goals for them. They are expected to go to college and to excel in school. C's and B's are not acceptable grades. Youth are not allowed to date until they are sixteen to eighteen years of age, and few work in McJobs outside of the home. Their job is to go to school.

Although there is often a cultural conflict between parents and their youth, and many youth grumble that their parents are too strict and hard on them, the statistics suggest something else. In California a much higher percentage of Asians go to college than do the other races.

It fascinates me to see how many Asian and Jewish children in Nashville are involved in music lessons, even though these culture groups comprise a very small percentage of the general population. At the Blair School of Music, almost half of the children involved in the Suzuki violin program have Jewish, Indian, Korean, or Chinese ancestry. While it cannot be said that music lessons are the tell-tale sign of parents' involvement with their children, it seems that in the long run the children who learn a particular discipline—such as playing the piano or the violin—develop skills that will lead to a lifetime of learning.

This is not to say that many other Americans do not support their children in ways such as taking them to church or involving them in sports and school activities. Among the tribal groups there seems to be a different perspective concerning children. Those who have recently immigrated see their children as bearing the fruit of their decision to come to America. What their children learn at an early age has long range implications. For them the American Dream is still an ideal to be grasped. They'll do anything to see that their child succeeds. But for many American-born Postmoderns whose families have been in the United States over a number of generations, the ideals of the dream have faded. Rather than having a culture of support and affirmation, they have had to figure things out on their own. In many ways they find themselves in a society that has failed to invest in their future.

Haves and Have Nots

Mike, age twenty-five, is the epitome of the racial ethnic diversity we have been talking about. But his story brings into focus even more pointedly that race is not the only thing that divides Postmoderns. Mike's father is Asian American and his mother is Euro-American. A college graduate, he is now a policeman in the Los Angeles Police Department, working in the heart of South Central Los Angeles. His daily route takes him right through the intersection where the Los Angeles riots began in 1992.

Q: What is the biggest issue you see in your work?

MIKE: Society is becoming more violent for many different reasons—cultural differences, a breakdown in family, and a lack of education are some I can think of. These are putting more pressure on people of my generation, which is causing more stress and life crises earlier in their lives compared to other generations. As a result they are not able to think through problems. They don't have problem-solving mechanisms in hand, so they have more negative reactions when things go wrong. Or they may join a gang, which provides peer support in a negative way.

Q: Do you feel that it is a war on the streets where you are working? Is that how the people you are working with feel?

MIKE: What I see is that people are being kept hostages in their homes. There is definitely a line between the good people and the not-so-good. The not-so-good are usually louder, more active, and more aggressive in keeping other people in their homes. Those who are good want to be left alone. It's limiting their lives. It's not getting better.

Q: What is the reason?

Q: How do you identify yourself— white, American, other?

Rick (seventeen, Fort Lauderdale): I think just as an American. When the Rodney King case came down, that touched off a lot of racial tension between black and white. That was interesting because we saw a change of character in our generation during that time. People were thinking "I'm white—this person is black," and they were looking at the differences, not the similarities. I feel that a person is a person, no matter the color, race, whatever, and the media kind of put the black community on the spot as being the problem, when really it's all of our problem. It's either all of us together or none at all.

MIKE: I think it is a lack of education. I have been working down in South Central in the inner city. I drive by the high schools and the elementary schools, and the conditions are extremely poor. I came from the suburbs in Los Angeles, and I used to think everybody had an equal chance. But after seeing some of these high schools and elementary schools in the inner city I can understand why they don't think they have another way out, or they don't get a proper education. I wouldn't expect myself to grow up with any type of career goals and motivation. I wouldn't expect anyone to come out with any other idea than that

Average earnings of full-time workers by education ages 25-35: 1993

Education Level	Male	Female
All Workers	$39,806	$26,165
Less than 9th Grade	15,860	13,051
9th to 12th (no diploma)	19,976	14,108
High School Graduate	25,532	19,151
Some College (no degree)	28,135	21,499
Associate Degree	31,355	23,990
Bachelor's Degree or more	42,296	32,154

Source: U.S. Bureau of the Census, *Current Population Report*, P60-188, *The American Almanac*, p. 479.

the world is against them, or thinking that they didn't have a chance of doing anything.

Q: Has this been an eye-opening experience for you?

MIKE: Definitely. I have been at this for two years, and it's changed my view of things. I used to think every kid had a chance. I thought a person who went to an inner-city school could have just as much chance of success as me, they just had to work at it. But now I don't blame them. I don't see how any of them get out. I see them now and I'll arrest some juveniles or younger adults, and I can almost understand why they are doing the violence they are doing. I'll arrest some blue-collar

worker who is doing something silly and there is no excuse for that. If they only realized the opportunities they have been given, that they were lucky enough to be born into or able to move into a better area. There's no excuse for them.

Q: What does this mean for your generation?

MIKE: I think it depends on where you are living. For the people I grew up with, it has leveled out and is getting better. People of my generation with whom I grew up are tired of the Generation X label, and have put it behind them. All my friends and acquaintances seem to be moving on and working hard. A lot of my friends are getting their educations, even their doctorates, as opposed to going to the work force and trying to come back. I think there is a high motivation to go for the big jobs, to excel young. I think it is a trend.

Q: Is that because there are no jobs to go to, or because a master's is equivalent to what used to be a four-year college degree?

MIKE: I totally agree that a master's degree is equivalent to what a college degree used to be. Almost no one I know can go and get a decent job with a bachelor's degree; you need a master's.

Q: So what I hear from you is that your generation is made up of the haves and have nots?

MIKE: Yes, you could say that. The part of my generation that I see every day does not have the same opportunities that I and my friends have had. For them it's getting worse because I don't see improvement in the local government or the schools.

Mike's experiences are a microcosm of the diversity Postmoderns face. Mike, who is biracial, finds himself working among poor blacks and Hispanics while his friends are pursuing their master's and doctoral degrees. His friends are headed toward success in careers while the people he sees every day seem to be heading for disaster. But even success for his friends is dependent on going beyond a bachelor's degree. They know that to get ahead in the increasingly competitive job market they will need advanced degrees. What does this mean for the Postmodern who has only a high school diploma? What does this mean for those who do not even graduate from high school?

Women and Equality

During the lifetime of the Postmoderns the image and the role of women have changed. Unlike previous generations women are increasingly being treated as equals. The 1996 Olympics was

Percent of recent high school graduates who enrolled in college: 1962-1992

	Total Enrolled	Males	Females
1962	49.0%	55.0%	43.5%
1972	49.2	52.7	45.9
1982	50.6	49.0	52.1
1992	61.7	59.6	63.8

Source: U.S. National Center for Education Statistics, *Digest of Education Statistics*, annual, *The American Almanac*, p. 178.

called the women's Olympics because of the number of medals won by American women in individual and team sports. In academia more women are earning bachelor's and master's degrees than men. Rene Denfeld, author of *The New Victorians*, comments:

I was born a year after the National Organization for Women was created in 1966, and I was a small child while many of the battles for women's rights were being fought. . . . For women of my generation, feminism is our birthright. While sexism may still permeate society, we know what it is to live without excessive confinement. We are the first generation to grow up expecting equal opportunity and equal education, as well as the freedom to express our sexuality. We are the first to assume what feminists had to force society to accept against its deeply ingrained prejudice: that we are the equals of any man. This belief may translate into the pursuit of a career or it may

Degrees earned: 1971-1992

	1971	1992	Males 1971	Females 1992
Bachelor	839,730	1,136,553	43.4%	54.2%
Master	230,509	352,838	40.1	54.1
Doctorate	32,107	40,659	14.3	37.1

Source: U.S. National Center for Education Statistics, *Digest of Education Statistics*, annual, *The American Almanac*, p. 191.

mean demanding respect for raising chil-dren—women of my generation believe in the right to choose.[22]

Although women in general do not yet receive equal pay in the work force, as Postmodern women move forward in the work force they will find themselves moving closer and closer to gender equality, perhaps even reversing it in their lifetime. When they move into their fifties and sixties, it's highly likely they will be paid as much or more than men.

In the 1993 and 1995 Spring Break Surveys, Postmoderns were asked who were the most successful members of their generation—men, women, or the same. While 48% of males said that men and women are equally successful, 52% of women said that women are more successful. Even more noteworthy, only 9% of women said men are the most successful, while 22% of men said that women are.

These results point to an interesting shift in relationships between the gen-ders. As Postmoderns were growing up, a whole series of books came out decrying the male half of the species. Advice on how to get rid of your husband, how to make it on your own, and other such top-ics were common fare. Women's studies became a major subject at colleges and universities; no one at that time even considered having a men's studies pro-gram. Because men were in power, why would they need empowerment?

So during the eighties and nineties, women in the work force have networked to support and mentor one another and to build careers and achievements. But men have been left to make it on their own. A great example of this is the Girls Day Out Program, in which parents are invited to take their daughters to work. This pro-gram was initiated in order to help young women get a greater vision for their life and their future. But what about young men? Why no day out for them?

Many Postmodern men have been raised with little or no positive male role models in the home. Instead they have to look to friends or to the media to find out what it means to be male. While the women's movement has in many ways positively empowered women to live bal-anced lives and to aspire to careers that contribute through family and work to the whole community, many young men have not had the same sources of support and mentoring. If violence and abuse is primar-ily a male endeavor, would it not make sense to pay just as much attention to the mentoring and support of young men?

In Pacoima, California, one group has taken such a stand. Out of the ashes of the Los Angeles riots, The United Methodist Church created *Shalom Zones*. One of these, a mile away from where the Rodney King beating took place, was created in Pacoima. Garth Gilliam, the program director, says their first priority was to focus on at-risk black young men, who in many ways are becoming an endangered species. They created a Mentoring and Rites of Passage Program for fatherless youth with the purpose of turning around the terrible results of drugs, violence, and gangs. Based on Judeo-Christian and Afrocentric themes, the program guides youth to confront three issues: *where we come from, where we are,* and *where are we going.* The goal is to help young black men build character and self-esteem, to learn conflict management skills, to learn how to set goals, to unleash the power of God in their lives, to respect their heritage, to learn financial management skills, and to value and pursue an education with the goal of maintaining a GPA of 3.0.

One year after its inception, young men in Pacoima have a new force in their lives. The *Shalom Zone* has a waiting list for the program. At the request of single-parent families they are in the process of developing a similar program for young women. The only thing holding them back is finding enough adult mentors to work with the youth. By making an investment in young men and women in Pacoima, the community has a chance for a better future. Instead of parents struggling as indi-

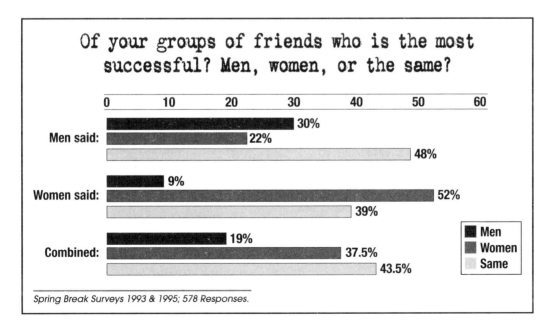

Of your groups of friends who is the most successful? Men, women, or the same?

	0	10	20	30	40	50	60

Men said: 30% / 22% / 48%

Women said: 9% / 52% / 39%

Combined: 19% / 37.5% / 43.5%

Legend: ■ Men ■ Women ▫ Same

Spring Break Surveys 1993 & 1995; 578 Responses.

viduals to raise their children, they have a place where they can work together.[23]

As we look at the issue of equality, it is important to see that while in older generations—such as the GI and Silent Generations—men hold most positions of power, in the Postmodern Generation equality between the sexes is an assumption shared by most men and women.

These trends reflect a change in assumptions about the importance of women, and in the relationships between men and women of this generation. Two students from Florida State University give us a deeper perspective on how they view "success" and the importance of equality.

Q: **Is there a difference in self-identity or success between men and women of your age group?**

BRUCE (twenty-one): Yes, I most definitely think so. I think that women of my generation are much more career-oriented than in the past. The male-dominated society of the past has begun the slow process of accepting equal status in the workplace.

Q: **Is this more threatening to the men because it causes more competition?**

BRUCE: There is more competition in the work place, but I think it makes for a better society. In the past when we excluded 50% of the possible work force, who knows what we lost in production

and insight and the like. Now I think it's healthy and fosters more positive emotional relationships between men and women if you look at a woman as your equal rather than down on her. In my personal relationships, I have been with people that I wouldn't consider my intellectual equal, and it's a rougher time than with someone that you can look to and admire. That's crucial.

NICK (twenty): My esteemed colleague speaks very eloquently. I happen to agree with a lot of what he said. Our generation has begun the move with an emphasis toward being more gender-sensitive and things like that. Here at college with our studies we have watched how people have moved to becoming more politically correct in their terms, and I think that's a very good thing. It is one of the key elements in bringing equality up to a certain level where we all need to be.

Q: **Would you say your generation is going to be more successful than previous ones? A lot of people say this is the first generation that's not going to do better than their parents.**

NICK: I disagree with that. We are in a lot more complex times than we were before. Things were a lot simpler way back when it was very established what each person does. It's more complex now, but I still think everything is moving toward achieving the most that you can, and I think that every generation does succeed in some ways over what the previous generation did.

BRUCE: I think the question about whether our generation is going to do better than the last, as far as success goes, depends on how you define the word "success." If you are talking about economic success, I am sure that I will make more money than my parents are going to. If you are talking about success as a generation—I think if we can think of ways to raise up women and minorities and people who are oppressed and have been oppressed and who are on the trail to equality—if we can further that along as a generation, I would consider that successful.

NICK: Part of those trends that include gender relations and relieving oppressed people have given me the impression that we are not in a decline. We are striving to be better and we are succeeding. It may be a lesser degree than we would like or than the media may state, but we are moving forward.

Sexual Orientation

Another aspect of diversity that is prominent among Postmoderns is sexual orientation. With the advent of AIDS in the early 1980's, an emerging gay and lesbian movement found its voice. Protesting against being blamed for the AIDS disease they sought equality and visibility for their group. ACT UP and gay parades around the country brought into the light a community that before had been largely invisible.

Today gays and lesbians are prominently featured in television shows and movies geared for young adults and youth. Television shows such as *Melrose Place* and *My So-Called Life* and movies such as *Clueless* feature gay characters. In the most popular television show for Postmoderns, *Friends*, gay and lesbian themes abound. In one of its most publicized shows, Ross's exwife marries her lover, a woman.

Karen Ritchie, in *Marketing to Generation X*, points out the following:

> The broad acceptance of sexual expression in the college-educated segment of twentysomethings is still largely unrecognized in the balance of American society. . . . According to Sarah Schulman, novelist, playwright, and gay activist, "If you come out in college there is an openly gay faculty member you can talk to and a gay student group, and you can even take Queer Studies 101."[24]

Although numbers are hard to come by, the *Sex in America* study designed by the University of Chicago's National Opinion Center found that 2.8% of the men and 1.4% of the women surveyed identified themselves as gay. When defined more broadly, 10.1% of men and 8.6% of women either identified themselves as gay, said they had had a sexual experience with someone of the same sex, or claimed to have had some physical attraction to members of the same sex.[25]

This points to another aspect of sexual orientation among Postmoderns. Rather than having clear boundaries, sexuality is seen as a continuum or a bell curve, with the large majority of heterosexuals in the center and gay and lesbians on the edges. Like so many other areas in the lives of Postmoderns, the boundaries of what is and is not acceptable behavior have become very fuzzy. The options are open for a person to explore.

In the 1996 season finale of *Friends*, Joey is up for an acting part in which he has to kiss a man. Throughout the show he is trying to see if one of his male friends will kiss him so he can practice for the part. When Ross kisses him at the end of the show, Joey replies that it's no surprise that his girlfriend Rachel loves him. In a previous show Joey was kissing the mother of one of his other friends. Is Joey gay, bisexual, heterosexual? Or is he just having fun?

One thing is clear: Compared to other generations there is a higher level of tolerance for—if not acceptance of—the gay lifestyle, especially among the college-

educated. For Postmoderns, sexual orientation is another aspect of human diversity that has to be figured out.

Genes and Diversity

One of the most controversial issues that underlies the sexuality debate is the question of whether homosexuality is a result of nature or nurture. Is homosexuality a product of genetics or of social influence combined with the individual's ability to choose?

In *A Separate Creation: The Search for the Biological Origins of Sexual Orientation*, Chandler Burr details the search for the gay gene. Citing both the proponents and the opponents of the notion that sexual orientation is a behavior trait, as is the trait that determines left-handedness, he focuses on what it means to have diversity. He raises the question of whether diversity is the result of biology or environment or a mixture of both.

For example, if a gene is found that predisposes an individual to a gay lifestyle, then the whole question of whether or not one chooses to have homosexual inclinations would be settled. But that would not be the end of the debate. Would this gene be considered to be a trait like having blue or brown eyes, or would it be considered defective, and thus in need of a cure? If it is a trait, would it be better for society to create in the womb more people who are homosexual in order to increase diversity? If it is a disease, then should society strive to wipe it out, as we did smallpox earlier this century?

The current work in genetics has implications far beyond the reach of just this one aspect of diversity. As scientists seek to decode our DNA and to find the genes that help determine who we are, everyone will be affected. Burr observes:

> *All knowledge is double-edged. . . . To the degree to which we learn to alter sexual orientation, we will learn, axiomatically, to alter lupus, ovarian cancer, sickle cell anemia, cystic fibrosis, left-handedness, hair loss, height, and on and on. It will mean the capacity for, if not the actual performance of, fetal sex selection and prenatal surgery, alteration of weight and eye color, the eradication of deafness, and, more slowly, the transformation of the physical race, enhancement of intelligence, and the coordinated biological management of violence.*[26]

Through genetic engineering, one drop of blood might tell your insurance agent what propensities for disease you have, tell your boss your sexual orientation, tell the police your gene map for violence, and so forth. While people can know more about you, will you want to know more about yourself? Do you really want to know that you are likely to die of cancer at an early age?

While great miracles will take place and great cures will become possible through the emerging application of genetic science, we are posed with a new dilemma. What happens to diversity when a parent can decide before the child is born its sex and the color of its eyes, skin, and hair? Will you choose your child as you would order a new car, with the latest accessories of intelligence, wit, and disposition?

In 1979 China embarked on a one-child-per-couple policy as a way to slow down its population growth. One result of this policy was unintended. By the year 2000 there will likely be a surplus of 70 million single young adult men. In the Chinese culture boys carry the family line forward and are their aging parents' social security, whereas girls leave the family at marriage to join the groom's family. As a result Chinese parents desire to have boys. Through the technology of ultrasound, the sex of a child is determined before birth. The use of this technology in China has lead to abortion when ultrasound determined that the child was female. Now China faces another problem. What do you do with 70 million single young men who have no hope of marrying and having a family? What do you do when you have lost the resources of almost 70 million women?[27]

While all of this sounds like science fiction, these are just some of the questions that will be asked and will be answered in some fashion or another in the 21st century. Postmoderns are the first generation who will find themselves faced with the choice of whether to take advantage of or overstep the bounds of the new medical sciences.

The Diversity Equation

For Postmoderns diversity is not a simple issue of black and white. Diversity is more about individual choices and opportunity than it is about race. Whites and blacks in poor communities have more in common with each other than with blacks and whites who are college graduates. As one African American student at Harvard remarked: "I don't think that labeling generations is realistic anymore. I think in our day and age you would be very hard pressed to call a twenty-year-old black living in an urban area, who has no family or dad or money, a Generation Xer, and call a black Harvard student, whose dad is a lawyer, the same thing. I think it's an anomaly."

Her point is well taken. Instead of the easy classification of one race as poor or rich, or one group as better than another, for Postmoderns economic opportunity, family background, educational attainment, gender, sexual preference, and place of birth all enter into the equation.

What makes diversity such a profound issue for Postmoderns is that while diversity can be a value to embrace, it also can be an issue over which people can be easily divided. Skin heads, Black Muslims, white supremacists, and gangs of every stripe and color are found among this generation. While for Boomers there was the Shangri-La time of "Let's all live together," for Postmoderns, living in diversity often leads to suspicion and division rather than acceptance.

When the economic pie is shrinking, and competition is expanding, when one group seems to be getting more benefits than the other, when people divide themselves according to their diversity, and differences are flaunted as rights, people are forced to take sides, whether they want to or not.

What has made America strong in its past has been its ability to receive the various talents and ambitions of people as they have come to this land. As each generation passed the baton on to the next, there was a resolve to see that their children had a better chance than they did. Many among the Postmodern Generation feel that this chain has been broken. Raised in a time of diminishing social investment, increasing violence, and increasing disruption of the family, Postmoderns find themselves in a survival mode. People in a survival mode normally do not see wide-open spaces into which to expand; but they see instead diminishing benefits that only a few people will enjoy.

But not all Postmoderns are content to leave it this way or to accept the prejudice of earlier generations that has divided them from their peers. As prom time approached, three students at South Penola High School in Batesville, Mississippi decided it was time to stop the tradition of separate proms for blacks and whites. Working with teachers and parents, they presented a plan wherein there would be one prom for all.

In a town of deeply rooted prejudice and division between blacks and whites the students at South Penola High School decided that enough was enough. "We go to school together," they challenged. "We eat lunch together. Someday we will all work together. Why can't we socialize together? We need to break the barriers that divide, and be united."[28]

The prom turned out to be a success. There were no fights, no arguments, no pointing out that one was better than the other. Instead they had fun together. They laughed. They reminisced about the good things that had happened at school that year. And they learned a couple of new dances from each other. Maybe this is as good a place to start as any.

From Religion to Spirituality

"Y ou are the first generation raised without religion," writes Douglas Coupland in his novel *Life After God*. Coupland, who coined the term "Generation X" in his first novel by the same name, talks about what it is like to grow up in an anesthetic middle class society, in which death is similar to something like recycling, and where young people who are "the children of the children of the pioneers" live "a life after God." In Coupland's vision of suburban life lived just this side of heaven, paradise was already found. Parents had paved the way, and he and his friends enjoyed the fruits of a trouble-free life. But life without God comes with a downside. He comments:

> I think the price we paid for our golden life was an inability to fully believe in love; instead we gained an irony that scorched everything it touched. And I wonder if this irony is the price we paid for the loss of God.[1]

"I have lived and grown up in the worst environment imaginable. A lot of stuff has happened to me. But when I found God my life was changed and became a lot easier. This generation is a hard, confused one."

Andy, 19,
San Diego, California

Coupland's insights move us to a topic that lies at the heart of the matter. For Postmoderns, God and spirituality are not trivial matters. In fact, this topic stands above the rest.

Postmodern Believers

While Coupland decries the loss of God, the vast majority of Postmoderns consider themselves to be believers. Seventy-nine percent of those questioned in the Spring Break Surveys said that in terms of religious beliefs, they are believers. Ten percent identified themselves as seekers, 6% as agnostic, and 5% as atheist. While it might be easy to write this off—anyone can say he or she is a believ-

Religious beliefs

Atheist 5%
Agnostic. 6
Seeker 10
Believer 79

Spring Break Surveys 1993 & 1995; 572 Responses.

er in something—those surveyed were fairly traditional in their beliefs.

The following graph shows the results of two questions asked of Postmoderns. The first asks: "Of the following, which do you believe?" Under this question you will see the list of different beliefs. Under the column (All) we see how the total group responded. All figures are percentiles.

The second question, listed at the top, asked Postmoderns: "How often do you attend religious services?" Beneath the question you see that 43% of those surveyed said they went weekly, and so forth. By comparing the two we see how attendance at religious services relates to what people believe.

A careful look at the correlation between the responses to these two questions reveals much about the beliefs of Postmoderns. First, a large majority (77%) assume the Judeo-Christian view of God as Creator. This is especially true of those who attend services weekly, of whom

Worship attendance and beliefs

| | | 2. How often do you attend religious services? | | | | |
1. Of the following, which do you believe?	All	Weekly (43%)	Twice a Month (10%)	Monthly (12%)	Yearly (18%)	Never (14%)
God is Creator. 77%		94%	88%	74%	71%	34%
Jesus is my Lord and Savior. 62		84	61	76	45	18
In the power of prayer 56		75	56	60	45	16
Angels exist 52		66	47	46	41	39
Only those who are saved will go to heaven 36		53	42	37	19	8
In ghosts. 21		12	19	29	32	31
Witchcraft is real 15		17	12	11	14	14
In reincarnation 13		7	10	16	18	20
All people will go to heaven. . . . 12		9	7	14	21	13
God is an energy source. 9		8	7	10	11	12

Spring Break Surveys 1993 & 1995; 600 Responses.

94% believe that God is Creator. A steady decline in this belief is seen as attendance goes down, dropping off to 34% among those who never attend religious services.

The second belief, Jesus is my Lord and Savior, describes those who identify themselves with the basic tenet of the Christian faith. Sixty-two percent affirmed this belief. Again the highest percentage was reported among those who attended weekly services (84%) as opposed to those who never attend, at 18%.

Fifty-six percent affirmed a belief in the power of prayer. Only 16% of those who never attend services agreed with this postulate.

Interestingly enough, the one belief that received the highest acceptance among those who never attend is the belief that angels exist. This may well be connected with the recent popularity of numerous books, movies, and television shows that deal with the subject of angels. One CBS surprise during the 1995-1996 season was the popularity of the show *Touched by An Angel*. In following seasons CBS plans to do spin-offs of the show. Angels seem to be a safe topic when treating the subject of religion.

The belief that "only those who are saved will go to heaven" has been one of the touchstones of evangelical and orthodox Christianity. Only 36% of those questioned agreed with this statement. Of those who attend weekly, a majority (53%) affirmed this belief, compared to only 8% of those who don't.

By putting these five questions together we get a picture of the range of basic beliefs as taught in the Christian tradition. In the 1993 Spring Break Survey respondents were also asked a couple of other questions relating to basic Christian doctrine. Sixty-one percent said they believed in the Holy Spirit, 60% said "people need to be forgiven of their sins," and 55% said that the "Bible is the inspired Word of God." Taken together we see that a majority have a basic agreement with Christian beliefs. The main exception is the much smaller group who believe that only the saved will go to heaven.

Other beliefs, such as the beliefs in ghosts and reincarnation, find higher agreement as you move from weekly attendance to nonattendance. The belief that "all people will go to heaven" remains fairly weak across the board.

Another question invited Postmoderns to identify the religious traditions in which they are active. This roughly corresponds with the 65% who attend religious services at least once a month (a combination of weekly, twice a month, and monthly attendance). Despite the syncretism of the Postmodern religious environment, it is interesting to note that, apart from Christianity, Postmoderns do not seem to be attracted in significant numbers to other religious traditions. Those who do not consider themselves Christians are much more likely to opt out of a particular faith than to be involved in a faith other than Christianity.

Are you active in any of the following religions?

Christianity	69.0%
None	22.0
Other	3.5
Muslim	1.5
Judaism	1.0
Buddhism	1.0
Mormon	1.0
New Age	0.5
Hinduism	0.01

Spring Break Surveys 1993 & 1995; 600 Responses.

The second largest response, at 22%, identifies those who claim no particular religious tradition.

As we look at this data, one conclusion stands out. Regular attendance makes a difference in the question of belief. The more regularly a person attends a religious service, the higher the likelihood of belief. The temptation here is to conclude that the answer to the church's problems is to simply increase attendance. Unfortunately, it is not this simple. For Postmoderns the nature of religion has changed. In their lifetimes they have seen the culture at large move from religion to spirituality. What made religion vital to the GI Generation no longer applies to Postmoderns. Rather than take an institutional approach to religion, most Postmoderns are more interested in developing their own spirituality as they seek to find God in the midst of the culture-shifts that define their lives. In some ways they may get to the same place as previous generations, but the route they take is very different.

For Postmoderns the words "secular" and "religious" have lost their meaning. For their grandparents there was a neat divide between the secular world and the world of religion. Each had its own separate compartment in which people participated on the correct occasions. People were educated in secular institutions, went to work on the days reserved for secular activities, and kept religion to themselves. The familiar phrase: "In polite conversation one never talks about religion or politics" was the rule of thumb.

On the Sabbath people in the 1950's and early 1960's went to receive religious instruction and to worship where the grand traditions of the faith were imparted. Churches and synagogues were the places to make connections with like-minded folks, where secular topics such as politics and personal problems were never discussed, where one attended religious ceremonies such as weddings and funerals, and where one learned the values necessary to make a person into a good citizen.

Each sphere had its own music. The religious institution had sacred songs, gospels, and hymns. At home people listened to big band, show tunes, or—if you were really hip—jazz.

Each sphere had its own creative arts.

The church had stained glass, vestments, and banners. The secular city had entertainment provided by movies, books, magazines, the theater, radio, and, increasingly, television. There were some crossover personalities such as Norman Vincent Peale and Billy Graham, who spoke on radio and television—but these were the exception and not the rule. Besides, their appeal had to do with religious edification, not with entertainment.

For Postmoderns, the religious and secular spheres have collapsed in a society that is highly spiritualized and mystical. Consider for example the MTV diva, Madonna, whose name is based on Mary, the mother of Jesus. When she first hit the scene in the early 1980's she adorned herself with religious symbols such as the cross. One of her first hits, "Like a Virgin," plays off the biblical description of Mary, the virgin mother of Jesus. Other songs, such as "Poppa Don't Preach" and "Like a Prayer," in which she makes love to a statue of Jesus in her music video, are laden with refracted religious symbolism.

While at first glance this looks like an all-out attack on Christianity, it reveals something even deeper in the culture: An attempt to take religious symbols and invest them with meaning, even if it appears demonic. Grunge rock groups such as Nirvana, and heavy metal groups such as Guns and Roses, went heavy on religious themes, mocking belief in anything while crying out at the same time for belief in something.

A World Without Religion

Coupland speaks about this paradox. He observes in his generation a desire for belief when there seems to be nothing that can be trusted:

I must remind myself we are living creatures—we have religious impulses—we must—and yet into what cracks do these impulses flow in a world without religion? It is something I think about every day. Sometimes I think it is the only thing I should be thinking about.[2]

"My religious experience helped me get in touch with God. Since then, though, I have questioned and denied—I have been more inclined to decide what God wants, not what I want."
Matthew, 17,
Fort Scott, Virginia

Perhaps, like me, you wonder what Coupland means when he says we live in a world without religion. First let's try to define the word religion. A religion is a system of thought and belief that gives followers a common understanding of the world and a way to experience the transcendent. Followers adhere to a particular set of beliefs and practices as a way to express their faith—their way of connecting with the extraordinary, the mysterious, and the supernatural. This belief system or pattern pulls them forward as a group, and offers hope for the future, usually pertaining to some kind of promise of an afterlife, a resurrection, or a returning to live again on the earth. The field of religious inquiry is the state of the soul and its relationship to the universe. Religion concerns itself with the ultimate question of the meaning of life.

Religion also calls for a common world-view that unites people. It offers believers a common vision of the future, and has a universal language of belief and action. It also offers believers a set of spiritual disciplines and practices that move the believer into a deeper understanding and appreciation of the faith.

But Coupland also brings up another point that we cannot afford to miss. Trust and religious faith go together. When trust in the leaders of the religion or in its precepts breaks down, religion becomes suspect.

No Fear

I discussed this subject with Leonard Sweet, author of *Faithquakes*, and dean of Drew Theological Seminary. Sweet noted that the slogan for the generation who graduated in the fifties was "no sweat," yet they are the generation that worked the hardest. The slogan for the generation who graduated in the sixties and seventies was "no problem," yet they are the generation that faced the most personal problems. The slogan for today's graduates is "no fear," yet they are the generation that seems to have the most to fear.

This fear is exhibited in many ways: black clothes and army boots; rock groups with names like Nine Inch Nails and Killing Joke; adrenaline-boosted extreme sports

such as snow surfing and bungee jumping; apocalyptic quasi-religious groups such as the Branch Davidians and the Michigan Militia; terrorist acts such as the bombing in Oklahoma and the bombing at the Olympics in Atlanta; phrases such as "drive-bys," "gang bangers," and "body piercing"; diseases such as "ecoli" and "AIDS"; broken relationships begun with "prenuptial agreements."

These images and descriptions speak to a universal sense of foreboding that coils just the other side of consciousness. Like a laugh track gone bad they bring out an ironic point of view expressed with heavy sarcasm, hoping that something might be real. Postmoderns wonder where everyday life and their belief in God fit together.

The Trivialization of Religion

In current American society the concept of religion runs counter to the experience of everyday life. Just the idea of belief is a struggle. Stephen L. Carter, in *The Culture of Disbelief*, points to how public media, laws, and politics trivialize those who are religious. Pointing out numerous instances in which religion has lost face in the public arena, Carter defines the problem with religious belief in America:

> *In contemporary American culture, the religions are more and more treated as just passing beliefs—almost as fads, older, stuffier, less liberal versions of so-*

called New Age—rather than as the fundaments upon which the devout build their lives. . . . And if religions are fundamental, well, too bad—at least if they're the wrong fundaments—if they are inconvenient, give them up! If you can't remarry because you have the wrong religious belief, well, hey, believe something else! If you can't take your exam because of a Holy Day, get a new Holy Day! If the government decides to destroy your sacred land, just make some other lands sacred! . . . And through all of this trivializing rhetoric runs the subtle but unmistakable message: pray if you like, worship if you must, but whatever you do, do not on any account take your religion seriously.[3]

This perspective is a direct result of modern rationalistic thinking. Anything that cannot be proven scientifically is considered void of verifiable truth. It is this perspective that laid the groundwork for the whole notion of the division between science and religion, and fuels the disrobing of religious belief in the name of rational discourse. What it has meant in the modern world, the world to which Postmoderns are reacting, is the tacit acceptance that religion is merely a private and subjective matter.

Thus the "world without religion" to which Postmoderns are reacting is the world in which the previous generations have tended to privatize religion into subjective, nonbinding preferences of the individual. It is also the world in which Postmoderns are bombarded with a plethora of images from different and even contradictory traditions. Yet with such apparent variety and relativity, Postmoderns seek a religious perspective that can genuinely make sense of the struggles and problems they face. Indeed, they want to take spiritual issues seriously.

The Secular City

In place of a religious society, modern theologians embraced the concept of a secular society in which the religious impulse came of age in secular work. Just as Postmoderns began entering the world in 1965, Harvey Cox wrote the theological work of his generation, *The Secular City*. Tracing humanity's evolution from the tribe to the city to the technopolis, Cox argued that a secular society can be based on biblical values that carry through into the culture even though the culture may not recognize it. The theoretical framework for the secular city is the understanding that religion and politics have their own places, each making room for the other. Secularization does not mean the complete elimination of religious practice and belief; rather, it allegedly allows room for faith and belief to grow.

In the mid-sixties this concept was widely embraced by mainline church denominations that were already moving into secularism. Since 1900 the church in America had found itself fighting a rearguard action against modernism—the post-Enlightenment worldview that increasingly reduced the claims of religion to the purely natural realm of the senses. People were increasingly comfortable believing in a God who is already present in human efforts toward moral and scientific progress; but to believe in a God who is transcendent, and who brings supernatural healing and revelation, was a throwback to old superstitions.

During the 20th century mainline seminaries sought to emulate the academic trends of the other professions. The miracles of Jesus, the Resurrection, the exorcisms, and the healings related in the Bible were simply stories of faith that were germane to New Testament times. The key to Christianity was to provide a professional clergy who could minister to the spiritual needs of the congregation and who could explain the faith in a way that appealed to the rational person in us all. Sermons were not utterances of divine proclamation as much as they were academic lectures used to convince the committed that the preacher knew what he or she was talking about.

The Problem with Secularism

While Cox painted a vision of secularization that promised to embrace religious practice, this dream has turned into a dysfunctional type of secularism. Today, in the name of secularism religious practices and beliefs are placed outside the public view. Even more troubling, in the name of secularism, the beliefs and practices of the Judeo-Christian tradition are being thrown

out in order to create a level playing field, while the practices of other faiths and belief systems are given free reign. Consider for example a recent conversation I had with my daughter who had just finished her first year as a student in the public school system.

Daughter: "Daddy, I need a dream catcher."

Dad: "What's a dream catcher?"

Daughter: "Well, I had some bad dreams last night, and I need a dream catcher to stop them from bothering me. Ms. Burns said that the parents of Indian children put dream catchers above their beds to stop the bad dreams and to let the good dreams come through."

Dad: "You really don't need a dream catcher. When you have bad dreams, ask Jesus to protect you and take them away."

Daughter: "But Daddy, before the Indians heard about Jesus they had dream catchers. Can I have a dream catcher?"

This conversation illustrates in a significant way the problem with "selective secularization." If my daughter were to say to her teacher: "Well, my Daddy says I don't need a dream catcher because we pray to Jesus," she would probably be told that in school we can't talk about Jesus. Christians also can't pray at school, can't sing Christmas carols, can't have an Easter pageant, and so forth. But we can celebrate Halloween—fill the school stage with witches, goblins, crystal balls, Ouija boards, and other objects of pagan and wicca practices—and invite the students to participate in this activity.

The Postmodern Generation is the first that has not been allowed to have voluntary prayer in the schools. In 1966 the U.S. Senate voted to prohibit voluntary prayer in public school. While earlier generations had a universal sense of spirituality rooted in the Judeo-Christian faith, Postmoderns have been raised in an atmosphere of eclectic spirituality in which a host of religious practices mix and multiply.

I say this not to make a case for or against school prayer. To do so would be to miss the more fundamental dilemma. Today a school prayer would not necessarily be based on the Judeo-Christian perspective. Any kind of prayer from any kind of perspective could become the norm in a given school. Who would be able to decide which prayer is the right one? Whose rights would be violated if a Hindu or New Age prayer were the norm? Even worse from my perspective as a Christian, a prayer of the week from many different religious persuasions might be used, further pushing the point that all spiritualities are the same.

The point is this: Rather than growing up with a particular faith and belief system that is shared by society as a whole, Postmoderns find themselves enticed, seduced, and informed by a wide variety of religious practices and beliefs. Any of these can be used or abused according to an individual's fancy.

As far as society goes the message is simple: Believe anything you want to. Have your private prayers, wear your beads, your icons, your religious symbols if you must. Go through your orders of worship, your rituals, and your practices. But by all means do not do anything about it. Pray, but don't believe too much. And most of all, accept all religions as equal. They are just different ways of getting to the same place. Don't push yours as being better or superior to someone else's, even if theirs is opposite to your own belief system. Keep your faith to yourself.

The question is whether or not Postmoderns are content with such an eclectic religious orientation, or are looking for a spirituality that goes deeper.

Rene Denfeld, in *The New Victorians*, devotes an entire chapter to the theme of "The Goddess Within," detailing how some feminists have been attracted to goddess religions.[4] She tells about classes on college campuses around the country that incorporate books and teachings on goddess religions as part of the curriculum for many women's studies classes. Denfeld reports: "One of the most popular ways of practicing the goddess religion is feminist witchcraft, or wicca."[5] Adherents celebrate Halloween as their high holy day and invite students to close class sessions with religious rituals from this movement. These believers see witchcraft as a return to the prepatriarchal religion in which women were the spiritual leaders and had equality with men.

Denfeld's concern about the identification of feminism with goddess religions is that

> . . . *women of all ages and backgrounds from traditional faiths find current feminism deeply insulting. . . . Many women with no strong religious affiliation find the feminist flight into fancy a waste of effort that draws energy away from reforms that would address real-world concerns.*[6]

As a woman of the Postmodern Generation Denfeld regards these practices as taking away from the real concerns of the feminist movement—equality with men, equal pay, and the concerns of balancing work and childcare.

Denfeld's account illustrates how one Postmodern reacts to the apparent trivializing and subjectivizing of spiritual issues. For her, religion needs above all to take seriously the practical and personal problems of life in the postmodern world. The hodgepodge of contemporary religious options does not fill the bill. The evidence shows that Postmoderns are not willing to accept the banishment of the traditional faiths from the world of education, work, and politics, while replacing them with a quasi-spirituality that accepts aliens, UFO's, Mayan prophecies, psychic hotlines, crystals, and I Ching indiscriminately, as though they were all one and the same thing.[7]

When religious truth claims cannot be taken seriously, then all religious practices are the same. Instead of having a common religion, or living in a secular-ized society in which religion and the secular have their places, the Postmodern Generation has been raised in a highly spiritualized culture in which anything and everything is all right because it all allegedly leads you to God, if that is what you want to believe. Yet Postmoderns are rejecting this relativistic approach, in search of a spirituality that has deeper roots and more staying power.

Spirituality on the Internet

A recent excursion on America Online, the most popular Internet provider, is worth pondering. As I logged on I was greeted by the main menu and was invited to take a look at *Extra,* an entertainment spot that was highlighting a new movie called *The Craft*. Underneath a picture that showed four teenage witches, a message said something like this: "Craig, we have a spell for you." I clicked on the picture and was lead to the *Extra* page. On the *Extra* page I was invited to explore *The Craft* even further through a number of features. I clicked *The Craft* and came to another page that allowed me to choose between a pagan chat room, a wicca chat room, or a look at other spiritualities. If you don't know, wicca is the religion of witchcraft. I clicked on other spiritualities, and found myself with the options of Christianity, Judaism, and Other Faiths. I clicked on Christianity, and eventually found myself exploring the cyberchurch, in which a hypertexted version of Psalm 23 allowed me to explore the passage in depth.

This experience leads me to the following observations. First, in the framework of the Internet medium, all spiritualities come across as equal. One is no better than another. Second, there is no judgment or, I dare say, discernment as to what might be a good spirituality or a bad one. Third, the avenue of access is through a page that specializes in entertainment news. The site was obviously set up to hype a new movie that featured teenage witches. As a sidenote, an interview on television made a big deal about the fact that one of the actresses in the movie owned her own occult bookstore, and that one of the advisors to the movie was a real witch. Fourth, Christianity was accessed by surfing through a number of different spiritualities. Fifth, at any point I could have entered a chat room and talked to like-minded individuals, guided only by my curiosity. Instead of ending up at the cyberchurch I could just as easily have entered the wicca chat room and had a conversation with a coven of witches, all in the safety of my own home.

This access to a wide variety of spiritual motifs is available throughout our culture. Bookstores abound with books on spirituality. Books such as *The Celestine Prophecy, Chicken Soup for the Soul, Embraced by the Light*, and—for young teens—the *Goosebumps* series, were among the top ten bestsellers in 1995.

Children's movies like *The Lion King*

reflect the heavy influence of New Age thinking. The Postmodern film trilogy *Star Wars* gave its own brand of religious dogma, proclaiming: "Let the force be with you."

None of these provides the seeker or believer with a wider frame of reference that comes from Judeo-Christian roots. Instead the follower is encouraged to choose for the moment, putting faith in whatever spiritual modality works at a particular time. In the midst of these options, Postmoderns seem to have a love-hate relationship with the spiritual claims of traditional faith.

The Danger of Nihilism

In 1965 Cox stated that the greatest danger secular society faces is nihilism:

> *Nihilism represents the adolescent phase of the relativization of values. It swings back and forth from a giddy celebration of the freedom man has when the gods are dead, to a wistful longing for the return of a world of secure and dependable meanings and norms.*[8]

Cox went on to paint a picture of the secular city in which God's movement of grace and freedom continues. Three decades later, however, our culture finds itself caught in the stage of nihilism, where derision of religion and longing for faith collide with a vengeance.

Alanis Morissette, whose alternative CD *Jagged Little Pill* won four Grammy Awards in 1996, including Album of the Year, expresses these conflicting emotions

Alternative music

Interview with Sean, age twenty-eight, music store manager and drummer for an alternative band.

Q: What is alternative music?
SEAN: The best way to describe it is that it has an edge to it. It's raw. It's not clean and neat like the electronic music sound of the 1980's, which was heavy with drum machines and synthesizers. Alternative is more acoustical. Real drums, acoustical guitars—that sort of thing.

Q: Is there a particular instrumentation that is used?
SEAN: You have your basic rock instruments like guitars and drums, but groups will use other instruments like mandolins, violins, or harmonicas as part of the mix. Each group does its own thing.

Q: You said the music was raw. What do you mean?
SEAN: For example, I play drums in an alternative group. I have to keep the rhythm going but the other instruments will play off it by not being quite in beat. Also alternative music needs to have a lot of back beat. So you'll hear songs that use other percussion instruments like tambourines or conga drums along with the regular drums. The music has to have a beat.

Q: What about the vocal? What makes it different than rock?
SEAN: Alternative singers don't have to have great voices. Unlike other kinds of music vocals don't stand out as much. What is important is how all the sounds fit together.

Q: What about the lyrics?
SEAN: That is the driver of alternative music. Instead of love songs, the alternative artist tries to tell a story. It's the story and the ideas that make a good song. That is what is making it popular among young people. They don't want easy answers. They want to experience the life of the person who is singing. They want something that is real.

in one cut on the CD called "Forgiven." The song talks about being raised a Catholic girl by loveless priests who taught that you can't have fun without guilt. She fulfilled her religious duties by singing in the choir and confessing her sins to a jealous man. Her problem, in the end, was that the questions she needed answered were regarded as stupid. While she rejected what she learned, she still believes. In the concluding chorus she sums up this desperate need to believe in something while those who impart the beliefs seem distant and untrustworthy.

We have to realize that, for Alanis Morissette and her generation, the leaders of religious institutions have come to symbolize the hypocrisy: "Do what I say, but not what I do." Need we rehearse the list of various scandals involving TV evangelists, priests, and ministers in local congregations who have been caught in abuse and sexual misconduct? Need we list the "lesser sins" of institutionalized sexism and racism that keep women and minorities out of leadership positions, and make Sunday morning worship one of the most segregated hours of the week? Or what of the comforting indifference and denial that closes churchly eyes to the hurts, needs, and changes swirling around us, as though everything were really "fine" and "okay" in our lonely, angry, and fragmented world?

As a result of this perception of religious institutions, the Postmodern Generation has a healthy skepticism about the church. Rather than buy into the needs of religious institutions to perpetuate themselves, Postmoderns seek to make an authentic connection with God. They are looking for places that intentionally include them in the journey. They need to know that their opinions and insights count. More than this, they are looking for places that will address their questions.

Those who wish to be in ministry with the Postmodern Generation have important choices to make. They can ignore Postmoderns and pretend they don't exist. They can skip over them and focus on the next group of kids, who "surely will turn out to be better." They can embrace them, lap up every element of their world-view and culture, become hip, and sing "rap" and "alternative" music in the church. They can judge them and say: "There's no hope for them, why bother?" Or they can listen to them, learn from them, and help them to become responsible adults. This, it seems, all present American generations need to do.

A Society of Siblings

Robert Bly, whose book *Iron John* helped launch the men's movement in the late 1980's, is now focusing on a topic worth considering. After three years of research Bly concludes that the best way to describe our situation is that we live in a society of siblings. Rather than venerate our elders and care for our children, we all seem to want to stay in adolescence.

We have all become half-adults. We want to play but we don't want to lead. We want to empathize with one another. No one has wisdom to share to help the young out. No one is an authority in anything. We all share the same playing field.

This is true not just for Postmoderns—it is seen across the generations. The GI Generation wants to reap its rewards by playing golf every day and going on cruises in the Bahamas. Baby Boomers and Silents want to stay perpetually young by getting hair transplants, slapping on wrinkle cream, playing rock till they drop, and getting facelifts as long as their skin will hang together. Postmoderns want to stay in the safety of the nest as long as possible before going out into the world.

Commercials love to venerate the young, the slim, and the athletic in an

"My generation should work on a vaccine for materialism."

Edward, 27,
Chula Vista, California

attempt to make us all into Energizer bunnies always on the go. As we all live in the now, no one has time to think about the past or the future.

The problem with living in a society of siblings is that everyone wants an equal share of the pie. Or, if we can get away with it, we want more. A brother or a sister has no more wisdom or knowledge than me. They are my competition for affection, attention, and resources.

Rather than being raised by adults, today's children are being raised by sib-

"Conquering bulimia has made me love and appreciate myself, my body, and my soul. The death of a friend made me realize that we are mortal and therefore we should appreciate life and love, and live to the fullest."

Tanya, 24,
Elmhurst, New York

lings who just happen to be a little older. One of the results of this is a deepening rage on the part of the unparented. Bly puts it this way:

> *The deepening rage of the unparented is becoming the mark of the sibling society. Of course, some children in our society feel well parented, and there is much adequate parenting; but there is also a new rage. A man said to me, "Having made it to the one-parent family, we are now on our way toward the zero-parent family." What the young need—stability, presence, attention, advice, good psychic food, unpolluted stories—is exactly what the sibling society won't give them.[9]*

Another mark of the sibling society is a constant need for the new. People stuck in half-adulthood are not interested in someone else's history. They want to make their own. They love the new, the bold, the unique, even the weird. Having little use for the wisdom of the past they want to create their own society. Bly points out that this was tolerable when adolescence lasted three or four years. But when it lasts from ages twelve to thir-

ty-five, then trouble begins. Elders vanish from view, children are left on their own, responsibility and tradition seem only to constrain the natural impulse.

Bly's insights push us to ask what it will take for us to grow up. One reason we refuse to grow up is that growing up means getting closer to our own mortality. Staying young means we are keeping the grim reaper at bay. But despite our attempt to ignore the reality of the human condition, images of death and destruction seep into our consciousness whether we want them to or not.

While Postmoderns wear their "No Fear" T-shirts, jeans, and shoes, the culture at large languishes in a mood of denial. We want things to be okay; but our sense of security rides on an undercurrent of anxiety. While this book has focused on the Postmodern Generation, the issues Postmoderns face will be compounded in the generation that follows. Some among the Millennial Generation are benefiting from the provision of well-heeled Baby Boomer parents. Still, the reality is that violence, births to unwed mothers, and poverty are not disappearing. In fact most experts on violent behavior predict that the crime rate will jump to higher levels when the more numerous Millennial Generation hits its teen years.

To say it another way, whatever we are doing or not doing for today's children will reap its own harvest. Neglect, poverty, disconnection from the society at large, and nonparenting does not result in a generation of givers, doers, and model citizens. Those we abandon now will not disappear, they will grow up with the scars and anger that abandonment breeds.

All is not lost. There are people who care. But as a society we cannot put our head in the sand. We must embrace the Postmodern Generation's challenge to tell it like it is. We must own up to our weaknesses, build on our strengths, and work together for the common good.

The problem seems to be that the organized church finds itself in the untenable position of trying to meet the needs of the generations who have already found their place inside the church, while at the same time owning up to its responsibility—or dare I say *call*—to be in ministry to those beyond its doors. The majority of mainline churches, such as United Methodist, Presbyterian, and Episcopalian, find themselves with aging congregations who are content with the way things are. At the same time some congregations sense the need to minister to the young, who are either opting out or flocking to independent churches. Some of these independent community churches are showing a better capacity to reach out in ways that effectively communicate to Postmoderns and other recent generations.

The group that seems most absent from the church is Postmoderns. As a result one of the myths surrounding Postmoderns is that they are not as religious as previous generations. They are not as

loyal to the church. They are an irreligious lot, in need of religion. They need us to help them. But in fact the opposite is true. The church needs Postmoderns at least as much as the Postmoderns need the church. Postmoderns have a focus on God that is not satisfied with empty platitudes, easy answers, rituals that do not make sense, or prayers devoid of action.

"I think there are people who are dealing with the issues of abuse, divorced parents, or whatever major personal issues are going on in their life. They go to church and they don't hear anything that resonates with their own life experience, or they feel that the church itself is denying something that is going on. That is in a way a betrayal of their own personal experience and they are not going to want to come back. I think that it is really important to face where our society really is and to be able to talk about things head-on—not like their families, where things get swept under the carpet. It has to be a place that speaks truth and honesty. If it doesn't, then it is not relevant. I guess that is one of the things I feel very strongly about."

Violet, 27, student at
Boston Theological Seminary

Unlike those caught in the secular/religious divide, Postmodern believers take their faith very seriously and want to know how it applies to all of life. Church is not just something you do on Sunday. To be real it must affect life at work, in the family, in the community, and—most important—one's relationships.

Healthy Relationships Count

Another factor that relates to church attendance drives home this point. By comparing attendance in religious services with a person's "parents' marital status" we get another view of how family, faith, and attendance are related.

Moving across the spectrum, from married parents to parents who are remarried, we see that weekly attendance drops from 51% to 26%. But this does not tell the whole story. By combining "yearly" and "never" the picture becomes clearer. While 25% of Postmoderns whose parents are married attend yearly or never, 38% of those whose parents are separated, 48% of those whose parents are divorced, and 56% of those whose parents are remarried attend religious services once a year or never. Fifty percent

of those whose parents are never married fit into the same category.

One more piece of the puzzle needs to be noted. When comparing beliefs among those whose parents are married, divorced, or remarried, another fact is revealed. The beliefs of Postmoderns in these categories vary by only about 10 to 14%. Sixty-five percent of those whose parents are married, 56% of those whose parents are divorced, and 56% of those whose parents are remarried believe in Jesus as their Lord and Savior. The same is basically true in the other categories.

What conclusions can be reached from this data? First, parenting plays a large role in a person's active participation in a church. Those whose families have stayed intact have a much greater likelihood of active church experience than those whose parents have gone through family transitions or breakdown.

When the family system breaks down, attendance breaks down as well. Those working with youth in the past ten years have noted how hard it is to find a regular

Parents' marital status and worship attendance

Attendance	Married	Separated	Divorced	Remarried	Never Married
Weekly	51%	37%	34%	26%	43%
Twice a month	12	3	10	8	—
Monthly	12	22	8	10	7
Yearly	15	22	21	31	14
Never	10	16	27	25	36

Spring Break Surveys 1993 & 1995; 568 Responses.

time to meet among those whose families have gone through a divorce. When parents have joint custody or visitation rights on weekends, the children involved lose a sense of continuity. They might be in different places each weekend. Just staying up with the schedules of two households is hard enough for most children.

Second, the church's response to divorce and remarriage also plays a part. When divorce takes place within a family involved in a faith community, one or both parents often leave. People who know the family can easily take sides. In some instances the whole family is banished because they are seen as having broken their covenant with God and the community of faith.

Lost in the theological and sociological wrangling are the children caught in the middle. Rather than provide a place to find hope and peace, the faith community sometimes finds itself taking sides in a battle that results in loss for all involved.

Third, for Postmoderns belief and attendance at religious services do not

necessarily equate. Many feel quite comfortable with the concept that they can

> *"Many of the problems of our society have been blamed on our generation (that is drugs, violence, apathy, and so forth). I find this interesting—especially in light of the fact that the generation ahead of us is the one that raised us! I believe (based on my own life and my wife's teaching experiences) that our nation's largest problem is the breakdown of family life, fueled by the lack of church attendance."*
>
> Jason, 24,
> Pearland, Texas

maintain their faith without being involved in a faith community. In the 1993 Spring Break Survey 40% said the church is the best place to grow in faith. While this closely relates to the 43% who attend weekly, 60% do not see the church as the best place to pursue their faith.

Fourth, and perhaps most important, the modern church has seen itself as pro-

Parents' marital status and beliefs

Beliefs	Married	Divorced	Remarried
God is Creator	82%	74%	68%
Jesus is my Lord and Savior	65	56	56
Belief in the power of prayer	62	47	55
Angels exist	57	47	58
Only those who are saved will go to heaven	39	32	32

Spring Break Surveys 1993 & 1995; 539 Responses.

viding models for the upright citizen who is comfortable in the "religious" world of the church and in the "secular" world of work, education, and family. In this regard "right beliefs" are those which enhance one's position in the community, support a middle-class society, and do not rock the boat. The modern church has tended to embrace those beliefs that confirm its own self-image of respectability, and to ignore those that require a hard look at our own brokenness. As a result, the modern church has also denied the real pain seen in the break-

 "My religious beliefs and experiences are dear to me because they make me who I am and what I am. There is hope. Pray!"

Jonah, 17,
Shreveport, Louisiana

"On many occasions I have been filled up by the Holy Spirit. I have experienced God's powerful healing of emotional scars and grief, and have felt his presence in my life in such an incredibly real, physical way that it changed my life."

Jeannie, 24,
Houston, Texas

down of families and the upturn of violence in society.

What the decline in worship attendance tells us in relationship to parenting and family background is that for many Postmoderns the number one issue is *having healthy relationships that mirror*

the faith that the church supposedly professes. When the family breaks down, trust in the church and its beliefs suffers as well. When a congregation becomes enveloped in personality conflicts and cycles of dysfunctionality, its values become suspect.

For Postmoderns spirituality and relationships go together. It is out of these relationships that faith and trust in God grow. For moderns, rational thought has been the hallmark of social and religious respectability. But rational thought can easily become rationalization. For Postmoderns, reason is just one part of the picture. God touches more than the mind. For spirituality to be real, it must lead to a quest that encompasses all aspects of a person's life—thoughts, emotions, and the deep yearning for wholeness and healing that all persons have at their core. For something to be believed, Postmoderns must experience it at *all* levels of their existence.

As the Postmodern Generation seeks God it has a variety of paths to explore— some traditional, some new, some ancient—each with its own claim to authority, and each with its proponents. While many religious perspectives have found a voice, each person is challenged to put together the puzzle pieces in his or her own way. Religion has evolved into a spirituality of which the one constant is the search. Salvation is not a one-step deal, it is an ongoing process of growth and development that lasts a lifetime.

From the Modern to the Post-modern Church

im Celek is pastor of Calvary-Newport Mesa Church in California, one of the most effective Christian churches in ministry with the Postmodern Generation. He says that in order to attract and retain Postmoderns the church must offer the most attractive alternative. Instead of standing on the street corner and proclaiming that we have the truth, the local church must create a place of integrity, compassion, and authenticity in which Postmoderns can find a safe place to seek God. He is convinced that once Postmoderns discover the power and excitement of the Christian alternative they will find the truth through faith in Jesus Christ.

Dieter Zander, founding pastor of New Song in Covina, California, and now on staff as a pastor at Willow Creek Community Church outside Chicago, brings into focus what the postmodern perspective brings when it comes to talking about Jesus Christ.

> *"We are faced with so many choices. Knowing about all the different avenues there are allows us to choose the correct one. If only more people knew the promise of our Lord and Savior. What a difference He has made in my life—every aspect. Without Him, I would be absolutely lost."*
> Alexis, 17,
> Scottsdale, Arizona

Q: What does the postmodern perspective mean when it comes to sharing faith?

ZANDER: Postmodernity is big because people need to understand that this is the first genera-tion that grew up without any absolutes any place along the line. That has a huge effect on the way you process truth. I don't know if there will ever be another time where we will process truth in a linear manner.

Q: **Can you speak to what it means to have no absolute truths?**

ZANDER: At one end there is no truth, while at the other end all truth is truth. In the middle of it they are letting go of the idea that humanity through technology is getting better, which was the big hope of previous generations. The big hope of the Boomers was: "We're going to have a better world because we are making it better." The Postmoderns are saying: "It ain't going to get better." This is just huge in terms of this generation's mindset. When you give up on technology and on the idea that humanity is making the world bet-ter, you get an increased investiga-tion into something beyond tech-nology and empiricism. Follow? In other words, for postmodern peo-ple, you do not have to prove it anymore for it to be real.

Q: **Which is the opposite of the modern perspective that said: "Prove it, then I'll believe." For Postmoderns, experience provides the key, right?**

ZANDER: Right, and that's huge. That opens a door for God because there's that aspect of God that you just can't prove. You see that Postmoderns are willing to enter into a dialogue about Chris-tianity, even when you can't prove it, per se. You come at it com-pletely different now. You don't start with: "This is true, therefore believe it." You start with: "This is attractive," and then you move toward: "This is relevant," and after you have established those two things, then you say: "You want to know why it's attractive or even why it's relevant?—because, it's true."

Q: **They have to validate it by their experience.**

ZANDER: They have to see how it touches their lives.

As the church moves into the future, the postmodern perspective will bring radical changes in the way believers share their faith, in the way they structure their faith community, and in the way they live out their faith together.

My research indicates several key fac-tors in churches that are effective in min-istry with Postmoderns. We are in danger, however, if we try to make this list into a prescription rather than simply listen deeply to what Postmoderns are saying about the church and faith. What Postmoderns will not tolerate is surface changes. They are quick to discern what is fake and smacks of hype. They also long for a place that takes them and their needs seriously.

These insights reveal something else of immense significance. What we see in the leading-edge churches is a pattern of church life that will motivate and retain Christian believers of the next century. Much of what we now do in church is an outgrowth of the modern way of doing things. The modern structure of the church was extremely hierarchical with committees and checks and balances up and down the line. Preaching had more to do with uplifting and consoling the saved rather than with teaching people how to live out the faith in a changing world. Relationships were built around the committee table or in task groups such as the choir. The minister did all the ministry, while the laity's job was to take care of the minister. When he or she did not do his or her job right, it was time for a change. The postmodern congregation turns these modes of operation on their head.

The Web of Inclusion

First and foremost, the postmodern church creates a web of inclusion that focuses on discipleship rather than on turning people into members. I asked Tim Celek how he defined membership in his church. He replied: "A member is someone who is active in a small group." Rather than focus on worship attendance

A conversation between a senior pastor and his new postmodern associate minister:

Senior Pastor: I want you to go help the youth become churched.

Associate Minister: I don't want to be churched. I don't want to be boxed in. If you are saying, 'Go share faith in Jesus Christ so youth can become disciples,' then that's what I would like to do.

Senior Pastor: Yes, that's it. Go share the faith so people can become disciples of Christ.

or participation in a committee, the number one priority of the postmodern congregation is to involve people in an accountability group—a small group of six to twelve persons who meet regularly for prayer, study, support, and mission. These groups are fundamentally discipleship groups in which participants learn how to live out the faith. The genius of these groups is that they specifically meet the needs of Postmoderns who are looking for healthy relationships. In a real sense these small groups become the participant's extended family.

The web of inclusion does not stop here. It takes into account a person's first experience with a congregation all the way up to that person's graduation from the congregation. In other words, the congregation has a specific discipleship system designed to help individuals grow in their faith. Classes on prayer, spiritual gifts, and how to share the Christian faith are given on a regular basis. While small groups help individuals put these spiritual disciplines into action, the congregation supplements this by offering ongoing classes on the basics of the faith.

The role of the pastor is to provide the vision, setting, and system in which discipleship can take place. The pastor's job is to be like the web master on the Internet, who manages a particular web site. The web master's job is to create new web sites, maintain the sites, and update them continually. In other words the role of pastoring in the postmodern congregation is not simply to get people to join and then place them on committees or in places of ministry such as teaching church school.

The main task is to create opportunities for discipleship and to develop leadership among the laity, who will in turn lead others to faith and growth as disciples of Christ. This means thinking of faith as a process of growth and development. The modern approach was to make sure someone was a good member. The postmodern approach is to encourage those who are considering following Jesus Christ to get involved in a lifelong process of personal salvation. You don't get saved and then go on to do something else. Faith in Christ moves the believer into a

lifetime of learning, growing, and giving.

The Postmodern Congregation: Using the Arts in Worship

In the book *Contemporary Worship for the 21st Century: Worship or Evangelism?*,[1] which I coauthored with Dan Benedict, we talk about three basic kinds of worship services used in congregations around the country. One of these is called the seeker service. This service uses secular songs, video, multimedia, drama, dance, and Bible-based teaching as worship elements. The goal of the seeker service is to create a place in which prechurched people can hear the message of the Christian faith. This is counterposed by two other services that are primarily for believers—the *Book of Common Worship,* which uses the traditional hymns and liturgies of the faith, and the *Book of Common Song,* which uses contemporary Christian music and teaching as its primary elements.

We argue that in order to reach the prechurched and seekers, congregations must offer seeker services or seeker-sensitive services that speak to people outside the church. I would like to take this one step further. In order to reach the believers of the future, congregations will have to learn to use all the arts, including electronic media, in order to communicate the faith.

What makes seeker services effective is that they communicate in a postmodern way. By using the various elements of the culture they speak in today's language. The next time you see a stained-glass window, take a close look at it and ask why stained-glass windows were created in the first place. Before people could read, the church communicated through the arts. Stained-glass windows, statues, intricate wood carvings, and paintings on church walls and ceilings were all created to tell the story of the faith. New converts were taught the faith not by reading about it, but by viewing the biblical stories through these various media.

The Sistine Chapel ceiling was not painted by Michelangelo so that the Vatican could have a nice piece of art. These paintings were rendered with bright colors and broad strokes so they would communicate the great truths of the faith. The art of the medieval church was the multimedia of its day.

Postmodern congregations use all the arts in their worship to communicate the gospel message. Video projectors and television monitors are used for more than just showing video clips of movies. At Christ United Methodist Church in Alexandria, Virginia, TV monitors installed in the worship center scroll through announcements before worship takes place. At Crosswoods Community Church in Birmingham, Alabama, a Bible story illustrated by an artist is projected on the screen to tell the Scripture lesson. At Bellevue Community Church in Tennessee, a Christian music video is used as a prelude to the worship service. At Ginghamsburg United Methodist in Tipp City, Ohio, video clips and images are projected on a screen to enhance key points of the sermon.

These tools of communication are not simply for seekers. They will become essential tools for communication as we enter the 21st century. Churches of the future will be able to downlink to a screen in their worship center a live interview with church members on a mission trip in Mexico or Kenya. Or the congregation will receive a live feed of Bethlehem as the pastor talks about the birth of Jesus. You get the picture.

The modern church has been content to use a small piece of the pie in the realm of communication. Its musical instruments of choice are the organ and piano. Its musical style is primarily classical compositions and hymns of the faith passed on from past generations. Its communication style is primarily lecture and the reading of texts such as written liturgies or prayers.

The main reason modern congregations use a small segment of the communication styles available is that they have locked into the Enlightenment view of truth as logical proof. This has led to a division between the secular and the religious, which in turn meant demoting religious claims to a subjective level beneath the allegedly hard claims of science. The postmodern congregation is not willing to give up any type of communication, viewing the ability to communicate in a variety of ways as a gift of God.

What has been regarded as secular can be redeemed and given new meaning through the lens of the Christian faith. For example, is the Baby Boomer classic *Bridge Over Troubled Water* secular or religious? It is neither. It is the expression of a deep spirituality. When used in worship it connects to the Christian belief that Jesus is the bridge that gets believers across the troubled waters of our lives.

Material created outside the Christian community often raises the common questions that concern people. A pastor who understands the postmodern perspective may use a video clip from the movie *Forest Gump* to raise relevant questions about life. The person operating purely on the modern mentality will see *Forest Gump* only as an example of recent moving-making; entertainment devoid of faith and meaning. The postmodern pastor, by contrast, will show the scene of Forest running ahead of a crowd who thinks he has the secret of life. When Forest quits and walks away, the crowd looks lost. After showing the video clip the pastor will ask the congregation: "What is it you are chasing after?" The video clip is incorporated into the message as a way to connect with people where they are living today. By using it in the context of worship, the scene is infused with new meaning. Whenever someone sees that scene again they will be reminded of the deeper questions that lead them to seek God.

But, in case you have missed the point, new technology is not the answer. While technology allows people to experience Christianity in a way they can understand it, technology cannot take the

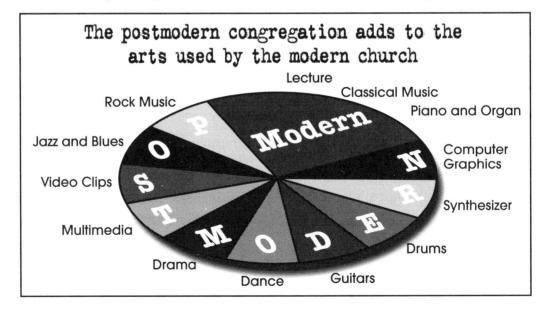

The postmodern congregation adds to the arts used by the modern church

place of real face-to-face experiences of prayer and ministry by people to people. What Postmoderns long for are real experiences of love and compassion, of opportunities to serve real people who are in need.

It's the Music!!!

An interview with Ross Kimura, music director at Ginghamsburg United Methodist Church in Tipp City, Ohio, shows how postmodern congregations use all the arts.

Q: **What kind of music do you need to speak to the twentysomething crowd?**

KIMURA: It depends on the kind of twentysomething you are talking about. For those who have come from a rough background it's a miracle that they are even willing to step into the church. It's exciting when that happens. The kind of music we are doing has a lot of backbeat. It has a heavy beat to it. We use a lot of seventies style music because they like a lot of the Boomer rock stars we grew up with.

Q: **What do congregations need to know about music? I think that in many ways music is more important than the sermon for this generation.**

KIMURA: I think you are right. Number one, I try not to be some-

thing I really am not. You need to be real. So the music is real to what we believe and the way we can communicate. Second, the music has to have excellence. My musicians have to be able to play the music. Third, I recommend that our musicians listen to a wide variety of music, even what's on VH1 or MTV. We listen to the Cranberries, Smashing Pumpkins, Ethridge, and to Pop Country. Listening helps us to duplicate some of the sounds that are being used. Fourth, we try to include youth and young adults in our music program. I try to design it so that they want to be in the adult choir. We will do a lot of choral music with solos and background, for example. The main thing is not to label people, but to treat them as individual persons, and to be a good example of what it means to be a Christian. We pray with people and for them. Those are the main things we are trying to do.

Q: **What are you looking to do in the future?**

KIMURA: We are going to try to add some of the alternative rock styles and inner-city music. Our choir is now ready to do some of the heavy rock gospel style. We also are going to do some of the acappella music that has Celtic

173

roots, and some Virginia mountain music. We are going to add some of the pure sounds like acoustic guitar, oboe, chimes, and rushing wind. I see us being in a process of constant improvement and updating. The main thing is not getting too far ahead of where the congregation is. We are not just a twentysomething congregation. Because we have a variety of age groups, we have to move at a pace that is challenging but not confrontational to the congregation. Openness and sensitivity have to go together.

Ross's comments shows the variety of artistic forms available to the postmodern congregation. Along with the organ and piano, these congregations use guitars, drums, synthesizers, conga drums, string, brass, woodwind instruments, marimbas, and so forth. They are limited only by their imagination. What about music styles? They use rock, classic rock, country, folk, Celtic, alternative, jazz, gospel, classical, and Christian contemporary, plus the various styles of world music such as Jamaican or Mariachi and the like. To communicate the message they add the use of drama, dance, projected art, and video to their primarily preaching style of teaching.

The postmodern congregation uses all communication devices available in an attempt to communicate the gospel to a culture in which electronic media and music are the norm. For example, the latest concept for baseball and football stadiums of the future have TV monitors at each seat so fans can watch the action on the field from the camera angle they wish to use. Each person will be able to play back the play he or she wants to see. Fans will be able to manipulate the data to give themselves an even more information-rich experience of the game. Congregations also need to find ways to enrich the experience of worship and faith development by tapping into the resources of the new communications technology and by rediscovering the arts of the historic church.

Team Players

One of the lessons we are learning about using a variety of arts in worship is the importance of teamwork. When Ginghamsburg moved to their new building, with a video screen and the technology that goes with it, worship planning changed as well. Instead of the preacher writing the sermon and then laying out a service of worship to accompany it, a team of six people puts the service together.

On Wednesday mornings the team meets to go over the theme for the weekend's services. They discuss the various media they may use to enhance the message. The preacher for that week goes to work on the outline of the message while the rest of the team puts together the drama, video clips, music, and projected illustrations that will go along with that weekend's services. Some team members are visually oriented, while others are more word oriented. Each has an opportunity for input. During the next two days the team meets to update its progress. Like putting together a play, the team members create a worship experience that will bring together a number of art forms and communication techniques. Their goal is to create an experience of the living God.

A key benefit of this kind of planning is that a whole host of people who have artistic, musical, computer-graphic, dramatic, and electronic media gifts are now invited to use them in worship. When a congregation limits itself to a small selection of media, only a few persons can participate. When a wide range of possibilities and gifts are used, the whole congregation benefits. Numbers of persons who felt excluded in the past now have a role in proclaiming their faith. This has the remarkable effect of deepening and energizing the faith of those who participate in this way.

On one occasion I took a group of pastors to visit Calvary-Newport Mesa Church. One of these was astounded to see a former member of her own church singing a hard rock song that challenged people to look at their relationships with one another. "I thought she had dropped out of the church completely," she exclaimed. "She had a number of personal problems she was dealing with. But look at her now! She is so alive. I never knew she could sing like that. Wow!"

Grace Community United Methodist Church of Shreveport, Louisiana, has two music teams—instead of a choir—that take turns leading worship. One team leads worship for a full month while the other takes that month off. During the time they are off, the teams have an opportunity to improve their music and add to their repertoire. Each team supports the other. Team members can substitute for one another if someone is gone on a particular week. If the bass player from Team A is gone, the bass player from Team B takes her place.

Team work does not stop at the worship service. In postmodern congregations work is organized into teams that have joint responsibility for various aspects of the congregation's life. Unlike committee work, in which members vote for some action and then leave it to one person to execute, the secret to teamwork is that decisions become the responsibility of the whole team.

Peter Block, in his book *Stewardship: Choosing Service Over Self-Interest*, says that one of the byproducts of teamwork is that individuals are empowered. This empowerment means people have their own ability to choose how to do the work, to define their purpose, and to realize that success and failure lie in their hands.

This creates two important dynamics. First, persons find that they have an emotional investment in the decisions made. This investment leads to commitment. Second, because decision making is in their own hands they experience increased freedom and their work becomes more creative. But teamwork only happens when the leadership of the organization supports team decisions. Rather than negate team decisions or seek to control them, leadership must enter into a partnership in which all benefit together.[2]

Options, Options, Options

Look around and you will see that almost everywhere you go you have options. Go to an athletic shoe store and you will have hundreds of choices for whatever sport you are participating in. The same is true in almost every business. Postmoderns are used to choices, and those congregations that offer a variety of options both in worship and in discipleship opportunities are best positioned to be in ministry with this generation.

Churches may think that in order to minister to Postmoderns they should get rid of their current style of worship. Nothing could be further from the truth. Instead of getting rid of things, congregations would be better advised to improve what they have. Not all Postmoderns are necessarily interested in a rock-style service. What they do require is a worship style that is well executed and that speaks to their everyday needs.

Postmodern congregations take seriously the desire of Postmoderns to have a variety of options. Duane Anders, pastor of Stillwater United Methodist Church in

Ohio, joined this small city congregation two years ago. Since then the church has changed its name, moved its location, and now offers four worship services—one on Saturday evening and three on Sunday mornings. Building on the strength of the congregation, Stillwater meets a variety of needs by offering worship services at multiple times and with multiple formats. When they moved to their new building they started with two services. Even though everyone could have fitted in the new sanctuary at one service, they began with two services—one contemporary and one traditional. Both services grew. Now they require four services to meet the needs of the growing congregation.

By creating options this congregation has grown in two years from 30 in worship to 400. By pursuing a vision that has moved them beyond their own comfort levels, they now find themselves in a growing, dynamic congregation that ministers to a whole new group of people primarily in their twenties and thirties.

San Jose Chinese Alliance has four worshiping congregations, each with its own pastor and language. Services are offered in Mandarin, Cantonese, Vietnamese (for ethnic Chinese from Vietnam), and English. Victor Quon, who works with the youth from each language group, must take into consideration the background of each person. For the Cantonese youth, classical music and karaoke are popular. Mandarin youth, primarily from Taiwan, prefer rock music and contemporary praise songs. For American-born Chinese a wide variety of Christian music and rock is popular. In each instance options are designed and implemented to meet the diverse needs of the 120 youth who are part of the congregation. As a result Chinese Alliance has about 950 people in worship on a weekend, and is one of the largest Chinese congregations in the country.

Options are not tied only to worship. Postmoderns also relish hands-on opportunities to be in service. Mission projects, community projects such as soup kitchens or building a house for Habitat for Humanity, or setting up a tutoring club for disadvantaged students are just some of the ways congregations bring together faith and action. Postmoderns are not content just to talk about their faith, they want opportunities to live it out in the world.

The Recycled Church

Unlike Baby Boomers, who like everything to be new, the church facility that attracts Postmoderns does not have to be brand new. In fact, congregations who are willing to combine the old with the new can use existing facilities for a whole new audience. Calvary-Newport Mesa Church got its start when a Baptist congregation hit hard times and donated its building to another church in the area. Rather than tear down the building, the new congregation added TV monitors, a new P.A. system, and theater lights to the sanctuary, which enhanced their ability to communicate in many different ways. The combination of old and the new meets the postmodern sensibility of using what is already there to its best advantage.

An ornate building with stained glass, organ pipes, and a beautiful altar can be updated by adding a video projector and screen, thus combining old and new, and giving the sanctuary an MTV unplugged feel. Although a modernist might see this as sacrilegious, it is no more sacrilegious than blessing another medium, a book, when it is placed in a position of honor on the altar. For Postmoderns, combining something ancient with something futuristic speaks to a mindset that is open to all. The key is not the medium, but the message.

Postmoderns Think Differently

An interview with Paul Tofte, communications specialist at United Seminary, points to a different way of interacting with knowledge. On the Internet hypertext is used to allow people to access many different kinds of information. Typically a word will be underlined like this, and when you click on it with your mouse you are taken to that particular idea or subject.

Q: What is important about the Internet and hypertext?

TOFTE: People that use the Internet are people that think differently. Most of us have been taught that you get an idea and you dig deeper and deeper into that idea. Hypertext says I can start with an idea, and if I see something else that interests me I can look at that instead and follow it from one idea to another. This is what is called nonlinear thinking. People are free to flow from one idea to another as they follow whatever interests them at the time.

Q: **What does this mean for preaching and communication?**

TOFTE: I think most people are used to getting up in the pulpit and placing down their manuscript and reading it from top to bottom until they are done. But the person who is listening might want to ask: "You just said 'Lord.' What does

"We don't know exactly what the Bible is saying, so if you could translate it into words we understand, we'd be a lot better off."

Julia, 14,
Hibbing, Minnesota

that mean?" If you were to answer them you might go into what the word "Lord" means, and the issues relating to gender and so forth, and end up at a totally different place than what you planned. That is nonlinear thinking.

Hypertext is really a statement about how we have been taught

by television to think. We don't watch just one thought for a long time. We can watch a Dodge commercial, and from a Dodge commercial we can go to someone doing surgery on somebody, to a Pepsi commercial, and we are not bothered by that at all.

Q: **So hypertext on the Internet takes this a step further, as it allows users to choose even smaller bits of information.**

TOFTE: So as a result we think differently. If we would give ourselves permission in the church to allow people to scratch all the itches that they have when the thoughts come to mind, rather than saying: "No, you have to listen till I'm done," we will be better able to communicate in the thought language of today.

Teaching Rather than Preaching

One result of nonlinear thinking is that preaching takes a different form in the postmodern world. Thus the role of preaching is to teach, rather than to confront, console, or convince. When I asked Duane Anders, pastor of Stillwater United Methodist Church, what he tries to offer people of his own generation he responded:

"One of the most important things we can do is to help people make application of the Scripture to their lives. I think a lot of people know the right stuff, they know they should read the Bible, they know God is good, and they agree with those beliefs. The problem is they don't live it.

"You ask people: 'Do you read your Bible?' and they say: 'Well, I don't know where it is.' You ask: 'Are you a good person?' and they say: 'When it's convenient for me to be so.' So how do you help people bring those values together? I think you have to take your own faith seriously and know what you believe as a Christian. Then you have to communicate the faith in real easy, how-to steps that they can apply to their lives."

The Message as a Guideline for Living

Common among postmodern congregations is the pastor who provides an outline of the message in the bulletin. In the modern church, the bulletin serves mainly as an index to the hymnal. In the postmodern congregation the bulletin includes a message outline (or a space to take notes), lists of small groups, and a statement of what the church believes and its vision for the future.

Here the outline becomes a communication tool. Instead of a throw-away message that people will forget by the time they get home, an outline provides an opportunity for people to interact with

the preacher. Commonly these outlines will include Scripture references under key points that the people are invited to read aloud with the pastor. The pastor might ask them to underline a specific point or to fill in a blank. During the sermon the pastor illustrates each point with stories, personal accounts about daily life, and biblical insights. He or she may even bring home a point with a video clip or a brief drama. After the service worshipers have something to which they can refer during the week. They can even use the outline as a tool to share the message with another person.

While an outline helps, it is not the key point. What is key is communicating in the heart-language of the people, so that the biblical message of salvation through faith in Jesus Christ is made real. What people are looking for in a message are guidelines and ideas for how to apply their faith to their life outside the church.

After a seminar on worship one pastor came up to me and asked: "My congregation thinks I am a little crazy. I always tell them stories and relate scenes from movies and television shows to the Bible. I am always thinking in images and pictures. Is that what you are saying?"

I responded to her: "You've got it. In a world of multimedia the gospel has to be communicated in a dramatic and vibrant way. Stories, personal examples out of your spiritual journey, and connections to the culture are what speak to people. They want to know you are living in the same world they are living in. They want to know that the God you believe in cares about them and their daily struggles and victories."

She replied: "Well, maybe I should do more of it. Maybe making connections with people is my gift."

Postmodern Christian Spirituality Is Deep

As Postmoderns look to the church they are looking for a faith that is deep, real, and alive. As I have talked with Postmoderns around the country they do not necessarily deride religious faith as much as they wonder how it applies to their lives. An even deeper question is how the church fits into their spiritual journey. Rather than ask: "Where are *they?*" congregations need to ask: "Where are *we?*"

Congregations who intentionally minister to Postmoderns find that Postmoderns add a whole new dimension to the life of the congregation. They give congregations an opportunity to engage the real questions people are asking, the "stupid" questions that no one is willing to talk about. They force congregations to put their faith into action and enable congregations to reach out to a wider audience of people who are seeking God.

One evening at a camp high up in the mountains of New Mexico I had the opportunity to listen in on a conversation between three postmodern pastors who were serving their first congregations. As they talked I recorded their remarks, and

share them with you now. I believe there is no better way to conclude this account of the changes Postmoderns have faced and their hopes for the future than to let you engage with this discussion among three spiritual leaders of their generation.

Marc, (twenty-nine, Albuquerque, New Mexico): "We are looking for a sense of the spiritual that is well done, genuine, and has high quality. It has to be authentic. Something a person doesn't have to know before they come."

Ann, (thirty, Crane, Texas): "Also it doesn't have to be generationally specific. Boomers are the only generation that thinks they have to be special. To have something just for them. Their younger children, the Millennial children, they probably will need something special for them too. People always say that they will take us into the 21st century. Postmoderns will be there before them."

Marc: "We are generally disenchanted with the solutions Boomers have offered. So we look for other options."

Keith (thirty, New Mexico): "What we want in our spirituality is something that is intensely deep."

Marc: "We don't want the sugar-coated Jesus. We want it to be real. The feel-good Jesus won't cut it. We have felt the sharp pain in our hand. We have seen the brokenness in our families, have had friends who have died. We know despair firsthand. So our faith has to be deep, to offer hope at a deep level."

Keith: "We have seen friends who

have been overwhelmed, have taken their own lives. Sometimes I feel it's just by the grace of God that I am here. It's not just that I want someone to help me. It's that I want the craziness to stop."

Marc: "When we were children and toddling around, we saw the images of Vietnam on TV. Now it is always there—Oklahoma—five people knocked off in a video store . . . ."

Keith: "One of my first memories as a kid was watching President Nixon resign. How does the President quit?"

Ann: "Now there is all this mindless violence."

Marc: "Life has gotten cheap."

Ann: "Another way to say it is that we are survivors."

Marc: "So I want to say, to scream out loud: 'It's Friday, but Sunday is coming.' The message of Holy Week—the Passion story—is our story. The healings are nice, the parables are helpful, but Holy Week is our week."

Ann: "I worked in a mental hospital for a time, and we played out the Lazarus story, and the kids yelled out: 'But our friends have not come back. They are still dead.'"

Marc: "If you go from the parade on Palm Sunday to the empty tomb on Easter you have missed it. The feel-good generation wants to skip over the pain of the cross. We want the whole story."

Ann: "It's nice to know that Jesus loves me, but what speaks to me is that Jesus feels your pain. He knows our lone-liness and despair. When I came to faith it was because here was someone who died for me before I was even born."

Keith: "But it's not leaving it at that. It's that Jesus can do something about it. It's more than self-help. It's the power of the Spirit and the Resurrection in our lives that makes the difference. Jesus is

"We are more than just one generation. I am a part of life. I am a mirror of earlier generations and a reflection for future generations as well. I am an individual."

Amanda, 16,
Los Altos, California

Friend, Lord, and Savior."

Marc: "For us friends are often as important as family. My friends have earned the right to be called my friend. Jesus has earned the right to be called friend in my life. As many times as I have betrayed Jesus he has never failed me."

Ann: "I think what is true is that we need a faith that is resilient, one which can stand taking a beating. The beating from doubt, despair, and hopelessness. Our faith has to be strong."

Keith: "When I look at my own life, family is something that I have had to look for. My own mother is on her third marriage. And hopefully her last. Last time she got married I said: 'This is the last time.'"

Ann: "You were parenting your mother."

Keith: "I remember when I was twelve I said this would never happen to me. But after four years of marriage I got a divorce. I found that I was trying to rescue my wife, but I couldn't. Now I am thirty and in my second marriage. I have a six-year-old from the first marriage and a seven-month-old from the second. When I got married the second time we worked at it and we looked for all kinds of ways to strengthen our marriage. But not just strengthen. We want to make sure that we are going to make it."

Ann: "So the question for many of us is what makes a healthy family."

Keith: "For many of us, family is not someone that we are biologically related to."

Ann: "For me, the church was my family."

Keith: "It was the third grade teacher who graduated with us, the youth counselor who was there for us, the friends from church who got me through the second breakup of my mom's family."

Marc: "But for me, what I felt betrayed by was the associate pastor who rejected my call or did not validate God's activity in my life. That's probably why I can't stand it when other generations confine and define what reality is for me. For example, when I wrote my credo of faith, the Boomer professor couldn't stand it. I poured my soul into it, but it was thrown away. It was rejected. And that left me bitter because he did not take seriously who I am or my life experiences."

Ann: "For me it was male peers who could not accept my call to become a pastor. Part of being from my generation is that the world may not affirm who you are or who you are called to be."

Keith: "That's true no matter who you want to be."

Marc: "So you have to depend on yourself and on that core group of friends on whom you depend."

Keith: "But now I realize that that is not enough because I personally can only take it to a certain point. I need God."

Marc: "So that is where the message of the church says: 'You are not alone. Christ is with you to be your Friend, Lord, and Savior.'"

Ann: "In my experience my faith stretches me to be in community with those who have let me down. It's through the Holy Spirit that we are able to be healed."

Marc: "We don't commit easily, but when we do it's for the long haul. That's why faith has to be real. It has to be deep *shalom*. That profound sense of the Holy Spirit."

Ann: "It's wholeness."

Marc: "Our words are inadequate. It's the power of the Spirit to make us whole."

Keith: "It has to be authentic. Not superficial."

Marc: "Not the feel-good Jesus. My faith starts with Jesus on the cross. The one who transforms our lives because of who he is."

Ann: "I want the eternal life that is found on the other side of suffering."

Keith: "I want faith that is real. The church that attracts people of our generation has to live out the faith that experiences the power and presence of the living Christ."

Marc: "It's more than just living it out. It has to be *shalom. Shalom* is more than knowing, it is being."

As American society wrestles with its core values, Postmoderns are saying: "Listen to us, maybe we have something you need." The generation who was raised in the midst of the culture-shifts that have rocked the world is now growing up. They have learned that relationships count, that God has not abandoned them, that they have something to give, and through hope and belief fears can be overcome. The question is whether we are willing to listen. For if we do, maybe

Now-here is my secret:

I tell it to you with an openness of heart that I doubt I shall ever achieve again, so I pray that you are in a quiet room as you hear these words. My secret is that I need God—that I am sick and can no longer make it alone. I need God to help me give, because I no longer seem to be capable of giving; to help me be kind, as I no longer seem capable of kindness; to help me love, as I seem beyond being able to love.

Reprinted with the permission of Pocket Books, a Division of Simon & Schuster from *Life After God* by Douglas Coupland, p 359.

we will learn something new about ourselves. Maybe the future will be better than we think.

E N D N O T E S

Chapter 1

1   William Dunn, *The Baby Bust: A Generation Comes of Age* (Ithaca, New York: American Demographics Books, 1993), p. 16.

2   S.K. Henshaw and J.Van Vort, eds., Abortion Factbook, 1992 Edition: Reading Trends, and State and Local Data to 1988. Table 110. Reported in *The American Almanac: Statistical Abstract of the United States, 1995-1996* (Austin, Texas: The Reference Press, Inc., 1996), p. 73.

3   Barry Glassner, *Career Crash: The New Crisis—and Who Survives* (New York: Simon & Schuster, 1994), p. 16.

4   Ronald Brownstein, "America's Anxiety Attack," *Los Angeles Times Magazine,* May 8, 1994, p. 17. Copyright 1996, *Los Angeles Times.* Reprinted by permission.

5   Brownstein, p. 17.

6   From: *The Quark and the Jaguar* by Gell-Mann. Copyright © 1994 by Murray Gell-Mann. Used with permission of W.H. Freeman & Company, p. 329.

7   Gell-Mann, pp. 24-25.

Chapter 2

1   From *Being Digital* by Nicholas Negroponte. Copyright © 1995 by Nicholas Negroponte. Reprinted by permission of Alfred A. Knopf, Inc., p. 14.

2   From *The Road Ahead* by Bill Gates. Copyright 1995 by William H. Gates III. Used by permission of Viking Penguin, a division of Penguin Books USA, Inc., p. 31.

3   Negroponte, p. 5.

4   The People's Chronology is licensed from Henry Holt and Company, Inc. Copyright ©1992 by James Trager. All rights reserved.

5   Reprinted by permission of The Putnam Publishing Group from *Reviving Ophelia: Saving the Selves of Adolescent Girls* by Mary Pipher, Ph.D. Copyright © 1994 by Mary Pipher, Ph.D., p. 244.

6   "Simpson Trial Trivia," *U.S. News & World Report,* October 16, 1995, p. 42.

7   Neil Postman, *Technopoly: The Surrender of Culture to Technology* (New York: Random House, Inc., 1993), p. 25.

8   Postman, p. 70.

9   Pipher, p. 244.

10 DeDe Lahman, "How Are You Dealing?" *Seventeen,* May 1996, p. 148.

11 Pipher, p. 208.

12 Jim Impoco, "TV's Frisky Family Values," *U.S. News & World Report,* April 15, 1996, pp. 58-62.

13 From *Marketing to Generation X* by Karen Ritchie. Copyright © 1995 by Karen Ritchie. Reprinted with permission of The Free Press, a division of Simon & Schuster, p. 157.

14 Philip Elmer-Dewitt, "The Amazing Video Game Boom," *Time,* September 23, 1993, pp. 66ff.

15 Nicholas, "The Future of the Book," *Wired,* February 1996, p. 188.

16 Philip Elmer-DeWitt, "Welcome to Cyberspace," *Time,* Spring 1995, p. 9.

17 "How Big Is the Net," *American Demographics,* February 1996, p. 8.

18 "The Internet Reconsidered," from *Road Warriors* by Daniel Burstein and David Kline. Copyright © 1995 by Daniel Burstein & David Kline. Used by permission of Dutton Signet, a division of Penguin Books USA Inc., pp. 105-106.

19 Steve Meloan, "Http 90210," *Wired,* November 1995, p. 68.

Chapter 3

1   Laurence Hooper, "Digital Hollywood: How Computers Are Remaking Movie Making," *Rolling Stone,* August 11, 1994, p. 58.

2   Reprinted by permission of The Putnam Publishing Group/Jeremy P. Tarcher, Inc. from *The Truth About the Truth* by Walter Truett Anderson. Copyright © 1995 by Walter Truett Anderson, p. 5.

3   Anderson, p. 6.

4   Anderson, p. 241.

5   Michael D'Antonio, "The New Generation Gap," *Los Angeles Times Magazine,* March 14, 1993, p. 16. Copyright 1996, *Los Angeles Times.* Reprinted by permission.

6   John Katz, "Guilty," *Wired,* September 1995, p. 128.

7   Stewart Brand, "Two Questions," *Special Edition: Wired Scenarios,* Fall 1995, p. 32.

8   Danny Hills, "The Millennium Clock," *Special Edition: Wired Scenarios,* Fall 1995, p. 52.

Chapter 4

1   "Murder Victims by Weapons Used," Department of Justice, Federal Bureau of Investigation, *Uniform Crime Reports for the United States,* 1991.

2   Figures compiled from the following sources: "Murder Victims, by Age, Sex, and Race: 1993," U.S. Federal Bureau of Investigation, Crime in the United States, annual. Reported in *The American Almanac: Statistical Abstract of the United States, 1995-1996* (Austin, Texas: The Reference Press, Inc., 1996), p. 202; "New Orleans, Washington Top List," *USA Today,* May 6, 1996, p. 8A, based on the Federal Bureau of investigation's preliminary data for 1995.

3   "Murder Victims, by Age, Sex, and Race: 1993," U.S. Federal Bureau of Investigation, Crime in the United States, annual. Reported in *The American Almanac: Statistical Abstract of the United States, 1995-1996* (Austin, Texas: The Reference Press, Inc., 1996), p. 202.

4   Reprinted with the permission of Simon & Schuster from *The Day America Told the Truth: What People Really Believe about Everything that Really Matters* by James Patterson and Peter Kim. Copyright © 1991 by James Patterson and Peter Kim, p. 6.

5   "Deaths, by Age and Leading Cause: 1992," U.S. National Center for Health Statistics, Vital Statistics of the United

States, annual; and unpublished data. Reported in *The American Almanac: Statistical Abstract of the United States, 1995-1996* (Austin, Texas: The Reference Press, Inc., 1996), p. 94.

6   "Homicide Rates for Black Males. Homicide Rates for White Males," National Center for Health Statistics. Reported in *Newsweek*, August 15, 1994, p. 32.

7   "Firearm Mortality Among Children, Youth, and Young Adults, 1 to 34 Years Old: 1992." Reported in *The American Almanac: Statistical Abstract of the United States, 1995-1996* (Austin, Texas: The Reference Press, Inc., 1996), p. 100.

8   "State Prison Inmates—Selected Characteristics: 1986 and 1991." *U.S. Bureau of Justice Statistics, Profile of State Prison Inmates, 1986 and 1991.*

9   "Adults on Probation, in Jail or Prison, or on Parole: 1980-1992." *U.S. Bureau of Justice Statistics, Correctional Populations in the United States, 1992.*

10   Scott Minerbrook, "Mission on the Mall: Save the Children," *U.S. News & World Report*, October 30, 1995, p. 10.

11   "Fatal Shootings in Classrooms on the Rise Across the Country," *The Tennessean*, March 3, 1996, p. 10A.

12   Harry F. Water, "Teenage Suicide: One Act Not to Follow," *Newsweek*, April 18, 1994, p. 49.

13   Jeff Giles, "The Poet of Alienation," *Newsweek*, April 18, 1994, p 46.

14   Tim Friend, "Teens' Use of Drugs Rises 78%," *USA Today*, August 20, 1996, p. 1A.

15   Monika Guttman, "The New Pot Culture," *USA Weekend*, February 16-18, 1996, pp. 4-7.

16   Mindy Fetterman, "School Enrollment Soars," *USA Today*, August 22, 1996, p. 1A.

Chapter 5

1   William Dunn, *The Baby Bust: A Generation Comes of Age* (Ithaca, New York: American Demographics Books, 1993), p. 16.

2   Sam Ward, "Children of Broken Homes," *USA Today*, January 25, 1996, p. 1D.

3   From *Open Marriage*. Copyright © 1972 by Nena O'Neill and George O'Neill. Copyright © 1984 by Nena O'Neill. Copyright © 1984 by Roger W. Libby. Reprinted by permission of M. Evans and Company, Inc., pp. 254-55.

4   Christopher Lasch, *Haven in a Heartless World: The Family Besieged*. Copyright © 1978 by Basic Books, Inc. Reprinted with permission of HarperCollins Publishers Inc., p. 139.

5   Nina J. Easton, "Life Without Father," *Los Angeles Times Magazine*, June 14, 1992, p. 16.

6   David M. Gross and Sophfronia Scott, "Proceeding with Caution," *Time*, July 16, 1990, p. 56.

7   *U.S. Census Bureau, National Center for Health Statistics.*

8   Barbara Dafoe Whitehead, "Dan Quayle Was Right." Copyright © 1993 Barbara Dafoe Whitehead, as first published in *The Atlantic Monthly*, April 1993.

9   Ibid.

10   "Children of Broken Homes," *USA Today*, January 25, 1996, p. 1A.

11   U.S. National Center for Health Statistics, Vital Statistics of the United States, annual; Monthly Vital Statistics Report, and unpublished data. Reported in *The American Almanac: Statistical Abstract of the United States, 1995-1996* (Austin, Texas: The Reference Press, Inc., 1996), p. 79.

12   Ibid.

13   *U.S. Census*, "Marital Status and Living Arrangements: March 1993."

14   *U.S. Census*, "Marital Status and Living Arrangements: March 1994."

15   Cheryl Russell, "Why Teen Births Boom," *American Demographics*, September 1995, p. 8.

16   Ibid.

17   David E. Bloom, "Women and Work," *American Demographics*, September 1986, p. 26.

Chapter 6

1   Eva Pomice, "Is your job cool? Or does it suck?" *P.O.V.*, May 1996, p. 61.

2   Copyright © 1995 by Harry Dent. From *Job Shock* by Harry Dent. Reprinted by permission of St. Martin's Press, Incorporated, p. 36.

3   Neil Howe and William Strauss, "The New Generation Gap," *The Atlantic Monthly*, December 1992, pp. 74-75.

4   Andrea Stone, "Parents, Pupils, Teachers Decry Aging Facilities," *USA Today*, May 14, 1996, p. 1A.

5   "Children and Seniors Below Poverty Level: 1970-1994," *U.S. Bureau of the Census*, Current Population Reports, pp. 60-88.

6   Peter G. Peterson, "Will America Grow Up Before It Grows Old?" *The Atlantic Monthly*, May 1996, pp. 71-72.

7   "Generation Debt," from *Revolution X* by Rob Nelson and Jon Cowan. Copyright © 1994 by Rob Nelson and Jon Cowan. Used by permission of Viking Penguin, a division of Penguin Books USA Inc., pp. 25-26.

Chapter 7

1   Steven V. Roberts, "Betty, Meet Ashley, A '90s Woman," *U.S. News & World Report*, April 1, 1996, pp. 10-11.

2   "Resident Population, by Hispanic Origin Status, 1980 to 1994; and Projections, 1995-2050." U.S. Bureau of the Census, Current Population Reports, P25-1095 and P25-1104; and Population Paper Listing 21. Reported in *The American Almanac: Statistical Abstract of the United States, 1995-1996* (Austin, Texas: The Reference Press, Inc., 1996), p. 19.

3   Chip Walker, "Can TV Save The Planet?" *American Demographics*, May 1996, pp. 42-48.

4   "World Population Change," from 1995 *Information Please Almanac*. Copyright © 1994 by Houghton Mifflin Company. Reprinted by permission of Houghton Mifflin Company. All rights reserved, p. 129.

5   "Components of Population Change, by Race and Hispanic Origin, 1990 to 1993; and Projections, 1995 and 2000," U.S. Bureau of the Census, Current Population Reports, P25-1104; and Population Paper Listing 21. Reported in *The American Almanac: Statistical Abstract of the United States, 1995-1996* (Austin, Texas: The Reference Press, Inc., 1996), p. 20.

6   Jill Smolowe, "Intermarried ... With Children," *Time, Special Issue: The New Face of America*, December 2, 1993, p. 64.

7   "Married Couples of Same or Mixed Races and Origins: 1970-1994," U.S. Bureau of the Census, Current Population Reports, P20-450. Reported in *The American Almanac: Statistical Abstract of the United States, 1995-1996* (Austin, Texas: The Reference Press, Inc., 1996), p. 55.

8   Ellis Cose, "One Drop of Bloody History," *Newsweek*, February 13, 1995, p. 70.

9   Sharon Begley, "Three Is Not Enough," *Newsweek*, February 13, 1995, p. 68.

10 Begley, p. 67.

11 Steven V. Roberts, "Uncle Sam Bar the Door," *U.S. News & World Report*, April 29, 1996, p. 29.

12 Susan Dentzer, "Adding and Subtracting," *U.S. News & World Report*, April 29, 1996, p. 37.

13 Dentzer, p. 38

14 *UC Davis Magazine*, Spring 1996, pp. 9, 12.

15 "Immigrants Admitted, by Leading Country of Birth and State: 1993," U.S. Immigration and Naturalization Service, Statistical Yearbook, annual. Reported in *The American Almanac: Statistical Abstract of the United States, 1995-1996* (Austin, Texas: The Reference Press, Inc., 1996), p. 13.

16 "Estimated Undocumented Immigrants, by Selected States and Countries of Origin: 1992 and 1994," U.S. Bureau of the Census. Reported in *The American Almanac: Statistical Abstract of the United States, 1995-1996* (Austin, Texas: The Reference Press, Inc., 1996), p. 12.

17 "Immigrants Admitted," p. 13.

18 "Estimated Undocumented Immigrants," p. 12.

19 From *Tribes* by Joel Kotkin. Copyright © 1993 by Joel Kotkin. Reprinted by permission of Random House, Inc., pp. 4-5.

20 Kotkin, p. 24.

21 Ibid.

22 Excerpts from *The New Victorians: A Young Woman's Challenge to the Old Feminist Order* by Rene Denfeld. Copyright © 1995 by Rene Denfeld. Reprinted by permission of Warner Books, Inc., New York. All rights reserved, pp. 1-2.

23 Garth Gilliam, "Smiling, Wide-eyed Boys Again," *Christian Social Action*, December, 1995, pp. 14-16.

24 From *Marketing to Generation X* by Karen Ritchie. Copyright © 1995 by Karen Ritchie. Reprinted with permission of The Free Press, a division of Simon & Schuster, p. 157.

25 Joanne M. Schrot, "Sex in America," *U.S. News & World Report*, October 17, 1994, p. 76.

26 From *A Separate Creation: The Search for the Biological Origins of Sexual Orientation* by Chandler Burr. Copyright © 1996 Chandler Burr. Reprinted with permission by Hyperion, p. 307.

27 Luise Cardarelli, "The Lost Girls," *Utne Reader*, May-June, 1996, p. 13.

28 Jim Wooten, "Listening to America," *World News Tonight with Peter Jennings*. Transmitted on May 16, 1996, 2:42 P.M. (ablistn7)

Chapter 8

1   Reprinted with the permission of Pocket Books, a division of Simon & Schuster from *Life After God* by Douglas Coupland. Copyright © 1994 by Douglas Campbell Coupland, p. 273.

2   Coupland, pp. 273-74.

3   Stephen L. Carter, *The Culture of Disbelief: How American Law and Politics Trivialize Religious Devotion* (New York: Basic Books, 1993), pp. 14-15. Copyright © by Stephen L. Carter. Reprinted by permission of HarperCollins Publishers Inc.

4   Excerpts from *The New Victorians: A Young Woman's Challenge to the Old Feminist Order* by Rene Denfeld. Copyright © 1995 by Rene Denfeld. Reprinted by permission of Warner Books, Inc., New York. All rights reserved, pp. 127-53.

5   Denfeld, p. 145.

6   Denfeld, p. 153.

7   See Craig Miller's book *Baby Boomer Spirituality: Ten Essential Values of a Generation* (Nashville: Discipleship Resources, 1992) for a fuller description of the New Age Movement.

8   Harvey Cox, *The Secular City: Twenty-fifth Anniversary Edition* (New York: Collier Books, 1990), p. 30.

9   Excerpt from *The Sibling Society* by Robert Bly. Copyright © 1996 by Robert Bly. Reprinted by permission of Addison-Wesley Longman Inc., p. 54.

Chapter 9

1   Daniel T. Benedict and Craig Kennet Miller, *Contemporary Worship for the 21st Century: Worship or Evangelism?* (Nashville: Discipleship Resources, 1994).

2   Reprinted with permission of the publisher. From *Stewardship: Choosing Service Over Self-Interest*. Copyright © 1993 by Peter Block, Berrett-Koehler Publishers, Inc., San Francisco, CA. All rights reserved, pp. 35-37.

Listed below are the questions used in the 1993 and 1995 Spring Break Surveys. Those questions that were used only on one survey are noted. All other questions were used in both surveys. The 1993 survey was for those ages twelve through twenty-eight. The 1995 survey was for those ages fourteen through thirty.

1993 and 1995 Spring Break Surveys of Young Men and Women

Thanks for taking part in this national survey of young adults that is being conducted as research for a new book that is being written by Dr. Craig Kennet Miller about your generation. Few books have asked you what you think about yourselves and your future. This is your chance to let your voice be heard!!! Please carefully and honestly answer the questions that follow. Be sure to answer the questions that are printed on all sections of the following pages. When finished please seal your survey and return it to a survey taker.

FIRST NAME:_____
CITY: _____STATE: _____
OCCUPATION/MAJOR:_____
SCHOOL: _____
PLACE OF BIRTH: _____

AGE: _____
SEX: ☐ Male ☐ Female
GRADE POINT AVERAGE:
☐ 2.0   ☐ 2.5
☐ 3.0   ☐ 3.5   ☐ 4.0

ARE YOU:
☐ Single (never married)   ☐ Married   ☐ Living together
☐ Divorced   ☐ Remarried   ☐ A parent

LIVING ARRANGEMENTS:
☐ With parent(s)   ☐ At college   ☐ With friend(s)
☐ My own house   ☐ Apartment   ☐ Own family

ETHNIC GROUP:
☐ Asian American   ☐ African American (black)
☐ Euro-American (white)   ☐ Hispanic/Latino American
☐ Native American   ☐ Multiethnic

CURRENT EDUCATION:
☐ In high school   ☐ High school graduate
☐ In college   ☐ College graduate   ☐ In graduate school

ARE YOUR PARENTS:
☐ Married   ☐ Separated   ☐ Divorced   ☐ Single (never married)
☐ Remarried (☐ Mom ☐ Dad ☐ Both)
☐ Other

DO YOU CONSIDER YOURSELF TO BE:
☐ Conservative   ☐ Moderate   ☐ Liberal

IN TERMS OF RELIGIOUS BELIEFS, ARE YOU:
☐ Atheist   ☐ Agnostic   ☐ Seeker   ☐ Believer

- -

1. (1993) What two events have had the most impact on your life?

☐ Watergate
☐ Reagan getting shot
☐ Challenger disaster
☐ Fall of the Berlin Wall
☐ Gulf War
☐ Trade Center bombing
☐ Other

☐ Breakup of Russia
☐ Computer revolution
☐ Birth of MTV
☐ Death of Len Bias
☐ Magic Johnson getting HIV

(1995) What two events have had the most impact on your life?

☐ Watergate
☐ Challenger disaster
☐ Fall of the Berlin Wall
☐ Gulf War
☐ Breakup of Russia
☐ Birth of MTV
☐ Other

☐ Anita Hill/Clarence Thomas hearings
☐ Magic Johnson getting HIV
☐ Rodney King and the L.A. riots/rebellion
☐ Suicide of Kurt Cobain
☐ O.J. Simpson murder trial
☐ Election of the Republican Congress

2. Which of the following have you experienced?

☐ Your parents' divorce
☐ Suicide attempt
☐ Leaving home
☐ Voting the first time
☐ Finding a full-time job
☐ Serving in the military
☐ Losing your virginity
☐ Victim of violent crime
☐ Rape
☐ Abuse:
    ☐ Physical
    ☐ Sexual
    ☐ Verbal

☐ Your divorce
☐ A satanic ritual
☐ Returning home to live
☐ Having a baby
☐ Losing a job
☐ Conquering an addiction
☐ Having an abortion
☐ A religious experience
☐ An addiction to:
    ☐ Alcohol
    ☐ Drugs
    ☐ Sex
    ☐ Other

☐ Death of a close friend
(How did they die?)

☐ Accident   ☐ Suicide   ☐ Overdose   ☐ Drunk driving
☐ Gunshot   ☐ Sickness   ☐ AIDS   ☐ Other

3. Which of the above has had the most impact on your life? (Please elaborate)

4. (1995) Have you done any of the following?

☐ Driven while drunk   ☐ Carried a gun   ☐ Smoked pot
☐ Ridden with a drunk driver   ☐ Been arrested   ☐ Tried other drugs
☐ Drank to get drunk   ☐ Smoked cigarettes on a regular basis

- - -

5. Your childhood family was (multiple choice):
☐ Traditional (Mom at home, Dad at work)   ☐ Dual-earning parents
☐ Single-parent mom   ☐ Single-parent dad
☐ Blended (two divorced families brought together)
☐ Other

6. (1993) As a preschooler where did you spend most of your day time?
☐ At home with parent   ☐ With a babysitter
☐ In daycare   ☐ With a neighbor
☐ Home of relative   ☐ By yourself

7. With (1) as the highest, rank the following from 1–5 as to from whom you have learned your core values:
☐ Family   ☐ Church   ☐ Media   ☐ School   ☐ Friends

8. How would you describe the Baby Boom Generation?
☐ Greedy and selfish   ☐ Hypocritical
☐ Giving and caring   ☐ Matured by experience and ready to lead

9. Of your group of friends, who has a better understanding of themselves and a direction for their life?
☐ Men   ☐ Women   ☐ Same

10. What do you expect to achieve by the time you are thirty years old?
☐ To own my own home   ☐ To be married   ☐ All of these
☐ To have a child   ☐ To have a secure job   ☐ None of these

11. Do you expect your generation to be:
☐ More successful than your parents' generation
☐ Less successful than your parents' generation

12. On a scale of 1–4 with (1) highest, how do you define success?
☐ Having fulfilling relationships with other people
☐ Owning a home and having a family
☐ Having enough money to meet all your needs
☐ Growing in knowledge and wisdom as you age

13. Are you active in any of the following religions?
☐ Buddhism   ☐ Hinduism   ☐ Mormon   ☐ Christianity
☐ Muslim   ☐ Judaism   ☐ New Age   ☐ Other

14. How often do you go to religious services?
☐ Weekly   ☐ Twice a month   ☐ Monthly   ☐ Yearly   ☐ Never

15. Of the following, which do you believe?

☐ God is the Creator ☐ In reincarnation ☐ In angels
☐ God is an energy force ☐ In ghosts ☐ Witchcraft is real
☐ All people will go to heaven ☐ In the power of prayer ☐ Jesus Christ is your Lord and Savior
☐ Only those who are saved will go to heaven

(1993):

☐ In the Holy Spirit ☐ The church is the best place to grow in faith
☐ People need to be forgiven of their sin ☐ I can find faith myself
☐ The Bible is the Word of God

16. (1993) On a scale of 1-6, with (1) highest, what is the greatest problem facing your generation?

☐ Paying the bills of previous generations ☐ Taking care of the environment
☐ Finding our own identity ☐ Stopping the violence of crime and drugs
☐ Overcoming the stress of rapid technological change ☐ Fighting racism and sexism

17. (1995) Do you agree (yes) or disagree (no) with the following?

The government is doing a good job running this country	☐ Yes	☐ No
The criminal justice system is fair	☐ Yes	☐ No
The school system produces successful students	☐ Yes	☐ No
Organized religion is in touch with people	☐ Yes	☐ No
The family is working well	☐ Yes	☐ No
It's okay to have children outside of marriage	☐ Yes	☐ No
It's easier than it used to be to find someone to marry	☐ Yes	☐ No
I am committed to having a long-term relationship	☐ Yes	☐ No
It's better to live together before marriage	☐ Yes	☐ No
My career options are better than they were a year ago	☐ Yes	☐ No
I believe I will stay in one career for my working life	☐ Yes	☐ No
Boomers understand our generation's needs at work	☐ Yes	☐ No
I will receive social security benefits when I retire	☐ Yes	☐ No
There is more violence in my community	☐ Yes	☐ No
People should be allowed to carry guns for protection	☐ Yes	☐ No
I believe in capital punishment	☐ Yes	☐ No
The media is responsible for violent behavior	☐ Yes	☐ No
The generation following us will have more opportunities	☐ Yes	☐ No
Children will have it better than we do when they are over 12	☐ Yes	☐ No
The government should cut back on welfare	☐ Yes	☐ No
Legal immigration should be reduced	☐ Yes	☐ No
Affirmative Action should be outlawed	☐ Yes	☐ No
The government's first priority should be to cut the deficit	☐ Yes	☐ No

18. (1995) What else do you have to say about your generation?

19. (1993) What is your greatest hope for the future?